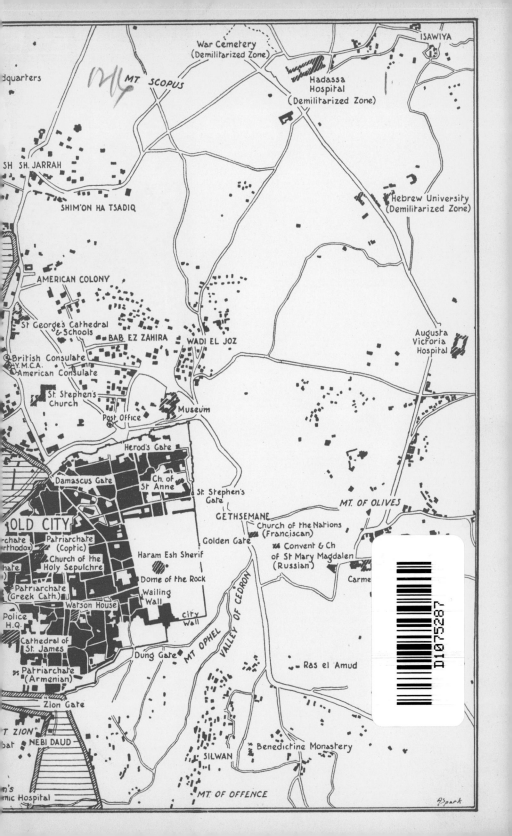

$1·00

THE ONE REMAINS

THE ONE
REMAINS

by

Stewart Perowne

London
HODDER & STOUGHTON

First printed April, 1954

*Made and Printed in Great Britain for Hodder and
Stoughton Limited by The Camelot Press Limited
London and Southampton*

The One remains, the many change and pass;
    Heaven's light for ever shines, Earth's shadows fly;
Life, like a dome of many-coloured glass,
    Stains the white radiance of Eternity.

P. B. SHELLEY, Adonais, lii.

List of Illustrations

Acknowledgments

I WISH to thank my old friend and colleague, Mr. Henry Knesevitch of the United Nations Relief and Works Agency, for his kindness in obtaining information and statistics from the Agency for me, and permission to publish them; Miss Ilse Muller, for her help in typing the manuscript; Messrs. Denis Baly, Richard Bird, Ronald Durrant, Elia Photograph Service, Humphrey Neame, The Director of the Palestine Museum, Cyril Silvester and Robert Walmsley for permission to publish their photographs, and, specially, Miss Mary Flack for typing the greater part of the book.

NOTE

I have used the terms "Mandate" or "Mandatory" as a general synonym for the British Civil Administration of Palestine.

The British Civil Administration succeeded the British Military Administration in 1920, with the appointment of Sir Herbert (later Viscount) Samuel as the first High Commissioner. On 25th April of that year, the Supreme Council, sitting at San Remo, allocated the Mandate to Great Britain. The final draft was tentatively confirmed by the League Council on 22nd July, 1922. It came into force on 29th September, 1923. It was abandoned on 15th May, 1948.

Fighting between Arabs and Zionists had already broken out. On 11th June, 1948, a truce was established, which lasted until 9th July. As a result of a Security Council Resolution of 15th July, a General Cease Fire came into effect on 18th July. A Cease Fire Agreement was signed at Rhodes on 3rd April, 1949.

STEWART PEROWNE

Jerusalem

St. George's Day—Feast of the Transfiguration, 1953.

Introduction

And when he was come near, he beheld the city, and wept over it, saying, if thou hadst known, even thou, at least in this thy day, the things which belong unto thy peace! But now they are hid from thine eyes.

LUKE xix. 41, 42.

FORTY years after Christ had spoken these words, the city over which He had wept lay desolate. Within a century, after a last desperate revolt against Rome, its very name was blotted out. A foreign settlement replaced it. The Tomb of Christ and the site of the Temple of His people were alike desecrated. Rome, it seemed, had closed her account with Jerusalem.

While the finishing touches were being given to the new Roman colony of Ælia Capitolina, which was to replace Jerusalem on the site of the city and in the minds of men, a Christian slave was writing a book in Rome. His name was Hermas, and his book is called *The Shepherd*. It is one of the earliest manuals of the Christian life, and so widely venerated was it that you find it bound up together with the books of the Old and New Testament in the great manuscript of the Bible called the *Codex Sinaiticus* which is now in the British Museum. The book is cast in the form of visions. In the first vision Hermas is visited by an old lady with white hair, who begins to tell him what he must do to be a good Christian. In the second and third visions, she gradually sheds the marks of age, until at the end of the fourth vision she appears as a young bride, clothed all in white. Hermas wonders who she may be, and at first takes her for the Sybil, the famous oracle of pagan Rome. But an angel tells him that she is the Church, old because she is from everlasting, but young and beautiful to those who have learned to know and to listen to her.

Jerusalem is like Hermas' Lady Church.

By the time that Hermas was writing, Jerusalem had already seen terrible vicissitudes. In the last three and a half thousand years, the city has changed hands more than twenty-five times. It has been utterly destroyed more than once, has been humbled often by famine, pestilence and earthquake. No other city in the world's history has suffered so much and achieved so much as Jerusalem. With the destruction of Jerusalem by Titus in A.D. 70 and its final razing sixty-five years later under Hadrian, its rôle as the centre of the Jewish faith and the site of the Jewish temple was ended. In another two hundred years it had become the official focus of Christian worship. Barely three hundred years after that, Jerusalem was captured by the forces of Islam, in their first volcanic eruption from Arabia. Ever since, except for the brief occupation of the Crusaders, it has been what it is to-day, a predominantly Islamic city, both in aspect and faith; and the holy rock, the threshing floor of Araunah the Jebusite which David bought to be the site of his temple, has known a longer history as a Moslem shrine than ever it did as a Jewish altar. No other city has known such changes, nor been loved by so many for so long. Only Jerusalem has commanded the devotion of the east and the west equally.

Hermas lived in Rome; in the language of Athens he wrote the message of Jerusalem. Rome, Athens and Jerusalem—these three cities have given us western civilization as we know it. The amalgamation of the strains of Athens and Rome was swift, easy and lasting. The spirit of the two cities was very different, and yet they had an hereditary affinity. They are both Mediterranean towns, and it was not difficult for Rome to assimilate Athens. It is no surprise that within fifty years of the conquest of Athens by the Roman general Sulla, the Roman poet Virgil is warning his countrymen to leave the arts and sciences of Greece to the Greeks, and Horace is decrying a suggestion that the capital of the Roman state be moved to Byzantium. Greece was winning all the time. The Greek language and Greek architecture became increasingly the vernaculars of Rome. In A.D. 330, the capital of the Roman Empire was moved to Byzantium, which for more than eleven hundred years was to rule as the heir of both Rome and Athens.

And of Jerusalem, too; for Constantine, the Emperor who established his capital in Byzantium, had already adopted the Christian faith and dedicated his new city to the Blessed Virgin. But the triumph of Jerusalem, its mingling with Rome and Athens, was by no means the easy and natural process which had produced the fusion of Athens and Rome. On the contrary, it is a story of conflict and bitterness, with the odds always seemingly against victory and peace, as the story of Jerusalem had been from the beginning, and has been to our own day.

Never, you would say, could so fierce, foreign and unforgiving a city, which had in any case been as utterly destroyed as Carthage itself, never could it succeed in identifying itself with Rome, or even in living on the sufferance of Rome. Yet it was to conquer Rome far more completely and permanently than Athens had done. From Jerusalem was to spring the generation that would give Rome her rulers, that would preserve Latin as the timeless and ever-living language of a Faith which Rome had tried to destroy, and would make her truly what her proud children were already calling her, the "Eternal City."

It is this strange, paradoxical achievement that gives Jerusalem its quality to-day. It is inhuman. Dean Inge went so far as to call it "indescribably grim and alien" after a visit to it. It wins you by no human gentleness, never makes you feel that "Jerusalem belongs to you." And yet it does possess you, and that completely. It has you in thrall. It is *La Belle Dame sans Merci* of cities.

It is of life in Jerusalem as it is to-day, that I shall try to tell you in this book. The life of ordinary people is what I shall try to describe, who we are, how we came here, what we do. But at the outset I must ask you to bear always in mind that, despite electricity, and aeroplanes, and politics and cinemas, Jerusalem is no ordinary city, that it is unlike any other city in the world, both in its nature and in its meaning. You may think that in telling my story, I live too much in the past. It is not the past, for the business of Jerusalem is eternity, and in eternity there are no years nor days. The whole of time is always around you. The present is the face only. I want you to see that as well as I can portray it for you. But we must take account of the bones underneath as well.

So first of all I shall try to describe Jerusalem as it is to-day, once again, as so often in the past, afflicted and distressed. Then I shall speak of its inhabitants, and how they fare. Thirdly, I shall give some account of what is being done by the Arab inhabitants of Jordan and by their friends and helpers of other races, to relieve and restore those who have been "minished and brought low, through oppression, affliction, and sorrow."

Politics I shall try to exclude, because it is things and people as they are that I want to describe, because it is hard to discuss politics without attributing motives or passing judgments, and because my work in Jerusalem is unconnected with any political aim.

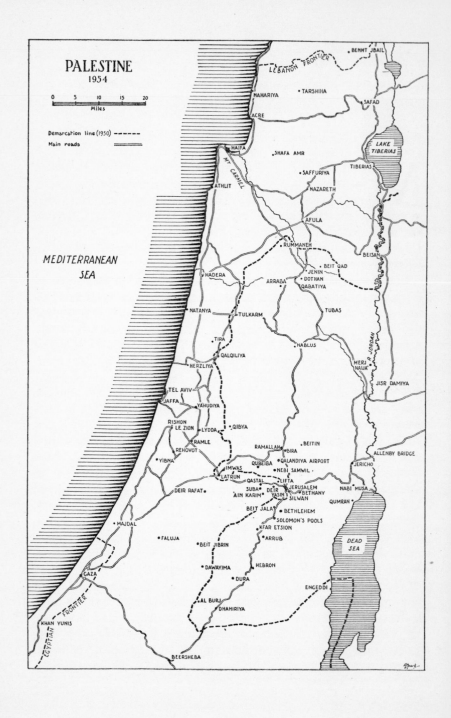

Chapter One

Howl, O gate; cry, O city; thou, whole Palestina, art dissolved.
ISAIAH xiv. 31.

MANY are the tribulations which have afflicted Jerusalem in its long and dolorous history: ruin, famine, massacre, earthquake, captivity, destruction—you would think that in our day it could cry like the last of the Habsburgs, "Nothing has been spared me!" But no; there was still, in the year 1948, a new and unprecedented trial to be borne: the Holy City was to be sawn in sunder.

In that year Britain gave up the Mandate which she had accepted from the League of Nations in 1923. (Already in 1920, in anticipation of the Mandate, a British civil administration had succeeded the British military administration established as British troops occupied the country in 1917 and 1918.) Theoretically, the Mandate was returned to the United Nations, who were thus made responsible for the future of Palestine. In fact, strife and bloodshed broke out between the Arabs and the Zionists, which after one abortive truce and the renewal of war, was finally brought to a stop by a second truce in 1948. In April, 1949, an armistice agreement was reached at a conference in the island of Rhodes, far from the battle-fronts. The line which it determined upon to separate the armies was only a modification of the "cease-fire" positions. It was an armistice line, not a frontier. Yet from that day to this it has served as a frontier, and in the year 1950 it was guaranteed by America, Britain and France from change by one side or the other. If you look at the map, you will see what an odd shape it is, and nowhere odder than in Jerusalem. In the country its effect is, very roughly, to leave to the Arabs the hill country, that is to say, what in days of old was Judæa and Israel, and to give to the Zionists the plains and the extreme south and north of Palestine, that is to say, Philistia, Galilee of the Gentiles and the Negeb of the Bedouin. In Jerusalem, the result has been to leave in Arab hands the whole of historic Jerusalem, and part of the northern suburb, and to place under Israeli control most of the modern town, which the Israelis hope, despite

United Nations resolutions in favour of a unified Jerusalem under international administration, to make into a capital. If they do so, it will be the first example on record of a state establishing its capital in the suburbs of a city belonging to another country.

"*Quidquid delirant reges, plectuntur Achivi*," wrote Horace: whatever madness the great ones of the earth commit, it is the poor peasants that suffer. So it has been in Palestine. As a result of the fighting, and of the truce which brought it to an end, hundreds of thousands of Palestine Arabs have been plunged into poverty and distress. Indeed, it is hard to find any family which has not been affected. There are three categories of sufferer. First, those who are officially designated refugees; secondly, those who are known as "economic refugees"; and, finally, the dwellers in the "frontier villages."

The word "refugee" has a depressing but all too familiar sound in our ears to-day. So many millions of mankind have been thrust forth from their homes and lands in these latter years that what is in truth a crime has come to be regarded as a mere process, just something which like hail or flood may overtake anyone at any time. Those whom the process affects become refugees, just as those who find employment become employees. The English word "refugee" was first used in 1685 to describe the Huguenots who fled from France and the Low Countries after the revocation of the Edict of Nantes. It was in England that the majority of them sought their refuge. England received them, and changed them from suppliants to citizens. In our own day, when much responsibility for the care of refugees is laid upon English men and women, they can take heart from the knowledge that they tackled their first "refugee" problem with humanity, and solved it to the abiding benefit of all concerned.

Official refugees are the charges of the United Nations Relief and Works Agency (U.N.R.W.A.), which has been appointed to look after them. The official definition of a refugee is as follows:

"a person who, through the Palestine conflict
"(*a*) lost his place of normal residence;
"(*b*) lost his means of livelihood;
"(*c*) is in need."

Of these refugees there are 864,636, each one of whom is registered with the Agency, and each one of whom, except new-born children,

A B C D E F G H I J K L M N O P Q

1 2 3 4 5 6 7 8 9 10 11 12

Augusta Victoria Hospital P.3
War Cemetery H.2
Museum I.5
St. George's C.5
Holy Sepulchre E.7
Haram esh Sherif (Temple Area) J.7
Gethsemane M.6
Nebi Daud ("Mount Zion") G.10
Silwan Village O.9
Citadel and Jaffa Gate D.8
Damascus Gate E.6
Watson House F½. 7¾5
Mandelbaum Gate B.5

(Elia)

Jerusalem from the air, looking north.

Jerusalem, 1948–54.

(R. Walmsley)

Refugees carrying water to a camp in the Jordan valley.

(D. Baly)

St. George's Cathedral and King Edward VII Tower from the School Playground, after rain.

is entitled to draw rations from the Agency. This is the total arrived at by the Agency itself; but to it must be added some 25,000 new refugees every year, the children of refugees. They are born refugees. From the first day of their lives they are "hungry and thirsty" and find "no city to dwell in." More than half of all the refugees, 476,201 (June, 1953), are to be found in Jordan. Almost another quarter of the total, 205,305, are huddled in what is called the Gaza strip, the portion of southern Palestine, about five miles wide and twenty-five long, which is now under Egyptian rule. The remainder are in Lebanon (103,305) and Syria (85,385).

Many of these refugees live in camps maintained by the Agency. Because so much has been written of the misery of the camps, it is commonly thought that all refugees live in camps. This is a mistake: In Jordan, only 138,367 are camp-dwellers, that is to say, less than one-third of those who are receiving rations. There are twenty-five camps altogether, distributed over the east and west banks of the Jordan, from the north to the south of the kingdom, the thickest concentration, nearly 70,000, being in the Jericho area. I mention this proportion of camp-dwellers not in order to minimize their distress, but because a solution of the camp problem, pressing though it is, will not in itself solve the refugee problem. The exact dwelling-place, and type of dwelling of every single refugee in Jordan is shown in Appendix I. The figures are for the month of June, 1953; but they vary little from month to month.

It is no good pretending that the camp-dwellers are not miserable. Despite all the care of the Agency, they are. Even the best tent is a poor substitute, in a Palestine winter, for the good stone houses in which these people formerly lived, many thousands of them on the coastal plain where even the winter is mild. The mere fact that they now live in camps and not in homes, that they are underfed and under-occupied, must lead to misery, and to progressive misery.

Many of the refugees who do not live in camps, have found shelter in caves or in ruined homes. I know some in Bethany, for instance, who are living in the ruins of houses which were made unfit for habitation by the earthquake of 1927. Some have found a lodging with relations, a very few have found a little work and are able to rent a room. But all are wretched, because all are dependent on the goodwill of others for their life. In tent, cave, or ruin they are kept from starvation only by a ration card. The ration card has become for the refugees more than a talisman, it is a fetish. Every

B

suggestion for their future is related to the ration card. If a proposal involves the loss, or possible loss, of the card, then it is damned in advance by the refugee between whom and starvation only his ration card stands.

This psychological attribute of the ration card is of the first importance, and there will be more to say of it when we come to the question of the future of the refugees and schemes for their permanent establishment. The Agency, naturally enough, must do its utmost to reduce the ration strength, for how else shall it justify itself in its annual report to the United Nations, who provide it with its funds? The amount of money voted for the maintenance of official refugees in 1953 was $5 million more than in 1952, namely $23 million. But this sum provides a monthly ration of only:

Flour	9 kilogrammes
Beans	500–800 grammes
Vegetable oil	175 ,,
Margarine	200 ,,
Sugar	500 ,,
Rice (sometimes)	400 ,,
Soap	100 ,,

In winter they also get:

Kerosene	1½ litres	⎫
Dates	500 grammes	⎬ monthly
Blankets	1 for each two persons	⎭

The Welfare section of the Agency has 180 milk distribution centres which daily give 19,000 shares of milk to mothers, babies and old people; and 13,000 underfed children get extra food on a doctor's prescription. For the sick, there are nearly 1,000 beds in twenty-one hospitals, mostly founded by government or voluntary agencies, but now run wholly or partly by the Agency, which also maintains thirty out-patient clinics and nineteen infant welfare centres.

Each complete monthly ration is estimated to cost $1.80. Judged by normal standards of healthy diet, it is not much. That is not the fault of the Agency. It would willingly give far more if it could. It simply has not the money, and it has not the money because the

United Nations of the world do not vote the money. A senior officer of the Agency told me that he had been administering relief for various agencies in different parts of the world for the past eight years, but that never had he been asked to feed refugees so meagrely as these Arab refugees of Palestine. To take but a single item, think what "one blanket for each two persons" means, in a tent, in a winter gale, in the hill country of Nablus.

Next, in this catalogue of misery, we come to the "economic refugees." By economic refugees I mean those who, though not coming within the definition of official refugee, are nevertheless suffering from the disruption of Palestine. Their number cannot be estimated. It would, I believe, be far easier to make a census of those who have not suffered in some way or degree. The list would not be long. First, among the economic refugees, come the professional and business classes. They must run into thousands. They include owners of house property in Jaffa, Haifa and modern Jerusalem, of orange groves and farms in the plain, of prosperous businesses and agencies. In most cases, these people have lost everything they possessed: money, plant, house and home. They have received no compensation or purchase price. They have had to start again from zero, and, as we shall see, the way they have done it is astonishing. But there are other economic refugees, people who never were rich, who held minor posts in the Mandatory Government, or had built up little shops or trades, or were just servants and gardeners and chauffeurs of their well-to-do countrymen and of the many British residents connected with government. Every village round Jerusalem had a number of families who were supported by such workers. All that is gone now, and the villagers are forced to look around for other means of livelihood. They do not often find it, and are hard put to it even to feed and clothe their families. Most lamentable has been the decline in the standard of education; but of this and other afflictions of the economic refugees, there will be more to say later on. Before passing to the frontier villages and their plight, let me cite one actual case to illustrate the state of the economic refugees, for they are largely anonymous, and yet they are also the majority. In the beautiful village of 'Ain Karim there lived a family of three sisters. 'Ain Karim is south-west of Jerusalem, and only a few miles from it. General Gordon hired a house there when he was living in Palestine, and both Roman Catholic and Russian convents have helped to adorn it with groves and gardens, for it is the traditional birthplace of St. John the Baptist. There was no more expressive and touching ceremony in days gone by, than the Feast of the Visitation at 'Ain Karim, for the Russian nuns on the Mount of Olives would come in procession with their Ikon of the Blessed Virgin, and would be met at the fountain of 'Ain Karim by a similar procession of the Russian nuns of the convent of St. Elizabeth there. The two Ikons, to the sound of solemn chants, would leave their respective frames, kiss, and then be borne in happy triumph up the flower-decked steps of the Russian convent, there to lodge together. It was a true visitation. During the last war, 'Ain Karim was the scene of a very different visitation, but a by no means unwelcome one. The Polish troops who were billeted there were gentlemanly and devout. They were liked by the villagers. One of these soldiers was billeted in the house of three sisters, Miss Rose, Miss Adèle and Miss Marie. All three were schoolteachers, of refined manners and Western ways, as their Christian names show. Their father had been a man of substance, and owned a large house, in which they were proud to make this European soldier welcome. But the poor soldier, undermined by his sufferings in Russia, developed consumption. The army had no more use for him. He became a civilian, a foreign civilian in a strange land. What was to be done? The three sisters had no hesitation. He must stay with them until he was well. So the soldier remained on in 'Ain Karim, and gradually got better. He had a little pension from the Polish Government. Then came 1948. The three sisters and their father became refugees overnight. They fled to Bethlehem, taking only the little that they could carry. But they took the Polish soldier as well. In Bethlehem, they found one poor room. The soldier's pension failed. So did the sisters' employment as schoolteachers; but not their care for their soldier. Only Miss Rose is now employed as a teacher, the others perhaps are too old, even if there were posts for them, which there are not. The soldier has no work either. But that little room in Bethlehem is one of the most happy and loving homes you can find. So strong is the bond of affliction, so deep the roots of charity.

Finally, we come to the frontier villages. These are the villages through which passes the truce-line. As I said, it was drawn in Rhodes, not Palestine, and on maps, not on the ground. The result was that the line has in many cases cut off villages from their lands. That means from their life, because from time immemorial, the village has been the unit of habitation in Palestine, and it has always lived by its land. The list of cities overthrown by Thutmosis III, which is carved on the pylons of the temple at Karnak, mentions 118 places in Palestine. They must have been small villages. That was just 3,400 years ago; but to this day the predominantly rural and agricultural scheme of life endures in Palestine. The peasants of to-day are the lineal descendants of the peasants of Biblical times. They have the same customs, the same psychology, the same proverbs—only the other day a Bedouin said to me: "We have a saying, 'the jealous man has a beam in his eye.'" They even have the same peculiarities of speech. The story of the word "Shibboleth" (Judges xii) is well known; the men of Ephraim "could not frame to pronounce it right," but said "Sibboleth" instead, and so the men of Gilead were able to identify them by their speech, and killed 42,000 at the ford of the Jordan river. To this day, in the land of Ephraim, that is to say, Samaria, "sh" is pronounced as "s." A short time ago I was listening to a class in a little school where illiterates are taught to read and write. One of the pupils, a grown-up woman, was called upon to read, which she did with great gusto. It happened that the exercise she was reading described the attributes of the "energetic peasant," which in Arabic is "al-fellah al-nashīt." She pronounced it "nasīt" throughout. These are the same people as they have always been; and if you want to understand their passionate devotion to their land, you have only to read the story of Naboth's vineyard (i Kings xxi). Naboth was offered either another, better, plot of land, or the "worth of it in money." Naboth refused to part with the inheritance of his fathers. But the Naboths of to-day like Naboth of old have had the inheritance of their fathers forcibly taken from them, and neither land nor money given in exchange. In village after village along the frontier, the ancestral lands have been shorn away by the truce-line. In some cases, thousands of acres have been lost, nearly the whole patrimony of the village, in others the line comes almost up to the houses of the village themselves. In one case, the line bisects a house. The villagers cannot be classed as refugees, because they have not lost their homes. But how are they to live? They have neither ration cards, nor land. In many cases their situation is made worse by the presence in the village of numbers of official refugees, for whom shelter has somehow to be found.

The moral depression of these poor villagers is increased by the very nearness of their property from which they are excluded.

They must sit in their houses, and watch others cultivate, or fail to cultivate, their lands under their eyes. The trees they planted, the groves they watered, all these they can still see; but if they venture to approach them, if they cross the line, they are liable to be shot as "marauders." Yet they have received no compensation, no price, for these lands and the fruits of their labours. Their property has just been taken from them and given to others.

Such in outline is the problem that confronts the Arabs of what was formerly Palestine. That problem is spread over the whole of the territory left in Arab hands, the area which is now known as the "West Bank" of the Hashemite Kingdom of Jordan. In Jerusalem itself, the problem is concentrated, for in Jerusalem you have both official refugees and economic refugees, and a truce-line that goes right through the city. If you look at the map you will see just how the line runs. Starting from the north, it comes in obliquely from the west, until it reaches the western spur of Mount Scopus, to the west of the main north road. It then runs down in a southerly direction, skirting the American Colony and St. George's, which remain in Jordan by a matter of yards, and so down to the Damascus Gate, which again is just within Jordan. Here the line turns south-west, and runs up the hill, along the old wall of the city, and so down nearly to the Jaffa Gate. Thence it runs again along the old city wall, to the south-west corner of it. Here it turns east, but only to just below the Zion Gate; then south again, down to the former Government House, and thence it gradually eases off to the west. On the eastern spur of Mount Scopus there is a demilitarized zone which comprises the Hebrew University, the Hadassah Hospital and the British War Cemetery. To this zone, including the cemetery, entry is forbidden, except for United Nations officials, and Israeli watchmen, who are relieved once a fortnight. Government House is United Nations property. Along most of the line, there is a no-man's-land of varying width, a swathe of desolation, dirt and neglect which increases the stricken aspect of the ruins which stand upon and beside it. For there are still scores of buildings that were damaged or gutted in the fighting and have not yet been rebuilt. The line crosses roads and closes thoroughfares. A street begins in one country, runs into the dirty jungle of no-man's-land, and ends in the other country. It is a single street; but it is easier for a citizen of the country at one end of it to go to any other land on earth than to the one at the other end of the street. The two territories are utterly separated.

And yet not separated. As I write, I can hear the siren blowing in Israeli Jerusalem, to give warning that the Sabbath is about to begin, for it is Friday evening. From the gateway of the Close, I can look into Israel. I see the houses, and the people: I see the buses, and all the life of a town. But that life has for me as much tangible reality as the image on the screen of a cinema. Nothing either living or inanimate may cross the line. Only death. The truce-line is not always silent. Firing is not infrequently heard. Two days ago, it lasted for several hours; and at the end ten Arabs had been killed and thirteen wounded.

Through this line there is only one official way, by which certain privileged people may pass between Jordan and Israel. It is the road just behind St. George's. Because it is near a house that belonged to a certain Mandelbaum, the crossing-point is called the "Mandelbaum Gate," but it is a gate only in the old English sense of a "way," not a door, for the street is quite open to the sky, and is obstructed only by the barriers that mark the limits of the respective states. It looks, in fact, just like a customs post on an obscure international frontier. On this side is the little hut flying the Jordan flag, then there is the inevitable stretch of no-man's-land, about a hundred yards of it, and then comes the hut with the Israeli flag over it. It generally has a deserted, forlorn look. For not many people use it. Sometimes you will see the white jeeps of the United Nations "observers," the officers responsible for seeing that the truce is respected, hurrying across, their drivers calling out the pass-number as they swirl round the dragon's-teeth barrier. Sometimes a consular car, with the flag of its country waving from a little flagstaff on the mudguard, will glide from one country to the other. And sometimes travellers, pilgrims or sight-seers, are allowed to cross. But they must have previously obtained leave from the authorities of both countries, and their names must appear on the list in the little hut, and their passports must be in order, and they must be there at the right time. When all has been arranged, you say farewell to them. They are on foot, and carry their own luggage. They look forsaken and alone, as they march away from you into no-man's-land. It is the same if you are meeting anyone. No car approaches, nor porters with luggage. Just one person, alone, a single soul, crosses towards you, on foot, and in silence. Little wonder that a sort of Moody and Sankey eschatology has grown up around this gap in the frontier. We refer to "the other side" and to "passing over" quite naturally.

A few days ago, as I was taking a pilgrim to the "gate," I said to the corporal on duty, in Arabic, "I have brought you a soul for the other world." He smiled and nodded: it seemed to him quite an ordinary way of putting it. And why not, in Jerusalem? For even at the Mandelbaum Gate, it is still Jerusalem that we are in, and Jerusalem, perhaps, in her heart of hearts, does not regard our unhappy divisions.

The most poignant sight of all at the "gate" is to be seen at the time of great Christian festivals, because Christian Arabs who still live in Israel may come over then to see their relations and friends. They are allowed forty-eight hours of joy and company, then they must go back. Again, you have the feeling of the other world. So many have assembled to meet those who are to come, there is so much happy expectation, such scanning of the narrow way along which they will appear. At last they arrive, like the spirits in Virgil's underworld, each begging to be ferried across first by old Charon, *"tendentesque manus ripae ulterioris amore,"* "stretching forth their hands in longing for the farther side."

Only Christian Arabs are so privileged. For the Moslem Arabs of Israel there is little hope either of return or of reunion. They must abide without respite amid the alien corn and concrete of Israel.

Chapter Two

*Ye have sown much, and bring in little; ye eat, but ye have not
enough; ye drink, but ye are not filled with drink; ye clothe you,
but there is none warm; and he that earneth wages earneth
wages to put it into a bag with holes.*

HAGGAI i. 6.

SO far, I have written of Jerusalem as seen from near the truce-
line and no-man's-land. But the effects of the truce, and of the
fighting that led up to it, can be seen in all parts of the town,
both inside the walls and outside. In this chapter, we will survey the
area outside; in the next, we will contemplate some of the gates.
In the fourth chapter, we will visit the Old City.

In the area of Arab Jerusalem outside the walls, the first thing that
strikes the returning denizen is that life and movement have been
intensified, that things are nearer together; and the second thing is
how neat and harmonious it all looks. It is as though some extra
passengers had been taken into a train which is already full, but full
of kind and friendly people. For instance, in the old fosse, between
the Damascus and Herod's Gates, except for a few squatters who
managed to evade or cajole the Mandatory authorities, I do not
remember that anything much existed. It certainly was not the
busy commercial centre it now is. First, next the Damascus Gate,
there is the bus station for the Bethlehem, Hebron, Jericho and
'Amman lines. There is the usual coming and going, backing and
filling, and the loud, jolly chaffering that surrounds eastern travel.
There are also those fascinating and mysterious bundles which the
travellers carry. They are so much more natural and interesting
than our regimented suitcases; and they must be so much easier to
pack and unpack. To the Arab, the bus is a natural development of
the caravan, so that he is much more at home in the vehicle than the
people of the west. He is neither harassed nor ill-tempered. The buses
of Jerusalem are often full, but they never look overcrowded. They
run to a fixed schedule, which is an excellent compromise between
Eastern leisure and Western pernicketiness. Last winter I was going
out for a Sunday afternoon walk with some visitors, and we wanted

to visit Nebi Samwil, the Mount Joy of the Crusaders, so-called because it is the hill from which the wayfarers from the west first viewed Jerusalem. The Ramallah bus (which leaves from another neat park, just opposite the Dominican Convent) could give us a good start. "When do the buses run?" I asked. "Every half-hour ... yes, there is a bus at half-past two, and one at three o'clock, and ..." "All right," I said, "We will catch the half-past two bus, if God wills." At two twenty-five, we were there, welcomed with smiles, and bowed into an empty bus, as though it were a royal box. By about a quarter to three, several other people had joined us; and I ventured to ask the manager or warden of the station, for he seemed to be neither driver nor conductor, whether we might now be expected to start, "For," I said gently, "this is the half-past two bus." He looked at me in pained reproof, and said, "True, O dear one; but how can a bus start until it is full?" I felt foolish for having asked.

Between the bus station and the roadway, there is a potter's stall. It spreads over the ground like a parade. There are platoons of pots, great and small. They come from Hebron. They are of many shapes, but all are graceful, and curiously, helplessly, human. You can understand, as you look at them, why Omar Al-Khayyám heard them talking, during his Ramadan walk, about the injustice of fate. They look as if they might get run over by one of the buses, unless their guardian restrained them. Next, in the late summer, there is the stall of the water-melon seller: great green globes piled high like cannon balls, with here and there one split to show its pink flesh framed in the white inner rind. Most people find the water-melon refreshing; but to me it always somehow suggests a cannibal feast, the flesh is so living and juicy. I prefer the grapes that you buy just inside Herod's Gate. Here, alas, Lucretius' dictum has come true: "*Cedit enim rerum novitate extrusa vetustas*"—antiquity has been thrust out by the new way of things. In the days of Nehemiah (iii. 1 and xii. 39), in the time of Our Lord (John v. 2), and right up to a few years ago, the Sheep Gate was at this point of the northern wall, and the sheep market, too. You would see the dusty flocks going home through it every evening, and in the morning the shepherds and merchants striking bargains just outside it. For this is the gate that gives the quickest access to the grazing-grounds, if such they may be called, on the hills to the north and east of the town. But at last the poor sheep and their shepherds have been ousted by the taxis. This is sad, but not as shocking as it might be. The sheep have not gone very far; in fact, only just round the corner. They now have their market in the fosse just to the south of the Storks' Tower, which is the tower at the north-east angle of the walls. And although Herod's Gate is flanked by two fuel stations, one on the east and the other on the west, they are trim and tidy, and the one on the west has a pretty garden. As I write, the owners of the station are enlarging their garden, so that it will extend right up to the gateway itself. The Municipality has encouraged them to do this, and has promised them free water for the flowers.

The Municipality has also planted trees on both sides of the road between the Damascus Gate and Herod's Gate, and protected them with wire cages; so that in years to come the fosse in which Godfrey de Bouillon erected the tower from which he, first of all the Crusaders, was to enter Jerusalem, will give a welcome shade to all who pass by.

Herod's Gate, and the quarter lying to the north to which it gave its name, used to be one of the quietest and most rural districts of Jerusalem *extra muros*. Two streets fanned out like spokes from the old fosse which carries the road to Jericho and 'Amman. There was a little coffee-house opposite the Gate, on the north-west road, and on the north-east stood, and still stands, the Rashidiya boys' school, the one good school building erected by the Turks—and it was many years before the Mandatory Government built one as good. There were a few houses and much open space. About three hundred yards along the north-west road was the group of buildings which housed the Government Arab College, and on its northern boundary the quiet road that formed the rim of the wheel, as it were, and joined the two roads from the Gate. On the other side of this road, balancing the Arab College, and on the line of the Third Wall of the ancient city, was the newly-built American School of Oriental Research. Then you came to an olive-grove and the playground of St. George's School, with the school buildings and the cathedral rising above the cypresses of the Bishop's garden. I lived and taught in the Arab College for three years. The buildings were primitive. We had neither electric light nor running water. The largest building, in which I had my room, had been a Turkish law court. All around us the ground was open. There was but little traffic or noise. There was plenty of room to play football and basketball, and still have space left over for walking about and reading (for the

Arab student is a born peripatetic). From my window, I could look across to the American School, and wonder if I should ever live to see the tiny trees in its garden grow up. Further along the transverse road I could see the Chief Secretary's house. Beyond, just round the corner, was a lovely old Arab house which was the home of one of the most gracious women in Jerusalem. To the east, you saw the great pine tree, the largest within miles, beneath which King Edward VII had camped when, as Prince of Wales, he had visited the Holy City with Dean Stanley in 1862.

The whole scene has been transformed now; but, as I suggested above, in a sociable sort of way. There has been no Draynflete brutality about it. Down by the Gate, there is another coffee-house, and on both roads there are shops. On the westerly road, beneath the old Moslem cemetery, there is a charming colonnade, simple and sheltering, which houses the post office, a book shop and a few others. We owe the colonnade to the insistence and good taste of the architect, Seyyid Yusuf Budeiri, who refused to be browbeaten by advisers who said that the colonnade was "un-economic." It is built of white stone, and with its plain surface, slender piers and pointed arches, wholly without ornament, it is in the best Arab tradition of modesty and proportion. Opposite this colonnade sit the porters. They are Hebronites, and form a sort of unofficial guild. If you want anything fetched or carried it is to them that you must apply. Whether it be a piano or an antique capital, they know just how it should be handled, but for your peace of mind it is better not to watch the actual process. The Arab College left its buildings before the war. One is now the Public Works Department, the others house a private school. In front of the main building has been built a row of shops and offices. On what used to be our playground there are houses, shops, a laundry-and-moneychanger, in whose window the clean garments vie with the clean notes, an air-line company, the Cleopatra Studio and the National Restaurant, where you get the best Arab food in Jerusalem. Opposite the old Arab College on the other side of the street are the Queen of Sheba souvenir shop, the Shahrazad Buffet and Tea-room, and a whole posse of tourist agencies, their windows bright with posters alluring you to fly to half the countries of four continents. All these offices and shops are refugees. In days gone by, the oldest of them had premises inside or just outside the Jaffa Gate. Later, they moved up into the boulevards and avenues of the New Jerusalem.

Their buildings are still there. So were their stock-in-trade, so were their bank accounts. They lost the lot. With a resilience that argues strongly in favour of Arab enterprise and durability, they have all started again. But it is on a much smaller scale. They will tell you that business is not what it used to be in the old days; and they wonder whether it ever will be again. Meanwhile, this is our commercial quarter, this little triangle that used to echo only to the voices of the teacher and the pupil.

You can hardly see the American School, the trees now are so tall and thick. The Chief Secretary's house is another hotel, the lovely old Arab house part of police headquarters; and on what remains of the playground a friend of mine is building a cinema. It will be a good cinema, because he is a good architect; but we already have one, all too near the cathedral, and another is being put up only a few hundred yards away from it. You would think we could hardly fill a third; but in an age which worships the shadow more willingly than the substance, I have no doubt that, poor as we are, all three shrines will be thronged continually with ardent congregations.

Only the pine tree remains aloof—more aloof than ever; because it now stands within the enclosing wall of the Rockefeller Museum and its grounds, which cover ten acres. The Museum is beautiful within and without. It is the gift of a munificent American. It was designed by an Englishman of genius. In 1927, Mr. John D. Rockefeller Junior offered a large sum of money to the Egyptian Government for the building of a national museum of antiquities. The offer was refused, perhaps as being offensive to "national pride." Mr. Rockefeller then offered up to $2,000,000 to the Palestine Government, who of course gratefully accepted it. Half of the sum was invested to provide an endowment, and the other was used for the construction of the Museum. It was the good fortune of the Palestine Government at that time to have as its chief architect one of the most original and gifted builders of his day, Mr. Austen Harrison. He designed schools, law courts, offices for them. He also built the fine Government House which still looks down, rather like Lot's wife, upon the city which is lost to it. In most cases, even when the Government was quite well off, Harrison was skimped for money. He was living in an age when money itself was considered to be of more importance than what you can buy with it. But here, in the museum, he was working not for a government, nor a treasurer, but for a patron, and a munificent and enlightened patron at that. The resulting building is one which has added a new lustre to the long tradition of Jerusalem's architecture. Its galleries are perfectly lighted, its lecture theatre has ideal acoustics, its reading-room invites study. All the fittings, such as showcases, windows, and floor-coverings are of the best.

The building consists of a central block built round a court-yard, with two triangular wings. The whole composition is sur-mounted, as you can see in the picture, by an octagonal tower, the inside of which is a circular dome over the hall. The great tower Psephinus which stood somewhere near the Russian Cathedral on the Jaffa Road, was also octagonal, Josephus tells us (*Wars*, V, iv, 3), and I imagine that it must have looked rather like Harrison's octagon. The courtyard is rectangular. On three sides of it there is a cloister; at the west end is a recess lined with tiles, patterned in blue and green and white, in which is a fountain. The recess is capped by a dome, above which appear the topmost branches of the famous old pine tree. The blue sky, the tree and the tiles harmonize perfectly with the lavender bushes which line the sunk pool on the axis of the rectangle, and with the lotuses which float upon its waters. Above the pointed arches of the cloisters, there are bas-reliefs by Eric Gill. The whole composition is living and beautiful, a modern expression of the architecture of repose, of which the Arabs in their hey-day were the masters.

Like most things Palestinian, Palestine archæology is austere. Not for Palestine nor for Jerusalem were the "gay religions full of pomp and gold" which Milton denounced in her neighbours. Not here will you find the glittering relics which enrich the museums of Cairo and Baghdad. And besides, the history of Palestine having been so stormy, nearly everything in the country has at one time or another been either broken or stolen. We must not look there-fore in the Rockefeller Museum for "objects," in the old-fashioned sense of the term.

Archæology is one of the few sciences that has gone up in the world in our time. Many sciences have gone down, and have been prostituted to base and evil ends, such as the invention of more destructive bombs, or more lethal poisons. But not so archæology. A hundred years ago, the science, and the word, were quite new. It was still the aim of the archæologist to collect, if necessary by guile or force, rarer and more costly objects than his rivals. Honest and public-spirited men such as Lord Elgin, who out of his own fortune had found the money, never wholly repaid, to save from destruction and preserve for posterity the unique marble sculptures of the Parthenon, were few. You have only to read the story of the quarrels, the stand-up fights indeed, which took place between the French and English agents on the mounds of ancient Assyria, to see what archæology meant in those days. The same sort of raiding went on for the same sort of prizes in Egypt. And when the loot was secured, it was drawn in triumph to the national temple, the British Museum, and Rossetti wrote an ode about it. It made you feel, not how great the Egyptians or the Assyrians had once been, but how great England now was.

That kind of archæology is a thing of the past. Modern archæologists co-operate internationally just as post offices do. The change is largely the work of a Briton, Sir Flinders Petrie, for it was he who made the discovery (among many others) that the most durable of man's earthly works are not silver nor gold, but pots. You can break the pot, but you cannot destroy it. So, if you can trace back the pots of mankind, even their broken ones, you can trace their history. It seems rather a come-down from winged bulls and marble friezes. But this study of potsherds has taught us far more than ever they did. Archæology has become almost a pure science. The archæologist talks a rare and dispassionate language, like those who study the higher mathematics. And he derives the same pure joy from his labours and calculations. In these last years, the isotopes have come to help in the work of dating, and when archæologists are assembled, besides talk of pots, you will hear mention made of "carbon fourteen."

You can see what a difference this new approach to archæology has made to Palestine. Palestine, so poor in so much, is exceedingly rich in pottery, because so many different people have invaded the country. Only last Sunday, I was at Dothan, where an enormous *tel* has long awaited excavation. This year, an American expedition from Wheaton College has made a beginning. So far, they have only dug on one part of one side: but there, within a few feet of the surface, they have come upon walls and pottery of the Middle Bronze age. Nothing later is laid over it. There it lies, so near to us in space, but separated from us by more than three thousand years in time. That is the sort of archæology which Palestine provides. And the days of the Mandate were, as Dr. Albright, the great American archæologist who was formerly Director of the American School, has written, the golden age of Palestine archæology.

It is in this spirit that we must approach the Rockefeller Museum. Unless, that is, we are archæologists ourselves. If we are, then we shall find laboratories, and photography rooms, and studies and every necessary aid and apparatus, even down to an infra-red camera. But it is for the layman that the galleries have been arranged. There are two of them, the South and the North. Each is divided into bays, dealing with one particular period. The periods themselves are clearly shown by large inscriptions painted in red on the wall above each bay, with big photographs to show typical sites of the period in question. For instance, the first bay in the South Gallery (which takes you from the Stone Age to the Late Bronze) is labelled: "Palæolithic Age, 200,000-12,000 years ago," and underneath are large pictures of the famous caves near Athlit, below Mount Carmel, where Miss Garrod found such a rich treasure of relics of primitive man between 1929 and 1934, and of another similar cave called al Kafzeh, south of Nazareth. The last bay in the North Gallery (which takes you from Early Iron Age to the Byzantines) is labelled: "Byzantine Period, A.D. 330-640," and the pictures are of the floor mosaics, about A.D. 540 from the Church of St. Peter and Paul at Jerash, now at Yale University, and of the fifth-century North Church at Isbeita, in northern Sinai. There are a few exhibits, and fine ones too, of the Crusader and Islamic period; but they have not yet been classified. The famous lintels from the Church of the Holy Sepulchre are in a little room apart.

You do not need a catalogue: as you enter each gallery, you pick up a copy of a "Gallery Book" which tells you all about each exhibit. If you use the guides, the objects, chiefly of pottery, in these two galleries will give you as good an outline of the history of man as you will find anywhere in the world.

I think the most tantalizing exhibit of all is a temporary one. Everyone has heard of the Dead Sea Scrolls, those ancient copies of the Scriptures and other ecclesiastical texts which were found in caves on the north-west shores of the Dead Sea some five years ago. Since that time, many other expeditions, both official and unofficial, have been made to discover more. These efforts have been successful. Not long ago the Jordan Government announced that it had allocated £15,000 for the purchase of scrolls in private hands— an outstanding example of putting first things first for such a poor

PAGE 29 *(Museum)*

The Rockefeller Museum, from the City Wall.

PAGE 30 *(Museum)*

The Rockefeller Museum, the Cloister pool.

PAGE 35 *(Elia)*

The Garden of Gethsemane and the Cedron Valley looking towards Siloam. The view has changed but little since the days of our Lord. The lower courses of the great eastern wall of the Temple Area and the monumental tomb (miscalled Absalom's Pillar) were both there in His day.

(*C. Silvester*)

The Church of the Nations in the Garden of Gethsemane from the west.

A souvenir postcard printed in honour of the Kaiser's visit to Jerusalem in 1898. The German text reads: "Peoples of Europe, guard your most holy possessions. Wilhelm, I.R."

exchequer. "Private hands" in this case means chiefly Bedouin of the Ta'amre tribe, in whose territory the caves lie. In days gone by, when there was a frontier between the east and west banks of the Jordan and the Dead Sea, these poor nomads made a scanty living as contrabandists. But with the merging of both banks in the Kingdom of Jordan they found their livelihood gone. So the scrolls have been a godsend to them. Most of those they have found have now been acquired by the proper authorities. But in March 1952 an official expedition, conducted by the American School, the Ecole Biblique and the Government Department of Antiquities, and led by Père Roland de Vaux, found in a cave at Khirbet Qumran, near the north end of the Dead Sea, two scrolls of bronze or copper. Apparently, to judge by nail holes along the edge of one of them, these scrolls were originally plates, affixed to the wall of some building. When its owners had taken to flight, they had rolled up their precious texts, hoping to take them along with them. But they were found too much of an encumbrance, and left for safety in a cave. That was in A.D. 133, perhaps, during the revolt of Bar Cochba. No one came for them until last year. They now lie on cotton wool in a special case in the museum. You can see that they bear writing in square Hebrew characters, but the writing is on the under side of the scrolls. Together, the two scrolls are 2·40 metres long; but what they say is still a mystery, for as yet no one knows how to unroll them without destroying them. One eminent scholar has told me that he thinks these two scrolls, or plates, must have come from the Temple itself, partly because he thinks he has discerned, through the back of the metal, the words "shekel" and "sacrifice," and partly because they were evidently of such sanctity that even in disaster and flight an effort was made to preserve them.

As you leave the Museum, you pause in the doorway. Before you is a spacious garden, brilliant with flowers, for the Curator, Mr. Yusuf Saad, is not only a genial expert in his profession, but also an enthusiastic gardener. Whatever the season, the lawns are green and the beds alive with colour. The garden is framed with a belt of olive trees. They look so big and strong that you wonder how they can be only twenty years old. The truth is that they are far older. When the Museum was building the experts said that you could not transplant grown-up olive trees; the fellahin said you could. The Museum authorities wisely took the advice of the fellahin, and there stands the grove to-day.

c

The Museum is an oasis of calm. You come out of it into the familiar glare of Jerusalem, to gaze once again on the familiar scene, on the walls, the domes, and beyond them the Mount of Olives. It seems sadder than ever, after the calm of those sleeping centuries within. And yet you feel refreshed. If man can do and suffer so much and yet preserve the line of his life unbroken, then why should man fix upon this particular bank and shoal of time rather than upon any other, either to hope too much, or to despair?

For the rest, our northern suburb is much as it was. The scanty remains of the olive grove by St. George's playground now accommodate a cement brickmaker's yard; and to the west, near the Armenian pottery, a smith is busy beating old tar barrels into roofing sheets. And St. George's School playground is still there. But it is being surrounded with a wall. For over fifty years it has been an open space, across which anyone was free to walk or to look. But now, such is the pressure brought about by our constriction, that unless it is enclosed, it is in danger of ceasing to be a playground altogether, and of becoming the haunt of dirt-track racers and amateur mechanics. Beyond St. George's is the American Colony. To the east, at the head of the Cedron valley, is the Wadi Joz, crowded with houses—small houses, which are all that Jerusalem can afford now. On each one, affliction and loss have laid their hand. To the north, on the Nablus road, you pass as of old the Nashashibi quarter, so called because it held the pleasant palaces of that family. Now, many of the houses are consulates. The British and American Consulates are nearer the city, the British being just opposite St. George's School, and the American a few yards to the south, separated from ours by the Y.M.C.A. The American Consulate has a little garden as brilliant as that of the Museum: it is a public amenity, which soothes the eyes all the more by contrast with the grisly desolation of no-man's-land at its back.

There are other bright gardens in Jerusalem. There is that of the Bishop's house, and that of the American Colony; beyond all, apart and above, there is the Garden of Gethsemane. Father Eugene Hoad has made this one of the most beautiful gardens in the world. More than fifty years ago, when it was being laid out, it was supplied with plants and flowers from Bishop Blyth's garden. This year, Father Eugene, always the most generous of men, gave us not only seeds for our own gardens, but lilies for the High Altar of St. George's Cathedral on Easter Day. Lilies from his garden, too, were included with the wild flowers from Palestine which were flown to Washington at Easter, to adorn the Presbyterian National Church in which President Eisenhower worshipped. The most brilliant part of the Garden of Gethsemane is the little plot among the old olive trees just north of the church. But the most serenely affecting portion of it lies just west of the road, down in the very valley of the Cedron itself. Here, you are alone with Jerusalem. The eastern wall of the Temple Area towers above you, just as it did in Our Lord's day. And, below us in the valley, we see as He and His disciples saw, the tomb which is called Absalom's pillar. At our feet, in the spring time, runs the little stream soon to be joined with "Siloa's brook that flows fast by the oracle of God" as Milton describes it. On our left hand, through the glade of olives, framed by the velvet of cypress trees, glow the golden mosaics of the Church of the Nations, the shrine that the Franciscans have built, on the site of a Byzantine basilica, over the Rock of the Agony, and above it the seven gilded domes of the Church of St. Mary Magdalen, built in 1888 by the Emperor Alexander III of Russia. Up on the slopes below the walls, they still plant and reap barley, as they always did. It is a country garden, wherein you hear only the call of the pigeons and the hum of the bees.

This cult of gardens, and their increasing beauty in Jerusalem, is one of the legacies of Britain. Not so much a legacy, as a requital. We are inclined to think that the English garden always existed. Bacon praises gardens, Shakespeare is full of flowers, and more than one of his scenes is set in a garden. But the garden as we know it, and as Jerusalem has come to know it, is a later product. "The Pleasure and Use of Gardens were unknown to our great Grandfathers; they were contented with potherbs; and did mind chiefly their Stables. But in the time of King Charles II, gardening was much improved and became common." John Aubrey, whose words I have cited, tells us that in the days of King Charles II, thousands of exotic plants were acclimatized in England. But the importations had started earlier, and it was from the Levant that they chiefly came. It was probably the Crusaders who took home with them the hollyhock, or holy hock (*Malva benedicta*), so called because it came from the Holy Land where it grows wild. Ogier Ghislain de Busbecq, the Flemish traveller who became the Emperor Ferdinand's ambassador to Suleiman the Magnificent, not only wrote a classic description of the almost liturgical veneration with which the Turks of Constantinople regarded their tulips, but introduced tulip bulbs into his native Low Countries. "Jessamines," Aubrey tells us, "came into England with Mary, the Queen-Mother," Henrietta Maria. They came from Persia, *via* the Levant. In Palestine, until recently, "they were contented with potherbs; and did mind chiefly their Stables." But now, as in the England of good King Charles II, "gardening is much improved and has become common." Violets, sweet peas, larkspurs, roses, marigolds, stocks, gillyflowers and snapdragons—these and many more have repaid the debt of the hollyhock, the jasmine and the tulip.

I said our northern suburb was much as it was: but there is one notable difference. We are no longer a capital city. Jerusalem has not always been a capital, by any means; on the other hand, it has in its day been the capital of pagan, Jewish, Christian and Moslem states—the only city in the world which has; in the latter days of Ottoman rule, Jerusalem was an independent Sanjak (i.e. it took its orders direct from Constantinople, and not through any provincial governor, or *wali*) under a *mutaserrif* of the first-class; and for thirty years it was the capital of British-administered Palestine. Now, we are a provincial town, with provincial offices. We have a mutaserrif, just like Nablus, Hebron, Kerak or Irbid. But he has his office in a small hired house in a little street behind the American School. So with the law courts, and the other government departments; they are all branch offices, in little side-streets, and often enough in little rooms up obscure stairways. The Moslem Sharia Law Court, which deals with personal affairs, is perched on the top of the *"Ecce Homo"* arch. Gone are the great Departments, the spacious, bustling headquarters, where citizens confronted the law's delay and the insolence of office. Gone are the directors, and the deputy directors, the collectors, the inspectors, the controllers and the secretaries. Gone, too, is the intrigue, the political gossip, which formerly made a Jerusalem conversation like a Disraeli novel without the wit. All the great world has left us and gone to 'Amman; and it is to 'Amman we must go if we want to see a minister or a member of parliament. Our present state, it is true, makes for quiet, for a certain detachment which accords well with a holy city. Nevertheless, we regret our former condition "for the comfortless troubles' sake of the needy, and because of the deep sighing of the poor."

One final note about dress. The veil has almost disappeared. So have "shorts"; so has the tarbush, or fez, a Turkish importation of

Austrian origin, which thirty years ago was worn even by pupils in class. Only on formal occasions is it now generally seen. For the rest, men either go bare-headed, or wear the traditional Arab head-dress, the white or coloured kerchief surmounted by the twin black woollen circlets, which is one of the most practical and becoming forms of headgear yet devised by man.

Chapter Three

Thy prophets have seen vain and foolish things for thee. . . . All that pass by clap their hands at thee; they hiss and wag their head at the daughter of Jerusalem, saying, Is this the city that men call The perfection of beauty, The joy of the whole earth?
LAMENTATIONS ii. 14, 15.

BEFORE we enter the Historic City of Jerusalem, let us pause to examine some of its gates, for Jerusalem is still one of the world's most excellent walled and gated cities.

The bisection of the town has deprived the Old City of the use of three of its gates, namely, the New Gate, the Jaffa Gate and the Zion Gate. The New Gate is merely a perforation of the city wall. It was built in 1887, in the reign of 'Abdul-hamid II, after whom it was originally named. It was recently blocked up with a barrier of stone and concrete. The other two gates are more venerable. The Zion Gate gave access to the group of buildings known as "Nebi Daud," the only structures outside the walls until the building of Bishop Gobat's School in 1853. It is related that the great Sultan Suleiman the Magnificent, who gave the walls their present aspect between 1536 and 1542, commanded his architect to bring Nebi Daud once more within their circuit (as it had been from 1192 to 1219 and again for a period at the beginning of the next century), and when he failed to do so, ordered his execution. The Zion Gate, or Gate of Nebi Daud, thus had some importance. Nebi Daud means the Prophet David. There is no credible tradition that the tomb of David is in the vicinity, and the ascription goes back only to the tenth or eleventh century. It is first mentioned, curiously enough, by a Moslem writer, Abu Ishaq al-Tha'leby (b. 1035) in his "History of the Prophets," and in such a way as to suggest that the tradition had existed for some time. When the Crusaders entered Jerusalem, in 1099, Raymond d'Aguilers, chaplain to the Count of Toulouse, mentions the Tomb of David as "among the holy things" in the Church of Sion. But the definite, circumstantial, localization of the Tomb must be ascribed to Benjamin of Tudela, a learned Rabbi of Navarre, who visited Jerusalem in 1163, and wrote an account in Hebrew of his travels. This is what he says:

"On Mount Zion are the graves of the House of David and of the kings that came after him. The site cannot, however, be identified, inasmuch as 15 years ago a wall of the church on Mount Zion fell in and the patriarch commanded the superintendent to restore the church, saying to him: 'Use the stones of the old wall of Zion for the building of the church'; and he did so. He hired about 20 workmen at fixed wages, who brought the stones from the base of the wall of Zion. Among these men were two friends who were confederates, and on a certain day the one entertained the other; after their meal they returned to their work, when the superintendent said to them: 'Why have you tarried?' They answered: 'Why need you complain! When our mates go to their meal we will do our work.' When the dinner-time arrived and their fellow-workmen had gone to their meal, they removed the stones and discovered the entrance to the cave. Thereupon one said to the other: 'Let us go in and see if any money is to be found there!' They entered the cave and found a chamber resting upon pillars of marble overlaid with silver and gold. In front was a chamber of gold and a sceptre and crown. This was the sepulchre of King David. On the left thereof was the sepulchre of King Solomon in like fashion. And then followed the sepulchres of all the kings that were buried there belonging to the kings of Judah. Closed coffers were also there, the contents of which no man knows. The two men essayed to enter the chamber when a fierce wind came forth from the entrance and smote them. They fell to the ground like dead men, and there they lay until evening. And there came another wind crying like a human voice: 'Arise and come forth from this place.' So the men hastily went forth in terror and they came unto the patriarch and related these facts to him. Thereupon the patriarch sent for Rabbi Abraham, the pious recluse of Constantine, who was one of the mourners of Jerusalem, and to him he related all these things according to the report of the two men who had come from the cave. Then Rabbi Abraham replied: 'These are the sepulchres of the House of David belonging to the Kings of Judah, and to-morrow let us enter the cave, I and you and these men, and find out what is to be seen there.' And on the morrow they sent for the two men and found each of them lying upon his bed terror-stricken. The men said: 'We will not enter there, for the Lord does not desire that any man should see the place.' Then the patriarch gave orders that the place should be closed up and hidden from the sight of man unto this day. All this was told me by the said Rabbi Abraham" (trans. Marcus N. Adler, *P.E.F.S.*, 1894).

Such is the sole "evidence" for the identification of the site of Nebi Daud with the tomb of King David. We notice that the first thing Rabbi Benjamin says about the site is that "it cannot be identified." Secondly, it is not even clear that the so-called tomb was on the site of the present shrine. The workmen were digging not at the church but at the base of the original wall of Zion, and it was presumably here that they found the cave, which led them to the hall. The tale itself might have come from *The Arabian Nights*. It was the report of two workmen who were confederates. No one else is said to have approached the cave, and they only once.

Where the tomb of David is, no one knows to this day. We learn from 1 Kings ii. 10 that David "was buried in the city of David." The site is unidentified; but from Nehemiah iii. 15, 16, it seems clear that it was near the stairs that went up from Siloam to Ophel. What we do know is that David's sepulchre was in existence at the time of the first Pentecost (Acts ii. 29), and that its site was known at least down to the time of Hadrian (Dion Cassius, LXIX, 14). Josephus tells us of two attempts to rob the tomb. The first was in the second century B.C., when "Hyrcanus opened the sepulchre of David, who was the richest of all kings, and took thence about three thousand talents in money" (*Wars*, I, ii, 5). The second occurred when Herod, having heard about Hyrcanus' raid, and that there was still more treasure left, "opened that sepulchre by night and went into it. . . . As for any money, he found none, as Hyrcanus had done, but that furniture of gold, and those precious goods that were laid up there; all of which he took away. However, he had a great desire to make a more diligent search, and to go further in, even as far as the bodies of David and Solomon; where two of his guards were slain, by a flame that burst out upon those that went in, as the report was. So he was terribly affrighted, and sent out, and built a propitiatory monument of that fright he had been in; and this of white stone, at the mouth of the sepulchre, and that at a great expense also" (*Antiquities*, XVI, vii, 1). There are some curious similarities between the report of Herod's escapade and that of the two workmen, which may well have struck the learned

Rabbi. Surely also he (and the Patriarch too) should have known the story, which is preserved not only by four Christian fathers but by the pagan historian Ammianus Marcellinus, that Julian the Apostate's attempt to restore the Jewish temple in 362 was frustrated by "balls of fire which burst out near the foundations"? Yet Rabbi Abraham seems to have accepted the workmen's testimony without corroboration, and, as he told Rabbi Benjamin fifteen years later, to have pronounced without more ado that the genuine tomb of David had been found. At the time of the alleged discovery, the Crusaders ruled Jerusalem. Benjamin of Tudela expressly tells us that Jews were allowed to visit the Western Wall of the Temple area to pray there. But the site of the Temple itself (the Dome of the Rock) was a Christian church, the church of the Knights Templar, in fact. Rabbi Abraham is described as "one of the mourners for Jerusalem." He may well have felt, as others may have felt after him, that at a time when the site of his Temple was in alien hands, a shrine on "Mount Zion" would be a convenient surrogate. Nor would the Patriarch have scorned to acquire another "Holy Place."

The chief, and oldest, association of these buildings is with the Cœnaculum, or Room of the Last Supper. The chamber now so called is not older than the fourteenth century, but the Christian tradition goes back at least a thousand years earlier. In the fourth century, before the building of the Church of the Holy Sepulchre, the Church of the Apostles, the world's first parish church, stood on "Mount Zion" on the site of the house of John Mark (Acts xii. 12). About 1130, the Crusaders rebuilt this church, and it is their structure which forms the core of the present Nebi Daud. The upper storey is hallowed as the room of the Last Supper, or "Cœnaculum." We have seen how the vaults below became associated with the "Tomb of David."

Although it was a Moslem writer who, as we have seen, first mentions the tradition that the tomb of David was on "Mount Zion," Moslems generally (like some Christians before them) held that King David was buried either on the Mount of Olives or in Bethlehem, the "City of David." It was only in the fifteenth century that the Moslems came to accept the "Mount Zion" tradition, but having accepted it, they defended it with tenacious veneration.

From 1333 to the sixteenth century, the Cœnaculum was part of a convent of the Franciscans. They were expelled in 1547, since when Nebi Daud has been a Moslem holy place, a consecrated mosque, to which however Christians were allowed access. When, during the adolescence of Fascism, in 1928, the Prince of Piedmont visited Jerusalem, an attempt was made to introduce the innocent prince into the chamber with his shoes on, in the hope of re-establishing a Christian claim to it. Through the vigilance of the British District Commissioner, the attempt was foiled. My own recollections of Nebi Daud are very pleasant. During Ramadan, as I shall tell later, it was the custom to pay visits upon Moslem friends by night. Twenty-five years ago, the *Mutaweli*, or Guardian of Nebi Daud, was a sheikh of great charm, a wealthy and benevolent man, who liked to make his many friends as happy as he could. During Ramadan, it was his custom to bring from Egypt one of the finest readers of the Quran in that country, to read to him and his callers. For me, he would choose the Sura, or chapter, relating to the Virgin Mary and the birth of Christ.

It may well be understood that the exclusion of this shrine, so dear to both Christians and Moslems, from part of the city in which they live, is a sad blow to them; and the sight of the Zion Gate, shut and barred and guarded, is a bitter reminder of it.

But to Britons, the present state of the Jaffa Gate is a source of more than sorrow, it is a standing reproach. For it is with the entry of British armed forces, and the inauguration of the brief period of British rule in Palestine, that this gate must for ever be associated in their minds and thoughts.

Traditionally, it is the Damascus Gate, not the Jaffa Gate, which was the gate of honour. During the Turkish régime, important persons, a new governor of the city, for instance, would enter by the Damascus Gate. The present structure stands on the remnants of a much older gate which we hope to examine later on. What we see to-day is the work of the Sultan Suleiman the Magnificent, who completed it, as an inscription records, in the year 944 of the Hegira, that is, the year beginning 10 June, 1537, during which in England the Pilgrimage of Grace was being barbarously suppressed. It represents the fine flower of Turkish architecture, and indeed the last great flowering of Islamic architecture in the Levant. In its style and ornament, the Damascus Gate is very different from the Jaffa Gate; yet by the irony of history, its symbolism is much the same, for both gates have celebrated false dawns and frustrated hopes.

The reign of Suleiman marked the zenith of the Ottoman power.

At his death, the Turkish Empire extended from the frontiers of Persia well nigh to those of Germany. His father, Selim I, in his short reign of eight years, had almost doubled the area of the Ottoman dominions. By crushing the Mamelukes, the strange slave dynasty which had ruled in Egypt since 1250, Selim acquired control over Palestine. He also obtained the title of Caliph, and so became the spiritual head of Islam. The Mongols had put an end to the Caliphate of Baghdad in 1258, since when the titular holders of that office had lived as impotent and indigent shadows in Cairo, under the protection of their Egyptian rulers. Mutawakkil, the last of the line, surrendered his title to his new master. That was in 1517. Three years later, Selim died, and his son Suleiman became Sultan-Caliph at the age of twenty-five.

For forty-six years, Suleiman was to make Turkey respected, admired and feared, in Europe and Asia, by land and sea. He seemed destined to inaugurate a new age of glory. The inscriptions he placed on his monuments proclaim his confidence. You may read them still, carved in the beautiful Arabic script called *neskh*, on the fountains with which he embellished Jerusalem. He is therein described as "Lord of the necks of the nations, Sultan of the Greeks, the Arabs and the Persians, the Glory of Islam and the Muslims, the Shadow of God in the Two Worlds, Protector of the Two Noble Sanctuaries, may God eternize his kingdom and authority, and prolong his justice and benevolence." He took part in thirteen great campaigns, ten in Europe and three in Asia. He codified the laws of the Empire, whence he is called in Arabic "al-Qanuni," the law-giver. For forty-six years this great man reigned. He lived to correspond with Queen Elizabeth I, whom he addressed as "a refreshing shower of rain." Well might he think that his work would survive him, that the foundations of future greatness were truly laid, and that his buildings would proclaim it to the world. For he was a great builder. As Caliph, he naturally felt a special concern for Jerusalem. Not only did he restore the walls in the form in which we now see them, he also repaired the Dome of the Rock, replacing the external mosaics, which time had proved to be incapable of withstanding the fierce winter storms, with the glorious integument of coloured tiles and contrasting marbles which has ever since given to the Dome its unique and distinctive aspect. In the Damascus Gate, he determined to erect a monument that should move every wayfarer who entered Jerusalem to admiration and praise.

In its design, Suleiman made two innovations. First, he was determined to make a clean break with the degenerate and over-ornamented style of the later Mamelukes. One of the astonishing qualities of all arts, sculpture or building, painting or music, is the speed with which perfection follows the initial invention, and the long-drawn-out proliferation of decay. Muslim architecture is no exception to this humiliating rule. You have only to look at the *Sebil*, or drinking fountain, of Qaitbai (A.D. 1482) which stands just inside the Gate of the Chain in the Haram esh Sherif, to realize how what was once strong and simple has been turned to favour and to prettiness. It looks more like a tea-cosy than a dome. For his new gate, therefore, Suleiman reverted to the older Islamic tradition, which depended on balance of mass, freedom of line, and proportion of plane with recess rather than on applied ornament. Ornament there is, but it is wholly subordinated to the structure. Secondly, Suleiman knew that the day of fortified gates was over. He lived in the age of artillery, of which he possessed one of the most effective forces of his time. Therefore, he built his gate mainly for show. He knew that though it might exclude thieves and raiders, it could not repel a well-equipped besieger. In view of this limitation, his achievement is all the more remarkable. If you look at the gate from the back, that is from inside the walls, you realize what a façade it is in its upper range. It looks almost like a stage set. But from the front, what strength it suggests, what grace. Its crenellation is light and airy, the belvederes are poised without effort, and the great pointed arch proclaims the function of the structure with quiet assurance. One of the most interesting details of the Gate are the plain round bosses on its northern face. It is sometimes assumed that these were intended to be carved, and that the work was never finished, but this is not so. These bosses are the vestigial representations of the columns that were often employed in antiquity (and by the Crusaders, as, for example, at Askalon and Byblos) to give strength to a wall, by acting as ties from the outer to the inner face. The ends of such columns extended to the outer surface, and so were clearly visible. The bosses on the Damascus Gate (and on the other gates and bastions of Suleiman's restoration) are simply carved on the stones that bear them; but they are intended to recall the old and familiar tie-columns, and so to induce an impression of strength. Genuine examples of these tie-columns may be seen in the east wall of the Haram esh Sherif. It was probably the presence of these that induced

Suleiman's architect to use the imitative bosses in his own work.

Such is the monument by which the greatest of the Turkish Sultans wished to commemorate his greatness, the liberation of the Holy Land from the yoke of the effete and unstable Mamelukes, and the inauguration of a Golden Age for Palestine. But alas for his hopes. When he died in 1566, he was succeeded by his son Selim, who is known to history as "the Sot." The new age never dawned, the long twilight of decay set in, and for nearly three hundred years not a single building of any note was erected in Jerusalem. When, in the early nineteenth century, the British wanted to build a consulate in Jerusalem, so wholly lost was the tradition of the Moslem builders of the great age, that it was necessary to bring masons from Malta. What had been designed as a beginning, proved to be but an end.

Such is the story of the Damascus Gate.

The Jaffa Gate has always been the gate of the foreigners. It is the only gate which faces west. It has had many names. It used to be called the Bethlehem Gate, and the Gate of the Mihrab (or Prayer Alcove) from the oratory of David in the adjacent castle. It is now called in Arabic the Gate of the Friend, that is, of Abraham, who was the friend of God, because the road to Hebron, where Abraham is buried, starts from this gate. An inscription which confronts those who enter, reminds us that "there is no God but God, and Abraham is his friend." But two of its most significant ancient names were the Gate of the Merchants, and the Gate of the Pilgrims. Always, since the city came under Moslem rule, it is in, through, and around this gate that contact has been made with the outside world. There was a time, indeed, when pilgrims might enter through no other gate. During the last century, when the west impinged more and more upon the city, it was at first just inside the Jaffa Gate, and later in a new suburb outside it, that the newcomers established themselves. With Victorian travellers, as with their predecessors, it was the routine to enter the city by the Jaffa Gate or to camp outside it if they arrived after dusk. For the gates of the city were shut at sunset, and also on Friday between noon and one, when the garrison were at prayer. By the end of the nineteenth century, some of the gates were still shut at night; but by then it had become the custom for the Jaffa Gate to remain open, so that those who lived in the new suburbs could communicate freely with their friends within the city.

The apotheosis of the Jaffa Gate, its entry by the man who seemed to be the world's most important foreigner, occurred in the year

1898. For reasons which do not belong to this chapter, England had by then lost to Germany the primacy of prestige and influence which she had formerly held in the Levant. It was the German Emperor himself who was paying a visit. And what a visit it was to be. Since 1816, when the Princess of Wales had visited the Holy City, many a European royalty had followed her; among them the next Prince of Wales, afterwards King Edward VII, his two sons, of whom the younger was to be King George V, the Austrian Emperor, and the King of Prussia, the Kaiser's grandfather. Now his grandson was to come as a reigning emperor, as The Reigning Emperor, in the eyes of many both in Europe and Asia. He was to be acclaimed as a sovereign, and as the Rising Star of the East.

The visit has passed into legend. And it deserved to; because in honour of the Kaiser, Palestine and Jerusalem were not only thoroughly cleaned up, they were largely renovated. The following is a short list of the works which were carried out before the Kaiser and his Empress arrived. A pier was constructed at Haifa for them to land at; the road from Haifa to Jaffa was made passable for carriages, and the bridges were repaired. Carriage roads were constructed from Jaffa to Jerusalem, and from Jerusalem to Bethlehem. In Bethlehem itself, new streets were opened, houses being torn down to give access to the German Lutheran church. A road was constructed to the Mount of Olives. The electric telegraph was extended from Jerusalem to Jericho, in case the All-Highest might wish to communicate with Europe from the city of palm trees. (As it turned out, he did not go there, so the telegraph was not used. One day the line was found cut, and thirty persons were imprisoned.) The old sheds which covered David and Christian streets were taken down, and the shop fronts were painted and whitewashed. In the Haram, the stonework of the arcades of the platform was plastered and painted in fantastic designs (since fortunately removed, though they are to be seen in old photographs), and the front of the Aqsa Mosque was daubed with yellow wash. For the first time, some of the streets outside the city were provided with lamps, which were kept burning all night—an extravagant innovation. The road to Nebi Daud, where the Kaiser was to take possession of the land on which the Church of the Dormition now stands, was widened. The beggars were rounded up and packed off to surrounding villages. Even the dogs were diminished. Never before or since has Palestine seen such a programme of public works and improvements carried out so speedily. And all for one man.

The Jaffa Gate was naturally included in the general renaissance. Up till then, no carriage way into the city had existed. But a plan had been drawn up for the construction of a broad, paved street, suitable for wheeled traffic, all the way from the Jaffa Gate to the Haram. Mercifully, it proved to be too costly. But two portions of it were made for the Kaiser. One, which puzzles visitors to this day, was the street outside the Lutheran Church of the Redeemer. Why, you wonder, is there this brief section of western street, wide enough for two carriages to pass, and with kerbstones and side walks, in the middle of the alleys and arches of the Old City? The answer is that it was part of the great plan. The street has been in existence for fifty-five years now, and has never yet known the touch of a wheel. But at the Jaffa Gate, a carriage road was not merely opened, but was used for fifty years. The top of the curtain wall that joined the gate to the Citadel was taken off, the ditch filled in, some other small walls removed, and a paved road laid down.

The Kaiser's visit to Jerusalem has become a type for all time of "hubris" and vainglory. I have before me as I write an album of photographs which make me doubt whether the half has been told. The streets are ablaze with Turkish and German flags, triumphal arches have been erected at intervals, the most splendid being that of the Jewish community, bearing in Hebrew and in German the inscription, "Blessed is he that cometh in the name of the Eternal. We greet him from the House of the Eternal." You can hardly see the street for decoration, and the long parade of brilliant, tightly-buttoned uniforms, gay with stars and ribbons. How pathetic they look, those important little men. They are all dead now, so that the uniforms seem more enduring than their wearers. It is a stifling day. The women cower beneath their sunshades. The men sweat with such dignity as they can summon up. There are scores of Turkish troops, a detachment of German sailors and the tall Uhlan body-guard, in their splendid white uniforms. A brass band, each player a Laocoön struggling with a vast serpent, goes before. The cavalcade is mounted. It is preceded by Arabs in their picturesque garb, carrying lances. But the most "Oriental" figure is that of the Kaiser himself. He, too, is in white. On his head he wears a shining helmet, surmounted by an eagle so large that you wonder how it can balance on so small a person. Its wings are outspread, as though it did not feel quite secure. From beneath this confection descends a long cloak, covering the neck, shoulders and torso. It was made, so an eye-witness has told me, of white silk shot with silver, so that it shimmered theatrically to every movement of its wearer. The Jaffa Gate is festooned with bunting, flanked by poles wreathed in foliage topped with spearheads which glint in the October sun. Above the gate is the most ominous-looking fowl imaginable. Its wings extend from one side of the great gate to the other. Its talons clutch the parapet from which it leans menacingly over the crowds below. From its gaping beak protrudes a long, writhing tongue. On its head is a great crown, and on top of the crown is a cross.

Such was the setting for the great entry. To the Holy Sepulchre, to the new Church of the Redeemer, of which his grandfather had laid the foundation stone, to the Mount of Olives, to St. George's Cathedral went this glistening actor. Throughout the whole of Jerusalem his personal standard preceded the All-Highest. Pilate had offended the deepest feelings of the Jews by introducing Roman standards into the Temple area (*Antiquities* XVIII, iii, 1). But the Kaiser had his carried to the very Dome itself. No one was very sorry when finally he stepped into the stuffy little train which was to take him away.

Twenty years later, the Kaiser was an exile. His kingdom and empire, and that of his Turkish ally, were overthrown. The two flags which had fluttered so bravely over the Jaffa Gate lay humbled in the dust. In December, 1917, another conqueror had passed through the Jaffa Gate, an Englishman this time. He entered on foot. It is hard now, and humiliating, to recall the enthusiasm which Allenby's capture of Jerusalem awakened among us. We showed, it is true, a good deal of smugness, of that instinctive sentimentality which foreigners mistake for deliberate hypocrisy. But that affects neither Allenby's greatness, nor the motives and principles of those who came after him.

Nearly ten years later, in the spring of 1927, Allenby returned to Palestine for the dedication of the War Cemeteries. At Ramleh and at Jerusalem, he spoke only of peace. In the strife in which he himself had led armies to victory, he had lost his only son; so that for him war held no glory, only bitterness. In Jerusalem, from the beautiful cemetery at the northern end of the Mount of Olives, he looked down over the city he had freed. The next morning, he laid

(R. Walmsley)

The Damascus Gate. For description and history see page 44.

(R. Walmsley)

The Cotton Market. "The finest bazaar in Syria" (Cresswell). Built in 1336 A.D. by the Emir Tenkiz, whose blazon it bears, for the Mameluke Sultan Mohammed-au-Nasir.

(*H. Neame*)

The approach to Watson House (on right) from the east.

the foundation stone of the Scottish memorial church of St. Andrew which stands on a little hill to the south of the Valley of Hinnom. I watched him closely throughout the ceremony. All the time, his eyes seem to be fixed on that gate through which he had entered Jerusalem ten years before. He knew, I thought, that it was there that his life's climax had been reached, and that nothing he had done since, or would do afterwards, could match that great hour. A friend who knew Allenby well told me that I was not wrong.

It was with high and godly hope that England's rule of Palestine was inaugurated. Great men were not lacking to direct it, nor good men to serve them. Samuel, Plumer, Chancellor—these names are still venerated in Palestine, as are those of countless of their subordinates, men and women who loved righteousness and hated iniquity. The story of what they did has been told by one of their number, Albert Hyamson in his *Palestine under the Mandate* It is a fair and honourable record; but now it is gone with the wind. The Jaffa Gate is desolate. The great door is shut, the street is silent. Grass grows between the cracked and dirty paving-stones. The roadway they made for the Kaiser is blocked with rusty wire and old barrels. On the Mount of Olives, the Cemetery is forsaken. It lies in a "demilitarized zone," and the United Nations guarantee that no mourner may enter it to pray or to remember.

> "Lo! All our pomp of yesterday
> Is one with Nineveh and Tyre."

How many of us who sung those lines really thought that it ever would be? But it is. And it lasted such a very little time, much less than either Nineveh or Tyre: only thirty years.

D

Chapter Four

Woe to Ariel, to Ariel, the city where David dwelt.
ISAIAH xxix. 1.

As you pass through the Damascus Gate into the Old City, you feel "the same, but not the same." The crowd seems to be the old familiar throng. There are the villagers, the priests, the sheikhs, the tourists, the guides, the merchants, the donkeys, all the kaleidoscope of the gate, and you say to yourself, "this, at least, has not changed." But you soon realize that it has. The very gateway itself, both above and below, proclaims our altered condition. Formerly, its walls, both outside and in, were as bare as those of a mosque. The only inhabitants of the actual gate were two fortune-tellers, who dwelt in two of its alcoves. They used trays of sand for their prognostications, and so reminded you of Our Lord's "writing on the ground," when the Scribes and Pharisees accused to Him the woman taken in adultery (John viii. 6, 8).

Now, on the rampart above the gateway, you see the pink head-dresses of the Arab Legionaries, as they pass behind the embrasures, looking out over no-man's-land. At night, after half past nine, you find the gate shut, as it never was in the first half of the century.

Below, in the entry itself, a little covered market has sprung up, to the benefit both of the inhabitants and of the municipality, which collects the rents. There is a grocer, a fruit-stall, two antique-mongers, a money-changer, a book-stall, a purveyor of knick-knacks, such as sun-glasses and torches, and two newspaper-sellers. These last certainly brighten the gate. The wares of one are chiefly journals from Cairo and Beirut, which in French and Arabic proclaim the iniquities of England and America, much as of old Isaiah or Ezekiel proclaimed those of Babylon and Tyre. The other sells American "pulps" and "westerns." Both have a highly-coloured, large selection of Arabic illustrated magazines and patriotic pictures. The money-changer's booth has its back to the northern wall, and so conceals the voussoirs of the old Hadrianic gateway which used to be visible. Fortunately, you can still see, to the right and left of the present gate, the great blocks of Roman stonework on which Suleiman founded his masterpiece, cleverly incising lines, to simulate joints, on the Roman stones, to make each one look as though it were not one but several smaller stones such as he himself used. For this gate is very old, as old, indeed, as Hadrian. And fortunately we know what it looked like. East of the Jordan, in Moab, there is a little town called Madeba. It is cited on the Moabite stone as belonging to Israel in the reign of Omri. Isaiah mentions it in "the burden of Moab" (xv. 2). In due time it became a Christian town, and the seat of a bishop. Then for many centuries it was deserted. In 1880, about 2,000 Christians migrated from Kerak to the old site, and on it built a new settlement. In the process of doing so, they uncovered some fine antique mosaics. The finest of all was found in the ruins of an old basilica, on which the Greek Church was being built. It was in the form of a map of Palestine and Egypt, and had a detailed representation of Jerusalem, as it was in the time of Justinian, that is to say in the middle of the sixth century. Unfortunately the map was considerably damaged before an intelligent prelate from Jerusalem realized its unique value; but enough still remains to show us what Jerusalem looked like at that time. And there you see Hadrian's gate, and just inside it a great pillar, like the one that his predecessor Trajan put up in Rome; and from the pillar, two colonnaded streets branch off like two fingers from a knuckle. The two streets are still there, and so is the Roman pavement of the more westerly, only a small distance below the present level. But the colonnades are gone, save for the fragment of a column here and there. And the pillar is gone. It must have been thrown down by the Persians, when they took Jerusalem in 614, for they spared nothing. And yet the name remains. We foreigners call the gate the Damascus Gate. But to the taxi-driver who takes you there, it is *Bab al 'Amoud*, the Gate of the Pillar. He could not tell you why he so calls it, but he would never think of calling it by any other name. So potent and tough is tradition in this city. The principal *suq* or market is little altered. All along Hadrian's street the shops are busy. And on the street of steps that leads up to the Dom Polski the vegetable-sellers still sit amid their wares. Here in the old markets, the shops are still of the old style, counters stretched across the opening of an arch. These shops bear the same relation to a modern store in London or New York as Punch and Judy does to Covent Garden or the Metropolitan Opera House. They have no windows; the goods are open to all who go by. At night, you shut up shop by coming out over or under the counter, drawing the shutters of wood or iron, locking the padlock on them, and going home with the key in your pocket. And formerly, everybody did go home. There was no electric light in the suqs until twenty years ago; only a few oil lamps at long intervals. Walking at night through these dim and deserted passages was like being in a very long and very silent cathedral, the silence seeming all the heavier by contrast with the concentrated babel and bustle of the day. I lived in the Old City, and night after night I would walk home without meeting a soul all the length of the market. Already by that time, the iron roll-shutter was beginning to displace the wooden one; so that at dusk, you would hear a noise like a waterfall as the shutters came down, and the clatter of commerce was suddenly stilled. Then came the dark, and the ghosts of the past, and all the sadness of the City's memory.

But that is gone, now. The covered markets are not so much affected, because from time immemorial they have catered for the peasants and the Bedu, with their coppersmiths, and their harness-makers and their textile sellers, their tripe-sellers and their cookshops. In many ways they can have been little altered from the days of the Crusaders, in which they were built. There is still one portion of the eastern range of the covered market which escaped the "improvements" of the Turks, where the little shops open, not sideways, like a cupboard, but up and down, like a mouth. The lower flap comes down on to a platform, and forms a comfortable counter not only for goods but for people to sit on and chat, while the upper is kept in place by a chain or a prop, and is used to hang things from. The Crusaders called the southern end of the middle aisle of the covered market "malcuisinat," "bad cookery street." The cookery is still there, but it has moved north, and it is certainly not bad. It probably never was; but the knights no doubt regarded it as "native." On the walls of this suq, you can still see in several places, carved in the stone, inscriptions such as "Sta Anna," showing that these shops belonged in those days to the Church of St. Anne, down by St. Stephen's Gate. Most of the little shops now have electric light, neon strips, which enable them to keep open after dark, and many have radios, too. And the streets are by no means deserted, because so many families who had formerly moved out of the Old City, have been compelled to move back again. It is the same with shops. Christian Street, which runs north and south above the Holy Sepulchre, had quite changed its character during the

Mandate. The big prosperous firms moved out into the new city, one by one, and their places were taken by little ones. The street had noticeably "gone down." So had others. Now, all their importance has returned to them, with an added sophistication that gives them a sort of arcade feeling. You buy nylons, and dress materials and lip-sticks, as well as spectacles and china. You even buy flowers. By the old western entrance to the Church of the Holy Sepulchre, long since blocked up, there are now two flower-stalls. One of them gets its flowers from the newly-planted garden by the Pools of Solomon, beyond Bethlehem; for in Jerusalem even innovations must conform to tradition.

The most assiduous night workers are the cobblers. In shop after shop you hear the tap of the cobbler's mallet, and see him and his apprentices bending over their work beneath the livid light. The leather they use is the famous leather of Damascus. The shoes they make for both men and women are good and cheap. But why do they work so late, and why are there so many of them? In a brief stroll the other night I counted twenty-seven. And there are many others in other streets. Where are their markets? This is a mystery; but their activity gives to Jerusalem by night a liveliness that formerly it lacked. In the eastern quarter, down on the Via Dolorosa, at its junction with the Valley, stood the Austrian Hospice, one of the most pleasant hostels in Jerusalem. Now it is the Government Hospital.

All this has happened north of David Street. To the south, the story is very different. This area was formerly occupied on the west by the Armenian quarter and on the east by the Jewish quarter, with some Moslem and Christian Arabs living between. The Armenians clustered round their convent. It was, and is, excellently administered, and in it stands their cathedral, which is the most stately and richly-furnished church in Jerusalem. The only difference here is that owing to the closing of the Jaffa Gate, no wheeled traffic can approach the convent, so that the locality is quieter. As we move east, we notice that the Arab streets are crowded to capacity, and that every house, every room, has its tenants. And so we come to the lane that runs just to the south of David Street, and above it, on the line of the old First Wall, built by King Solomon. And here we see, beneath an arch, a fine stone doorway, adorned with the blazons of the Order of St. John of Jerusalem. This is Watson House. It consists of an old Arab house, built round a cloistered courtyard, underneath which is the cistern, with western additions on the east side. It is of two stories, and, unique in the old city, it has a garden. The house, together with that next door, was formerly the property of the London Jews Society, and was at one time during the last century inhabited and thoroughly investigated by the famous Dr. Schick. He found that both the house and the garden are supported on a series of vaults, the lowest of which are so far below the present level of the city that he could not explore them. From the garden, raised as it is on the ruins of antiquity, you look out over the city, to the Holy Sepulchre, to the Temple Area, to the Mount of Olives beyond, and to the roofs at your feet.

This house is now the Ophthalmic Hospital of the Venerable Order of St. John of Jerusalem; and it has become so by a curious chain of events. Sir Charles Watson was a distinguished Sapper, much of whose life had been passed in Egypt. He had occupied Cairo after the battle of Tel-el-Kebir in 1882, and he had been a close friend of Gordon. Lady Watson told me once how, when Gordon was about to set out on his last journey to Khartoum, she had mended his socks. Her husband had wanted to go with him; but Gordon had refused—he would not take a married man, he said. So they went together to Cairo railway station to see him off, with a foreboding that they would never see him again. Although his professional life was largely spent in Egypt, both Sir Charles Watson and his wife had always loved Jerusalem. He was an active participant in the Palestine Exploration Fund. In 1912, appeared a book in the Medieval Town series published by Messrs. Dent & Sons, entitled "Jerusalem, by Colonel Sir C. M. Watson, K.C.M.G., C.B., M.A., etc. Illustrated by Geneviève Watson." The book had been largely written in Jerusalem itself. During the First War, Sir Charles died. His widow came back to Jerusalem as soon as she could. She lived for a time in the guard chamber over the Damascus Gate, and then succeeded in buying from the London Jews Society one of the houses which they no longer needed. She put into it nearly all her slender savings, and when she had paid for it, she was very poor. But she was very happy. She called the house Watson House, and placed in the cloister a beautiful plaque, made of Jerusalem tiles, recording its dedication. Then she bequeathed the property to the Order, of which her husband had been so devoted a knight. Lady Watson was very old by then—how old no one knew, because she never told, and very seldom spoke of herself, always of her husband. All we know was that she was an Alsatian by birth. She worked as a volunteer in the linen room of the Ophthalmic Hospital, whose fine premises near the railway station, damaged by the Turks in the war, had now been rebuilt and enlarged so that it was one of the finest hospitals of the whole Levant.

The house was far too large for one occupant, so to fill it, and to augment her little income, Lady Watson used to let rooms to favoured lodgers. Twenty years ago, I was one of them. To live there, in the heart of Jerusalem, was an experience and a privilege that is not to be forgotten. And Lady Watson told me that I could do as I wanted to with the garden. So I arranged it as best I could. There were a number of pieces of antique sculpture and decoration lying about, pieces that Schick had collected. These we set up here and there. And loads of good earth and manure were brought in by donkeys, for the garden is really a "roof-garden" being supported on medieval vaults. Plants were brought in too, and seeds and bulbs were obtained from England. The passion flower that to-day covers the whole fence between the garden and David Street below, is the progeny of a single sprig that I brought back one afternoon from the Benedictine abbey at Abu Ghosh. From the garden an old bridge led over David Street on to the roof of the Crusaders' Fowl Market, and I would sometimes go that way to work. The flat roofs around were used by dyers for spreading their cloths upon to dry, and in the spring you would sometimes see a sheep tethered, to crop, while it lasted, "the grass upon the house-tops which withereth afore it be plucked up; whereof the mower filleth not his hand, neither he that bindeth up the sheaves his bosom" (Psalms cxxix. 6, 7). Nearby is a coffee-house. It was once a Byzantine church, and I have been told that it is haunted by the ghost of a priest with a censer, but this I have only at second-hand from the caretaker, through another. In Ramadan, I would sometimes look down through the little window in the dome, upon the group below, where a story-teller would entertain his audience, as they sipped their coffee and smoked their pipes, with some old tale of heroes and fair women, always breaking off at a point of such suspense that he could be sure of his audience the following night —just like Shahrazad.

Lady Watson died on the last day of 1936. To the end she lived in Watson House. She refused an apartment in Hampton Court Palace, thereby, as she said, "making two people happy, me, and the next one on the list." "I shall stay here till I move to Mount Zion" (meaning the cemetery) she would say. And stay she did. But when she had gone, the Order were at a loss what to do with what was now their property. So they let it to the Government, who used the old part as an infant welfare clinic, and the new part as quarters for British policemen. Thus things went on until the end of the Mandate. The truce line places the fine hospital buildings down by the station in Zionist hands. No Arab patients can get there. Whereas Watson House is now surrounded by poor and needy Arabs, both citizens and refugees; and it is accessible from any part of Jordan. In the end, therefore, what seemed as though it might be a white elephant has become a godsend. There are beds for twenty-eight in-patients—the old hospital had over seventy. A new room has been skilfully added to the house by Sayyid Yusuf Budeiri, whose cousin Khalil is on the surgical staff of the hospital, and there every day between seven and fourteen hundred patients find relief, the number varying according as the season is damp or dusty. The garden is far better stocked and cared for than ever it was in my time. And how happy Geneviève Watson must be. She was right after all. She generally was.

Finally, down below the Byzantine coffee-house, we come to what was formerly the Jewish quarter. Just when it became the Jewish quarter, it is hard to know. During the Crusades, Benjamin of Tudela says that 200 Jewish families (the only ones he mentions) lived near the citadel. But there must have been others, because a part of the north-eastern quarter was called *la juiverie*. At some period after the Crusades, the south-eastern part of the city became the Jewish quarter. It was bounded on the south by the city wall, on the north by David Street, on the east by the Tyropæan valley and on the west by the Armenian quarter.

If you look down on Jerusalem from the Mount of Olives to-day, you see it chiefly as a mosaic of amber or honey-coloured stone, with the angles of the houses, and the lines of the roofs standing out hard and clear in the strong light. But the left-hand bottom corner of the picture seemed smudged and blurred, the lines are indistinct, and the colour seems to have faded from amber to dirty white. This is the Jewish quarter, and the reason for the change is that much of it is in ruins. It was the scene of heavy fighting during 1948, and many buildings were damaged. New mounds have been added to the strata of Jerusalem, and as you walk over them you see how soon contours can be changed, and how quickly and mysteriously what was stone but a short while ago is transmuted into dust and mud, into the earth of which every *tel* seems to be chiefly made. A new network of little paths, winding between pits and rocks, has in places obliterated the old streets. The quarter was inhabited by Jews; but the houses were largely the property of Arabs. It is the Arabs who have suffered most. Not only have the property-owners had their wealth destroyed; but houses that might have given asylum to refugees from beyond the line, can now afford them little or no relief. The ruins have been cleaned up remarkably well, and every standing roof is sheltering someone. But it is a sad area. Grown-ups and children alike seem depressed and miserable. Bedraggled, ætiolated boys and girls run in and out of low doorways. The quarter was always squalid, because the Jews who lived here were very poor. But the ruin of war has added to its squalor, and to its misery.

In the census of 1922, the inhabitants of Jerusalem, Old and New, numbered 62,578; in 1931 (the last census taken) 90,503. By the end of the mandate, the total population must have been well over 100,000, of whom considerably more than half would be Jews. The majority of all races lived outside the walls. Yet the present population of Arab Jerusalem is estimated at 80,000, of whom the majority live in the Old City. These figures give some idea both of the pressure of the refugees on the capital, and of the present density of population within the walls. Yet here is a remarkable thing: the city is cleaner than it has ever been. Everyone remarks on it, citizens and foreigners alike. I have heard it commended as far afield as Baghdad. It is a great credit to our Mayor, Haj Omar al-Wa'ari, his Town Clerk, Sayyid Anton Safiyeh, and their efficient staff. But everywhere you notice this pressure. There seem to be more shoe-shine boys than ever—three will compete for one pair of shoes—more guides, more corner-boys in the car-parks. And there are also more boys selling ice-cream in the form of "popsicles." These are carried around in neat white insulated boxes, either on foot or by bicycle. The boxes have written on them, in Arabic, "Everest," which has for several years been the name of our local brand; but the boys cry out "E-e-e-skimo," the generic name, which comes, I believe, from "Eskimo pie," a delicious form of ice-cream covered with chocolate, which I remember as something of an innovation in New England in 1923. But the traditional drink-sellers still hawk their wares. Still they cry, to the accompaniment of their clashing brass bowls, "Drink O thirsty one," "Sweeten

thy mouth with tamarind," as with easy virtuosity, in an arc like a
rainbow, they pour from their glittering brass urns just enough
to fill the bowl without spilling a drop. And still by night is heard
the clink of the coffee-cups, like that of castanets, as the coffee seller
goes his rounds to refresh the yawning watchmen.

Although the Old City is so full of people, fuller than it has been
for at least a century, parts of it are still open fields. If you stand on
the site of the old Palace of the Hasmoneans, on the northern bank of
the Tyropæan valley, opposite the Temple area, you see below you
a field of barley; and there is another to the south. In the far north-
eastern corner, too, by the Storks' tower, you will find the land
under crops, not houses. The fact is that those few who can build,
prefer, as they have done for the past fifty years and more, to build
outside the walls. The suburbs reflect this trend. They are all of them
expanding, Silwan most of all. Its inhabitants are a hardy race, who
boast with justice that near as they were, and still are, to the Zionist
lines, they never budged. Their village has climbed right out of the
Cedron valley, and has moved over towards Bethany, and along
the new road to Bethlehem. On the north, many new houses are
springing up along the main north road, between Scopus and the
airport at Qalandia, on what is still open country. This in itself is a
proof of another blessing that may seem unexpected: our security.
Despite the poverty, and the displacement of so many people, and
the habitation of so many remote and isolated sites, security, like
cleanliness, is better than it ever was, and that not only in Jerusalem, but
throughout Jordan. The old Palestine Police were good; but the Arab
Legion are better. Provided they are well trained, and proud of their
tradition and their honour, as the Arab Legion are, a national force
will always prove superior to a foreign force, however good, if only
because they know their fellows better than any outsider ever can.

Two old Jerusalem customs, both of them charged with significant
interest, have now been pretermitted, probably for ever. In each case,
however, the Second War contributed to their desuetude.

The first is the "Nebi Musa Festival." The prophet Moses, as we
know from Deuteronomy xxxiv, "died there" (i.e. near Mount
Nebo) "in the land of Moab, over against Beth Peor: but no man
knoweth of his sepulchre unto this day." Nevertheless, at some time
in the Middle Ages, a shrine of the "Prophet Moses," in Arabic
"Nebi Musa," was established five miles to the west of the north
end of the Dead Sea. There is no notice of this earlier than the

thirteenth century. Like other shrines, this one attracted its annual
pilgrimage, which took place about the time of Easter. Gradually,
the pilgrimage became more and more elaborately organized, until,
by the middle of the last century, it was regarded by the Turks as a
convenient counterpoise to the ever increasing number of foreign
Christian pilgrims who flocked to Jerusalem for Easter, specially
for the Eastern Easter. "Nebi Musa," therefore, although a Moslem
festival, came to be regulated by the Eastern Christian calendar.
From beginning to end, the proceedings lasted eight days. First, on
the Thursday before Palm Sunday, the Nablus contingent arrived.
They assembled in front of the American Colony, and at nine in the
morning, they trooped down through the Damascus Gate to the
Haram. The following morning more would come in, and all then
called on the District Commissioner who would "bless" their
banners. After midday prayers, the procession started out from the
Haram, down through St. Stephen's Gate, past Gethsemane, and
up to the corner above Silwan, called Ras al 'Amud (the Head
of the Column) where the Mayor had pitched a pavilion, and a
brief formal reception was held. Thence, in buses, or on donkeys or
on foot, the pilgrims went down to the shrine. On Saturday, the
Hebronites assembled at the convent of Mar Elias, half-way between
Jerusalem and Bethlehem, and next morning they made their
formal entry. They came in through the Jaffa Gate, and, after
spending the night in the Haram, proceeded on the Monday in
Holy Week, together with smaller contingents from the neighbourhood, to join their Nablusi brethren at Nebi Musa. There all the
pilgrims stayed, feasting and praying, until Maundy Thursday, when
they made a united Return, through St. Stephen's Gate, to the Haram.
On Good Friday, after prayers, they all dispersed to their homes.

"Nebi Musa" was par excellence a peasant festival. It was the one
occasion in the year when Jerusalem could see the clothes, the
customs and above all the dances of the villagers right in the heart
of the capital. Naturally, the assembly of so many folk from the two
towns that were the traditional strongholds of Islamic enthusiasm
caused some anxiety to the police, and indeed on more than one
occasion the parades had been known to degenerate into riots. There
was always the danger of an "incident," of some accidental collision,
the spreading of some false rumour, which, at the time of the Feast
might lead, as it did in the case of Paul, to a general uproar (Acts xxi.
27 et seq.). The slogans which the procession chanted were supposed

to be approved by the authorities, but there was always the possibility of an impromptu. In general, this feeling of contingent danger only heightened, as it does with other sporting events, the excitement and fervour of the scene. The entry of the Hebronites was the climax. Every tower and house and wall around the Jaffa Gate was crowded with spectators. The roadways were blocked. In swept the milling, surging crowd. It was not a military procession, all of a piece; it consisted of a number of articulated groups, each one with its sword-dancers, or wrestlers, or morris-dancers, and each trying to hold as long as it could, which was until the police moved it on, the attention of the spectators. Every now and then you would see a peasant apparently running to and fro over the heads of his fellows, a phenomenon effected by one man's carrying another on his shoulders, clamping his ankles to his own neck with his crossed arms, and then gliding up and down a lane which the crowd had cleared for him. The most beautiful were the dancers of the *dabki* or national dance of Palestine. It is a form of morris-dance, with the dancers dancing in a circle, holding hands, swaying in unison, stamping, leaping, shuffling in perfect accord, the leader waving his stick or his coloured kerchief above his head. Every now and then, the group, formed into a curved line, would start to glide round on the arc of a circle, and then glide back again, as though it moved not on human feet, but mounted on the rim of a wheel, such as you see in the escapement of a "hundred day" clock. The countenances of the dancers were fixed, almost hypnotized. You saw here the very essence of the ritual dance, of the "dance before the Lord." The music was provided by shepherds' flutes. These are like primitive oboes. They have the same orgiastic plangency. They consist of twin pipes, one much longer than the other, to give the chanter effect, made of bamboo, and with a reed in each of the twin mouth-pieces. These are placed wholly within the mouth of the player, who, if he is an expert, will breathe in through his nose and out through his mouth, thus producing an even and continuous note, like a bag-pipe. The dancers wore new clothes, shining striped robes like cassocks, and their best shoes. They were a fine and thrilling sight, and the spectators felt one with them in their excitement, as they turned and glistened in the bright spring sun.

All is silent now. Two days ago I saw some soldiers bargaining for a pipe, at the stall where they are sold, not far from the Holy Sepulchre. I was glad that among the undertones of war may *still* be heard the voice of melody and the sound of the dance. But the festival is no more. It has been abolished by adversity. There was talk of reviving it this year. The Mayor even spread his pavilion at Ras al 'Amoud. But it remained empty and forlorn. The peasants were too poor, too sad to keep holiday.

Nebi Musa was a festival of the sun: the other custom whose passing I lament was of the moon, I mean the "Ramadan calls." Ramadan is the name of the ninth month of the Moslem year. It is mentioned by name (the only month that is) in the Quran, which prescribes it as a month of fasting (Sura II, vv. 185-7). During this month the Moslem must fast from the moment when day-break enables him to distinguish a white thread from a black thread until dusk. Those who are sick or are on a journey may break the fast, substituting an equal number of days later on. Those who can keep the fast and do not, must redeem their neglect by maintaining a poor man. The Moslem calendar is lunar, not solar like ours, and the months contain 29 and 30 days alternately. There are thus 354 days in the year or 355 in a leap year, of which there are four in every cycle of thirty years. The new year, therefore (and the beginnings of all the later months), falls about 11 days earlier each successive year until in the course of about thirty-three years, each month makes a complete circuit of the seasons. (I say "about," because neither the lunar year nor the solar year exactly coincides with the earth's annual orbit around the sun.) In short, Ramadan may fall in the depth of winter or in the height of summer. This year, it started on the 13th May. To fast during our summer days, to take neither food nor drink, not even to swallow your own spittle, is a very strict discipline. Yet many thousands of Moslems support it. In the night season, it is permitted to eat and drink. A gun announces nightfall, and, towards the end of the night, another warns you to eat your last meal. A third announces the onset of the new day. The minarets of the mosques are illuminated during Ramadan. In days gone by they were lighted by rows of little olive oil lamps, each of which had been tended and set in order by a human hand. They twinkled with a living light. Now, the turn of an electric switch is enough; but the light it releases is cold and dead by comparison.

The night being thus the period of relaxation, it is the custom not only to eat and drink, but also to hear readings from the Quran, or some secular story, examples of both of which I have already

cited. It was also in former days the custom, during the second week
of the Fast, to receive visits from your friends. During these visits,
Jerusalem slipped back into the Middle Ages. The noises of the
western day were hushed, the sights of the modern world were
shrouded. You walked through the silence of the Old City, by the
light of the waxing moon. I used to go calling with my Moslem
friends, generally accompanied by the Aide-de-Camp of the High
Commissioner, whose good wishes he bore. First, we would visit
the Sheikh Khalil al-Khalidi. He was old when I first knew him,
and most venerable, for not only was he the head of his very ancient
and illustrious family, but the President of the Moslem Court of
Appeal, the senior dignitary of Islam in Jerusalem. He was a ripe
scholar, and a great gentleman. We would find him enthroned in
the middle of his diwan, the picture of repose and dignity. He wore
a long black robe and an old-fashioned white turban. Before and on
either side of him, as though attending his court with him as sole
judge, sat the members of the al-Khalidi family. They were of the
next generation, men of vivacity and talent. One was my Principal
at the Arab College, Ahmed Samih, a born educator, an original
thinker and a great leader, whose untimely death two years ago is
daily lamented by all who knew him. His brothers were doctors.
One of them is now the Foreign Minister of the Kingdom. In
ordinary surroundings, all three were by no means either still or
silent; but in the presence of the Head of the Family they sat like
statues, their hands on their knees, and their heads inclined in
reverence. It was patriarchal, and it was good.

Sheikh Khalil's house was just outside the north-west corner of
the Haram. From his door, we stepped down into the little passage
that leads to the Gate of the Shepherds, by the former Tower of
Antonia. Suddenly, as we rounded the corner, the Haram was
before us, vast, peaceful, and bathed in an ice-blue light. The contrast
with the obscure tunnel is unforgettable. Our next call was to be
on the Mufti, whose diwan was above the western cloister. On the
way, we could look our fill upon the dim, shimmering glories of
the Haram and the Dome of the Rock. By daylight the Dome is
one of the most beautiful buildings in the world; by moonlight it
is so beautiful that it seems not to be of this world at all. It is

> "Held in lunar synthesis,
> Whispering lunar incantations."

It will be gone with the day, you feel, so lightly does it seem to float upon the wide white expanse of the *Sahn* or platform which sustains it. Through the luminous silence we would walk to the rampart, and look down over the Cedron valley. It always reminded me, and still does, of the lines in the *Dies Iræ*,

> "*Tuba mirum spargens sonum*
> *Per sepulcra regionum,*
> *Coget omnes ante thronum.*"

for there below, glistening and cold, are myriads of white-topped Jewish tombs, which seem to be waiting until the trumpet shall sound.

There were other calls to pay, including the one to Nebi Daud which I have mentioned; and then we would walk back again through the mother-of-pearl landscape into our ordinary lives, while the little drums which poor men beat to call the faithful to their devotions throbbed through the shadows.

That, too, is gone.

But there is one change that is stranger, more ironical, more paradoxical, than any other: there are now no Jews in Historic Jerusalem. The "Return," the "Ingathering" has resulted in this. No longer do you see the wizened Yemenite porters, bent beneath their loads of crates, nor the pale young Poles, hurrying to their *Yeshivah* (or Rabbinical school) clutching their sacred books, arrayed in fur-girt hats and trailing robes, such as some noble patron had flung to their forbears long ago to keep out the cold of a Warsaw winter. No more do you meet the canny merchants from the outside world, talking Arabic with an Ashkenazi accent, nor the "modern" young Zionists, self-consciously sightseeing where their ancestors were content to worship. Nor, alas for the loss, do you see Leo Mayer, of the Hebrew University, that beloved scholar, with whom to walk through Jerusalem was an education. Such is his love of Islamic architecture and art, on certain aspects of which he is the greatest living authority, that every stone, as he hailed it, had a sermon for him and for those who were privileged to bear him company. It is Leo Mayer's contention, and his knowledge will make it good to anyone who doubts it, that, in addition to all its other distinctions, Jerusalem is one of the richest and most important examples of a medieval Islamic city which we possess. Not to see the eager smile of this great man, not to hear his gentle voice, as he explains the beauty and significance of a monument in Arabic, English, German, French, Hebrew, or one of several other languages, is a deprivation which almost daily brings home to me the evil times on which we have fallen.

The Wailing Wall echoes no longer to the murmurs of the mourners over Zion. As we have seen, Benjamin of Tudela records that the Jews resorted to it in his time. In 1625, an anonymous traveller from Carpi, near Modena, writes of specially arranged prayers being offered there. In 1928 occurred before the Wall the incident which was one of the causes of the 1929 riots, and in the next year an international commission settled the rights of the Moslems and Jews in regard to it. It was the only commission that ever did finally settle any dispute throughout the whole period of the British Mandate; and ironically enough it was the only dispute of which the essential factors no longer exist. For to-day, only the voices of little Arab children at play and the twittering of sparrows disturb the tranquillity of this famous and ancient Wall.

There have before been periods during which Jews were excluded from Jerusalem. During the Captivity (587-539 B.C.), though the walls were razed, and a large number of the inhabitants had either fled to Egypt or were deported to Babylon, a capital was established at Mizpah (Tel el-Nasbeh, on the Ramallah road, just north of the airfield), and the conquerors "left the poor of the land to be vine-dressers and husbandmen" (2 Kings xxv. 12). There was no rigid decree of exclusion. During the siege of the city by Titus in A.D. 70 thousands of the inhabitants died of starvation, and Josephus even cites an example of cannibalism (*Wars*, VI, iv, 4). Of the survivors, many of the younger were sold as slaves, and the elder either given away to be killed in the theatres of friendly cities, or sent to work in the Egyptian mines. On the ruins of the city the Tenth Legion established their camp. During the revolt of Bar Cochba, sixty-two years later, Jerusalem suffered still further. The leader, whose headquarters were near the Dead Sea, probably occupied the city for a time.

After the revolt had been crushed, Hadrian built his pagan city, Ælia Capitolina, on the site of Jerusalem, heathen colonists were introduced, and the Jews were by formal decree prohibited from entering. This seems to be the first, definite, legal exclusion of the Jews from Jerusalem. But even this edict was not strictly observed, for though it was in force when Eusebius wrote his history in 312,

(D. Baly)

The view from Watson House, looking east. Roofs of covered markets (Crusader) in foreground. Beyond the Haram esh Sherif, the Mount of Olives with (left to right) the Augusta Victoria Hospital, Greek Patriarch's house, and Russian Tower.

(R. Durrant)

The Dome of the Rock, with the Mount of Olives beyond, from the minaret of the Gate of the Chain.

(Elia)

The Sacred Rock. Originally the threshing floor of Araunah the Jebusite, then the Altar of the Jewish Temple. Note (top right) hole for drainage and (bottom left) ramp whereby priests ascended (Exod. xx. 26). Steps of Templar altar on right front. Grille is Crusader Ironwork, left *in situ* by Saladin.

(Elia)

Jerusalem from Ras al 'Amoud, showing the Haram esh Sherif and Herodian substructures ("Solomon's stables") on right. In foreground, "Minx-of-all-work."

the *Bordeaux Pilgrim*, only twenty-one years later, tells us that the Jews were allowed to visit annually "the pierced stone" (probably the present Rock of the Dome of the Rock). When Chosroes II attacked Jerusalem in 614, he is reported to have been aided by 24,000 Jews. There is a tradition, that in 362, Julian the Apostate gave the Jews permission to rebuild the Temple, but that the plan was frustrated (see page 41, above). In 629, the Emperor Heraclius renewed the edict of banishment. In 637, Omar conquered Jerusalem, and when 'Abdul-melik came to build the Dome of the Rock in 688, we are told, by Mujir-ud-Din, that ten Jewish families helped in the building, and that another company of Jews were among the servants of the shrine, as well as some Christians, but that both were later removed.

In 985, Al-Muqaddasi complains that in Jerusalem, Christians and Jews have the upper hand. In 1047, Nasir-i-Khusrau records that both Jews and Christians make pilgrimages to Jerusalem.

With the coming of the Crusaders, the lot of the Jews must at first have changed for the worse; but, as we have seen, they remained in Jerusalem. In 1031 there was already a Yeshivah, and six years later we have a record of a synagogue and also of the assembly of the Jews on the Mount of Olives at certain festivals. In 1156, a Petrus Judæus is mentioned as swearing allegiance to King Baldwin III.

In 1210 a wholly new development took place, for in that year Rabbi Samuel ben Simon made a pilgrimage to Palestine as the forerunner of 300 and more rabbis from the South of England and France who went to Palestine the next year. In 1267, when Nahman-ides visited the City, he seems to have found only two brothers, dyers, actually living in the city, though on festivals they gathered their brethren from nearby villages. He reorganized the community and acquired a new synagogue, near the Zion Gate, showing that by his time the modern "Jewish Quarter" had already become the abode of the Jews. Nahmanides, or Moses ben Nahman of Gerona, was a very famous scholar, well known throughout and beyond Spain, which he had been forced to leave as the result of the cele-brated Disputation which he had had with Pablo Christiani, a con-verted Jew, before King James of Aragon.

It is often thought by Gentiles that the Ashkenazim, or German and German-influenced Jews, did not establish themselves in Palestine until the nineteenth century. In fact, they were settled in Jerusalem in the fourteenth, at the latest. They were a separate

E

community, but worshipped with the Sephardim, or indigenous and Mediterranean Jews, in the same synagogue. The expulsion of the Jews from Spain in 1492 naturally sent many of them to Palestine, and the Sephardi community increased considerably. In the course of time all the Arabic-speaking Jews joined the Sephardim, which resulted in the formation of the two main communities, the Sephardic and the Ashkenazi.

The fortunes of Jerusalem Jewry undulated during the next four centuries, with the changing winds of politics. Generally speaking, the Sephardim got along with their Turkish and Arab neighbours, whereas the Ashkenazim were not always so fortunate, which resulted in their feeling bitter against the Sephardim. So strong did the feeling against the Ashkenazim become, that they gradually withdrew from Jerusalem and made Safad their headquarters. In 1721, the Ashkenazi synagogue in Jerusalem was attacked by the Moslems, and the woodwork and books burned. At the beginning of the nineteenth century, Ashkenazim who came from Safad to Jerusalem to avoid the plague, would sometimes wear Sephardi clothing in order to escape the hatred of the Moslems. Things had become so bad for them, that at one time the Ashkenazim could not muster a *minyan*, or the ten heads of families necessary to constitute a synagogue.

The expansion of the Jewish Community in Jerusalem, particularly the Ashkenazi section, during the nineteenth century is a well-known story. It reached its zenith and climax under the Mandate. And now that story, too, is ended, and, for the first time for many centuries not a single Jew is to be found in Historic Jerusalem.

But it is no edict that excludes the Jews now: it is acts and facts. A state of war, suspended only by the thin, five-year old truce, exists between the Zionists and their neighbours. As I write, it is just a month and a day since Zionist bullets killed ten of Jerusalem's citizens and wounded more than that number as they went about their peaceable business in the afternoon. Two nights ago, three villages near Emmaus were assaulted by Sten guns from beyond the line. An American friend of mine told me this morning that he had seen three of the casualties in Ramallah, an old man shot through the side of the head, a young man with both legs shattered, and a little boy shot through the mouth.

Chapter Five

We commend to thy fatherly goodness all those, who are any ways afflicted or distressed in mind, body, or estate; that it may please thee to comfort and relieve them, according to their several necessities, giving them patience under their sufferings, and a happy issue out of all their afflictions.

Collect or Prayer for all Conditions
of men, BOOK OF COMMON PRAYER.

AS usual, the Prayer Book sums up the whole situation in a sentence. The words which were designed to fit the circumstances of sixteenth- and seventeenth-century England, apply no less aptly to Jerusalem and Palestine in 1953.

The problem is still threefold, first to comfort and relieve, then to inspire patience (which must be founded on hope) and thirdly to provide a happy issue out of affliction. I shall try, in this and the following chapters, to describe briefly what has so far been achieved in these three stages, both as it affects the "official refugees" and the "economic refugees." I shall mention what is being done by private individuals, by government and international agencies, and lastly by voluntary organizations, including the Christian Churches.

Let us begin with the individual. Already, I hope, some impression has been conveyed of the astonishing resilience of the individual Arab. The way in which so many have established new lives, often in new lands, has surprised many friends who thought they knew them well. But in truth, the process is characteristic. The Arab is a fierce individualist. In the west, we have tended during the last three centuries to retreat from individualism, and to become more and more like sheep. So deep is our horror of the individual, in his crudest manifestation of tyrant or dictator, of which unfortunately Europe has produced a destructive number in the last three hundred years, that we have shrunk to the opposite extreme, and now pay semi-divine honours to committees and other elected bodies. The Arab would rather deal with an individual than a committee any day. To him, what you are is more important than what you do, style more essential than fashion, survival the great end of all policy. When confronted with a disaster such as the present one, the individual Arab shows instinctive vigour and initiative. Of the new businesses that Jerusalem has acquired, I have already said something. But there are two other ways in which this resourcefulness has been shown. The first is emigration. The Arabs have from time immemorial been great travellers. Not only have they produced famous travellers like Ibn Batuta and Ibn Jubayr; the ordinary citizen regards travelling as quite normal. His ancestors travelled yearly, from grazing-ground to grazing-ground, or as merchants along the great trade-routes from the spice-lands of the south to the markets of the north. Every Moslem is required by his religion to perform the pilgrimage to Mecca at least once (Quran III, 97). That injunction has always been a great stimulus to travel, and still is. Arabs travelled by sea not only to the West, but to the Far East, too. They sailed from Basra to India and Ceylon. They were very early established in China, whence they were the first to bring news of novelties which have now become household commodities, including tea itself. They settled in the East Indies, which still has close family ties with South Arabia. They settled in East Africa and West Africa. They have settled also in Cardiff and South Shields, in both of which cities I have visited them and found them to be regarded by the authorities as model citizens. They have settled in South America, in Central America and in North America, where it is said that more Arabic newspapers are published than in all Arabia.

Many of these spheres of settlement are now either closed or severely restricted; though only the other day two aeroplanes left Jerusalem each with twenty emigrants aboard bound for Brazil, whither they hope their families may follow them soon. But it happens that new outlets, of less scope admittedly, have to some extent supplied that deficiency. In Libya, with the disappearance of the Italian overlord and his British "caretaker" successor, it has not been easy to create a full-fledged indigenous administration. Palestine Arabs have helped to overcome the difficulty. The key men in many departments are Palestinians, trained under the Mandate. Libya is a poor country, and it cannot afford a very large or expanding civil service, nor is there much commercial development to call for skilled and trustworthy men and women. But in the Oil Lands of the Gulf, there is. From the point of view of Palestine, the discovery and exploitation of the Gulf oil has been of great benefit. Hundreds of Palestinians are there, earning good salaries, in the government, in the oil company, in the contracting firms, in local enterprise. There is one village near Nablus called Burin, which lived not by agriculture, but on the labours of its excellent artisans. With the end of the Mandate, it seemed doomed; to-day it prospers, on the remittances which its sons send back from Kuwait.

For no Arab would dream of emigrating for himself alone. There is probably no race on earth which more readily accepts responsibility for relations close or distant. It is an extension, or projection of the individual. If you ask an Arab how many souls he has to maintain, you will be surprised at the answer, more surprised when you analyse it. Often enough a little lad seeking his first job, as a messenger or an under-servant, will tell you that he has to keep eight people, either wholly or partly. The eight may include his widowed mother or his infirm father, his brothers and sisters, and probably old Auntie Fatima as well. So strong is this obligation to maintain not only ascendants and descendants but collaterals also, that during the war the British troops in Baghdad accepted it in determining who should benefit under the workmen's compensation regulations. It was the custom, and the law, of Iraq.

So now, many a home in Jerusalem is brightened by the remittance that comes from Kuwait or Qatar, and nearly every day someone applies for help in getting there. But an immigrant can only go there at the request of some friend or relative, already in Kuwait, who will guarantee to maintain him until he can fend for himself.

For the present and the immediate future, this emigration has been a boon. But if we take the long view, it is the reverse: for naturally many of the best brains have gone farthest, the brains that the homeland can least afford to lose.

Politically, the British Mandate was a resounding failure; administratively, it was a success. As long ago as 1902, Mr. Joseph Chamberlain, an imperialist if ever there was one, had seen the danger: "The weary Titan," he said in a famous speech, speaking of England, "struggles under the too vast orb of its fate." Twenty years later, the Titan was certainly no less weary, yet the orb of its fate had become vaster. Ten years before, Mr. Theodore Roosevelt, after his tour through Africa, which included Egypt, uttered his terse advice—"Govern or get out." We did neither; but we took on new responsibilities in East Africa, in West Africa, in Palestine and in

Iraq. The emperor Hadrian had ensured the Antonine age of peace and prosperity by contracting the frontiers of the empire, not by expanding them. We were to enjoy no Antonine age, least of all in Palestine. Nevertheless, our political ineptitude should not be allowed to obliterate our administrative success: at the outbreak of the Second War, Palestine was probably the best-administered country in Asia. There was security, except when politics destroyed it; there was justice. Agriculture, health, roads and education had all made sound progress; and a generation of Palestinian officials, competent and energetic, able and enterprising, had grown up in every department. In two departments especially, the two which affect the citizen most closely—health and education—Britain had succeeded admirably. The Department of Health through almost the whole of the Mandate was directed by Colonel, later Sir, George Heron, a man who had learnt the art of tropical medicine in Egypt before the First War. He was a firm and just administrator, and a man who could not accept or compromise with the second-rate. He knew the necessity of discipline, but was one of the most genial of men. He was quite unaffected by agitation or public clamour. He knew what was best, and did it. The results of his policy were remarkable. Death from malaria had become almost unknown within a few years. Colonel Heron simply made the mosquito illegal, both in the towns and the villages. Every house-holder in a town had a supply of printed and prepaid postcards, which hung behind his front door. If a mosquito occurred, you just posted a card. Round came an inquisitor in uniform the next day, and the offending mosquito would be found, either on your premises or your neighbour's, and eradicated. Those who were harbouring him were warned of what to expect if they offended again. They seldom did, because they knew that the Department of Health would accept no excuses. In the villages it was the same. As an assistant district commissioner I used to ride round villages far from any road or town. The only departmental officer I could be sure of meeting was the inspector of the Health Department, who would report anyone whose cistern lacked its iron lid. This was Heron's gift to Palestine, this, and the encouragement of gardening, for in his spare time Colonel Heron was the moving spirit of the Jerusalem Horticultural Society. He has retired now; but the work which he did lives, and so does the spirit by which he worked, in the standards and ideals of those whom he trained.

Medical services and education are the necessity of everyone, but of the two, you need education more continuously; because even if a child is born healthy, it is bound to be born ignorant. No department of government therefore is more sensitively in touch with the people. Here again, Palestine was very fortunate. Humphrey Bowman, the first Director of Education, was a man of great natural sympathy, charm and humour. And he had the gift of being able to attach first-rate people to himself. He soon collected a staff which set itself the task of building up an Arabic educational system which was to be the best in existence. And it succeeded. The aim of the Palestine education department was to teach Arabs through the medium of their own language, up to at least a matriculation standard. This had never been attempted anywhere before. In Palestine it was achieved only by the Education Department of the Government. This was constantly denounced as "colonizing" by the so-called "national" organizations, whose own schools, where they had any, taught their secondary classes through the medium of English. It was easier, less trouble; because when the Government started out on its new policy, the necessary Arab text books simply did not exist. When I was at the Arab College, I would see my Palestinian colleagues working late into the night, translating their next day's lectures from English into Arabic. English itself was taught as a second language, at first with an Englishman to help his Arab colleague. The staff of the department was almost wholly Arab. Miss Hilda Ridler was in charge of women's education, and in her training college she had two English assistants. But all the girls' schools which she founded, and directed for twenty years, were staffed by Palestinians. In the Arab College, there was one Englishman, but only for a few years: not long after I had left the College, my place was taken by one of my own pupils, 'Abdurrahman Bushnaq, one of the most responsive boys I ever taught. He took an honours degree in English at Cambridge, and has a far better knowledge of English literature than I can ever hope to acquire. At the Headquarters, there were four Englishmen only, the Director, his deputy, the director of physical training, and the chief clerk. Among the Arabs, were men of great ability, notably Jibrail Katul, and Ahmed al-Khalidi.

The fine flowering of Palestine Arab education was due to a collaboration between Ahmed al-Khalidi and an equally remarkable Briton, Jerome Farrell, who succeeded Bowman as Director of

Education in 1937, having been his deputy for ten years before that. Farrell and Khalidi between them created the Arab College and the whole solid pyramid that underlay it. They were both men wholly dedicated to the cause of education. They sprang from utterly different societies. Farrell was trained by the Jesuits and by Cambridge. He was a first-class classic. Ahmed al-Khalidi was the son of an ancient and illustrious Arab Moslem family, educated at St. George's School and the American University of Beirut. Farrell was shy, Ahmed a born extrovert. But theirs was the perfect partnership. Each had a great respect and affection for the other. Farrell now lives in active retirement in Ireland. Ahmed, alas! died two years ago. Between them, they perfected a system of education which, by using Arabic as the language of instruction, produced pupils, alert, fluent and accurate in Arabic and English both, who were among the best instructed and best mannered youths in Asia. And they were the best trained teachers in the whole Arab world.

Where are they now? Scattered to the four winds. Some of them, all the more honour to them, have remained in their country. The late Minister for Reconstruction, Anwar Nuseibeh, was at the Arab College before he went to the Persse School and Queens'. During his short tenure of the office, which he doubled with that of Defence Minister, he wrought wonders, and gave an entirely new direction to the Government's development policy. He has been succeeded by another Arab College old boy, Anwar al-Khatib, of Hebron, who first showed his mettle as Mayor of Jerusalem in very difficult days. The new Education Minister is Ahmed Tuqan, bearer of a time-honoured name and a former colleague on the Arab College staff, who had already proved himself an educator of great ability and a worthy disciple of Ahmed al-Khalidi. These have remained, and others with them. The Director General of Forests, Ya 'qub Salti, is a former pupil of mine; the Director of the Tourist Department, Ahmed Sab'a, was at the Arab College a little later. Both are noted for their energy and enterprise. As I go about the country nothing gives me more pleasure than to meet former pupils of the Arab College, upholding its honour and tradition. Their "doyen" is Ihsan Hashim, who, after a distinguished career in the Mandatory Government, has now become Under-Secretary for Foreign Affairs, a position which he adorns with ability, geniality and that gift for being equally and sincerely at home and friendly with his own countrymen and with those of other countries which is one of the hallmarks of the Arab College. But the College itself is gone. Its second, permanent home, specially built for it near Government House, is in a "demilitarized" zone. During the fighting it was looted and defiled, its library scattered. Now the building stands, or is supposed to stand, empty. I have dwelt at length on this subject of education, because in no one particular have the assets of Arab Palestine suffered a more grievous diminution than in the loss of the Arab College, and the "diaspora," as one of them described it, of its trained teachers.

"Exoriare aliquis nostris ex ossibus ultor": as a result of Ahmed Tuqan's energetic initiative a new Teachers' Training College has arisen, on a commanding hill above 'Amman, with a model demonstration school alongside it, and a magnificent industrial school nearby. The Women's Training College is at Ramallah. In the provision of these splendid buildings and their equipment, Point Four has notably helped. Most important of all, Ahmed Tuqan has induced more than twenty of the country's best teachers to return. The great tradition is being maintained.

The second means through which the individual sufferer has improved his own and others' lot is the land. Here the gain has been absolute, with no alloy of loss. All over the country, but specially on the West Bank, new farms have come into existence, and old ones have been extended.

This is the culmination of a process which was started nearly a century ago, the reclamation of the soil of Palestine. Just how productive the land had formerly been, it is hard to judge. In one asset, namely, trees, it seems always to have been poor. There were a few localities, such as Carmel and Tabor, which were covered with trees, both of old and until recent times; but in general the country even in antiquity seems to have been bare. Solomon's importation of timber from Lebanon may have been a matter of taste rather than necessity; but the rapidity with which, according to Josephus, the Roman armies denuded the environs of Jerusalem, suggests that at the time of the siege, in A.D. 70, Judea was not thickly afforested. The siege lasted altogether 134 days, between April and September. Within a fortnight of its being begun, Titus ordered his troops to collect timber to make banks, as a result of which "the suburbs were left naked" (*Wars*, V, vi, 2). By the 20th Ab (22nd August), we are told that every tree within a radius of twelve miles had been stripped of its branches (*Id.*, VI, viii, 1). The ravages of the Persians in the seventh century must have still further ruined the country. In A.D. 1047, we learn from Nasir-i-Khusrau that "round about the city there are no trees." When the Crusaders came to besiege the city, they were worse off even than the Romans, for they had to import the timber for their engines from Europe. Later travellers speak of the barrenness of the Judæan landscape. Further damage was done during the nineteenth century by the Turkish tree-tax, and right down to the time of the First War, when hundreds of olive trees were cut down by the Turks to provide fuel for their trains.

But since the sixties of last century, a regeneration has been in progress. It owes its origin to Christian devotion. The reclamation of the waste places was started by the Lutheran Templars, who came to Palestine from Germany in 1869, and established not only the "German Colonies" in Haifa, Jaffa and Jerusalem which are still models of planning, but also farming villages at Sarona and Wilhelma near Jaffa and at the northern Bethlehem near Nazareth. Next came Jewish colonists, whose great agricultural school at Mikveh Israel, near Jaffa, was to be the precursor of many more. It was here that the first eucalyptus trees were grown in Palestine, from seeds given by Mr. Spafford, founder of the American Colony, to whom they had been sent by a friend in Tasmania. The planting of the hill country was carried on by Christian communities—of whom the pioneer was Father Müller at Qubeibeh, who in the first years of this century transformed an absolutely bare hilltop into a pine grove whose fame is now world-wide. The Lutherans were doing the same on the Mount of Olives, and the Russians and the Greeks also. Later the Russians and the Franciscans were to regenerate the Garden of Gethsemane, the Salesians, the Dominicans and the Benedictines all of them to contribute to the restoration of the woods of Judæa. A comparison of a photograph of fifty years ago with the same scene to-day will show how abundantly they have succeeded.

The coming of the British administration greatly extended and accelerated the good work. Twenty-five years ago, the screes of Bab-el-Wad, where the road from Jaffa enters the hills, were bare; yet I remember that Canon Hanauer had told me that when he was a boy in the fifties of the last century, he had been afraid to go down it at night because of the wild animals in its thickets. To-day, thanks to the planting of new trees by the Mandatory Government, it is once more wooded. Near the towns, householders, Arab and Jew alike, were quick to take advantage of the new piped water supplies to plant trees.

In the countryside, the change took longer to come about, largely due to a pernicious habit of the fellahin, whose customary form of revenge was to cut down their enemies' fruit trees. It was not worth planting and tending for years an orchard of which you might be deprived in a single night. This ruinous form of crime was put an end to by the "Collective Punishments Ordinance," which made the villagers collectively responsible for any malicious damage inflicted by one of their number on the trees of another. In effect, it made the whole village into an insurance society, whose underwriters, that is to say every adult male, were constantly on the alert to forestall claims. That was in the early thirties; by the outbreak of war, this law, combined with an energetic programme of agricultural education and demonstration, and, very notably, the example of the Christian and Jewish settlements, had started a transformation of the hill country of Judæa and Samaria. On all sides, new vineyards, olive-groves, and fig-groves had sprung up. Apples and plums were being introduced, and hill after hill formerly bare and shivering, was being clothed with branches, blossom and fruit. Old terraces were being reclaimed, new enclosures built.

Under the press of affliction, this salutary process has been extended even further. Some of the farms are very large, such as the fine fruit farms of Sayyid Wafa Dajany near Sweileh, and at Mejdal on the Jerash road, both on the east bank. Many are just little gardens, such as you might find beside an English cottage. At Qalqilya, on the Tulkarm plain, where the villagers have lost nearly the whole of their rich orange groves, by reason of the truce-line, new wells have been sunk, and new gardens laid out. Near Jerusalem, land which had been left uncultivated for years, because the city offered employments more profitable than agriculture, has now come once more under the plough. And every day seems to witness the extension of the walls and the terraces and the trees. In this respect, if in no other, good has come out of evil.

We come now to the Government's help to the refugees. One of the first acts of King Husein, on returning to his country from Harrow and Sandhurst, even before he assumed his constitutional powers, was to visit one of the largest refugee camps, near Jericho, and tell its occupants that he would always have their welfare at heart. Some months earlier, the Prime Minister, Sayyid Tewfiq

Abulhuda, had announced that Jordan considered all the refugees within its borders as citizens. But the Government's sympathy has gone far beyond words.

In 1952, the British Government made a loan of £1½ million to the Jordan Government, which thereupon set up a Development Board, with the Prime Minister as Chairman, and the Minister of Economics as Vice-Chairman. In the present cabinet, the Minister of Economics is also Minister of Development. It also, very wisely, obtained the services of Mr. J. C. Eyre, of the British Middle East Office. This Office, or B.M.E.O., as it is called, is the relic of the wartime Minister of State's office in Cairo, and a very beneficent relic it is. It is a sort of "Universal Aunts" to the Levant. Any state which wants the services of an economist, a farmer, a welfare worker or such, has only to apply to B.M.E.O., and the requisite man or woman will be forthcoming. Mr. Eyre has worked in agriculture in many parts of Africa. He was also for five years an officer of the Agricultural Department of the Mandatory Government of Palestine. After surveying the situation, he suggested to the Board that the citizens most in need of help were the inhabitants of the frontier villages, and that the best way to help them would be to go over the line, village by village, see what had been lost, and what left, how many extra mouths there were to feed, and then see how many could be fed, and by what means. Thus came into existence the "Frontier Village Loans Committee," and £190,000 odd from the British loan was allocated for its work. In 1953, the British Government granted Jordan another loan of £1½ million. Three-fifths of this is to go towards the current budget, leaving £½ million for development. Some of this £½ million no doubt will also be allocated to the Frontier Village Loans Committee.

The principal objects of the Committee are, to make the land more productive by terracing and restoration, to increase irrigation where possible, and to provide mules and tractors. The number of mules available in the country could not be increased overnight; so, to avoid fruitless competition for those there were, the Committee arranged to import eighty from Cyprus.

So far, I have mentioned the Frontier villages only in generalities; now that we have come to the work of the Committee, let us examine one or two of the villages through their eyes. I have named Qalqilya, near Tulkarm, as an example of enterprise. Qalqilya has a population of 7,020. It used to own and farm 7,000 acres, much of which was irrigated by means of pumps, and grew crops of oranges and grape-fruit. Its citizens were well known for their skill as farmers. They were left with only 2,600 acres, hardly any of which was previously irrigated. Nothing daunted, these people set to work to sink new wells. Twenty-three were started, mostly dug by means of open shafts, cut by hand, the spoil being raised to the surface on a rope drawn by a camel. Only twelve were finished: the other eleven were left incomplete for lack of money. But wherever there is water available, the farmers of Qalqilya have planted citrus to restart the citrus industry they lost. It is an amazing example of faith and courage. Thirty of them have clubbed together and with a loan from the Committee have bought an engine and a pump. By this means they can nurture their own citrus trees, and during the years before they come to maturity they can grow a crop of vegetables on the same land which will reach the market after the Jordan valley crop, which is seven weeks ahead of the hills, and before that of the hills themselves.

But no loan, no Committee, with the best intentions and the best application, can alter the fact that Qalqilya is no longer able to support its inhabitants. Only a fraction of the land left to Qalqilya can be irrigated, and it is clear that the total acreage remaining to the village can support less than a quarter of its present population on a reasonable standard of living.

Or take a little village on the southern edge of the Plain of Esdraelon, perched on the southern foothills of the Carmel spur, between ancient Taanach and Megiddo. Its modern name is Rummaneh, which means pomegranate; but the prophet Zechariah (xii. 11) makes clear its ancient connection with Rimmon. The present population is 1,060, which includes 650 classified refugees, who receive half rations from U.N.R.W.A. Originally, Rummaneh possessed 5,500 acres. Now, the truce-line has slashed away more than half, and of what is left the majority is rocky waste. Only 900 fertile acres remain. These are unirrigated. It takes 33 acres of dry-farmed land to maintain a family. You can gauge the plight of Rummaneh from these figures. The people have sold all their movable property, their furniture and their trinkets, their animals and their ploughs, in order to live. The Loans Committee has given what help it can. But the future for these people also is not bright.

Coming south, we touch on the village of Emmaus (Imwas), just below Bab-el-Wad, on the Ramleh plain. It, too, is a foothill village.

It looks out over what used to be the best fox-hunting country in Palestine, in the days of the "Ramleh Vale" hounds. Now, all that country is closed to it, and the foreground of the view is defaced by acres and acres of good land run to rack and ruin, where "thistles grow instead of wheat and cockle instead of barley." This is the product of the truce-line. What Tacitus said of the Romans, has been brought to pass by the United Nations: "they create a desert, and call it peace." The immediate sufferers have been the villagers of Emmaus. Its 1,740 inhabitants formerly owned 4,300 acres. They now have 620, and of those, only 580 can be farmed. The good Trappist Fathers whose monastery of Latrun is adjacent to the village do what they can for these poor people. The Loans Committee are helping here, too, to bring the little remnant of land into the best possible use and profit.

Finally, to end this melancholy catalogue, let us take a village in the far south, El Burj, "The Tower," which is south-west of Hebron, on the way to Beersheba. Harvests here have never been plentiful, for the rainfall is capricious and inadequate. Yet somehow, by farming on a very extensive scale, its two thousand inhabitants contrived to live. Altogether, they made some use of about ten or eleven thousand acres, much of which was down near Beersheba itself. Now, they are confined to one thousand, of which more than a quarter is useless, and their one well is "on the other side."

Such is the story of the "frontier villages." There are sixty-three of them altogether, and in each one this sad tale is being acted out. For those who prefer statistics, Appendix II tells the hapless story in official figures. You can see how hard a problem these villages present. But you can see also what a difference to them the Frontier Village Loans Committee is making. For what can be done to help them will be done—that is what the committee are proving. And it is the Government that is doing it.

From the first loan, £75,000 was allocated to Jerusalem, £25,000 to the municipality for specific schemes which are now being worked out, and £50,000 for the development of small industries. This £50,000 for the encouragement of small industries has stimulated an amazing variety of enterprises: garages, clothing factories, mechanics, blacksmiths, carpenters, dairies, flour mills, a cold-storage plant, a sweet manufacturer, a sausage-maker. Most characteristic of all, it has helped to buy Bibles for workers to cover with olive-wood boards. These will gladden homes all over the world.

Jerusalem has also benefited from the main block of the loan by the construction of two new roads and an improvement of the airfield. The old direct road to Bethlehem, only five miles long, is severed by the truce line. During the fighting a military road was hastily made, which was precipitous and long, for it had perforce to pass through the fringe of the wilderness. But just before Christmas 1952 an excellent new road, only ten miles long, was constructed by the District Engineer, Khalid al-Khalidi. A direct road has also been opened between the city and the Mount of Olives, over the Cedron and the Wadi Joz. Jerusalem's airport is at Qalandia, 10 km. north on the Ramallah road. Originally this was merely an emergency landing-strip. In 1926, Imperial Airways brought thither a new "airliner" the "City of Jerusalem." It was a gala day. Lord and Lady Plumer, and many of their staff, and a selection of "notables" and hangers-on were taken up for little tours over Jerusalem. For many of us it was the first flight of our lives; and never shall I forget the sensation of leaving the earth, and then almost at once looking down upon the Temple Area and the Mount of Olives. This airport is being completely reconstructed from loan funds, and will soon be able to accommodate four-engined planes.

The loans to Jerusalem, like the frontier village loans, are administered by the Committee's Jerusalem office, which is directed by Mr. Ibrahim Ka'ibni. Mr. Ka'ibni was a colleague of mine in the Mandatory Government. He was our chief Arabic translator. He has a remarkable knowledge of the country and its citizens, is a man of absolute integrity, shrewd but sympathetic. On his own estate near Ramallah, he has given a practical demonstration of what can be done in turning a rocky hillside into a productive fruit farm, on which he employs six refugee families.

The psychological effect of this care by Government for those of its citizens who are in the "economic front line" is great. And it is not the only thing the Government is doing in the front line either. It is building new settlements. The first, on the western brow of the mountains north-west of Hebron, is now nearly finished. It consists of eighty houses, built in a little village on the site of a former Zionist one. The old Zionist huts were mostly made of plaster, the new houses are made of stone. Each house has two barrel-vaulted little rooms, with a kitchen, and a little cistern and a latrine of its own. There is land for the inhabitants to farm in the valley below. It is a great experiment, the first of its kind. This is being built from funds provided by U.N.R.W.A. and put at the disposal of the Minister of Reconstruction and Development. Others are to follow it, in different parts of the frontier.

Which brings us to U.N.R.W.A.—the "United Nations Relief and Works Agency," to give it once again its full title.

A great deal has been written and said about U.N.R.W.A.—about its aims and hopes, about its staff and salaries, about its plans and shortcomings. All that concerns us here is what it has done and is doing. Of its past I would say only this: it was created, all of a sudden, by a resolution of the General Assembly of the United Nations on 1st May, 1950. Although the Resolution created the name and the body, it could not create the staff who were to bring it to life and work. It is hard enough, as we all know, to expand the staff of an already existing ministry or army, and at the same time to preserve its efficiency, honesty and economy; to create a wholly new creature out of nothing is far harder. No wonder that at first there were misfits and fumbles. But that has been overcome. U.N.R.W.A. is an Agency, not an autonomous body. This is hardly worth writing perhaps—it is so obvious. But it is often overlooked, partly, I think, because in English we always call the organization by its initials, slurred into the horrible name of "Unrah," as though it were some minor Egyptian god. In Arabic, its nature and function are preserved in common speech, which refers to it as "the Agency." Poor Unrah, it is quite ungodlike, for it can do nothing at all of itself. If, therefore, it is not doing something which people think it ought to be doing, it is not fair to blame it: we should blame the General Assembly of the United Nations whose Agency it is, and that means blaming the United Nations, which means ultimately blaming you and me.

The Agency has a double function—to provide relief, and to undertake works. The original idea was perfectly logical—the refugees must all be settled in new homes, which U.N.R.W.A. would provide, and meanwhile, while the homes were being found and made ready, U.N.R.W.A. would feed those who would shortly be moving into them. That was three years ago. So far, U.N.R.W.A. has settled only 2,369 bread-winners, say 12,000 people, which isn't much, out of the 864,000 on the Agency's ration roll, plus the natural increase, at the rate of 25,000 babies a year.

Clearly, something has gone wrong. But before we come to discuss it, since it comes under the heading "works," it may be helpful if we look over the "relief" side of the Agency's operations because those come first, and are being carried on daily and successfully.

Of the actual camps, and of the rations that are distributed in them and outside them, I have said something above in chapter one. I also said that less than one-third of the official refugees live in camps, so that even if you were to get rid of the camps, you would still not have solved the problem. This point is so important, that I do not apologize for rubbing it in. The camps are awful: squalid, hopeless, canvas slums for the most part; so that it is a natural and proper instinct to want to do away with them, and to concentrate attention on the camps. But even if all twenty-five of them were to disappear from the face of Jordan to-morrow, there would still be 338,000 official refugees left. U.N.R.W.A. knows that as well as anyone, and so we find that the Agency's operations spread far beyond the mere maintenance of the camps. With the assistance of U.N.E.S.C.O., they maintain sixty elementary schools, for 17,000 pupils, and there are another 11,500 awaiting admission. (U.N.E.S.C.O. is another creation of the United Nations. It sounds like a Rumanian statesman or a Latin verb, but it is really short for United Nations Educational, Social and Cultural Organization.) The mere fact that there are such places as refugees' schools, and that thousands of children know no other education than what is to be had therein is itself a melancholy indication of the break-up of the Mandatory educational system. The teachers in these schools are themselves refugees, and seldom have either adequate training or superior qualifications. But for these, too, U.N.R.W.A. is doing a good work: in conjunction with the famous American Friends' Schools at Ramallah, it organizes summer training courses for its own school-teachers, both men and women. There was one last year, and there is to be another this year.

The Agency has its own health service. It is excellent. Schools you can build in camps, hospitals you cannot. The hospital must be in the right place, that is in as healthy and as accessible a spot as possible, and it must be equipped. Also, if a schoolmaster is ignorant, his pupils do not necessarily suffer irretrievably; but if a doctor is, his patients easily may. What the Agency did, therefore, was to come to arrangements with existing hospitals, whereby their work should continue, or perhaps be expanded, through assistance given by the Agency. By this means, twenty-one hospitals have been

F

helped to carry on and 949 beds are available for in-patients. Not all patients need to go to hospital: a visit to a clinic is often enough, and in any case it is a necessary first step, because not nearly all those who should go to hospital can find room there, so that it is important that all those who can be treated on their feet should be. There are thirty clinics, and two mobile ones. And for the little children there are nineteen health centres.

These institutions are all run by Palestinians. The clinic I know best is the one just inside Herod's Gate, in what used to be a hospice for Indian troops, and before that for Indian Moslem pilgrims. It is this clinic that refugees living in Jerusalem and its environs attend. The doctor in charge is another of the ubiquitous al-Khalidis, Dr. Ragheb, the brother of Khalid. The refugee hospital for Jerusalem is that operated by the Lutheran World Federation in the former Kaiserin Augusta Victoria Stiftung on the Mount of Olives. This imposing building has had a short but hectic history.

When the Kaiser and Kaiserin were here in 1898, they went up the specially made new carriage road, to visit the Russian convent on the Mount of Olives. Stretching out her arm over the famous landscape, the Kaiserin (so one who was present has told me) said how much she would love to own some land on so sacred and commanding a hill. Her wish was overheard, and granted. A subscription was started, under the auspices of the German branch of the Order of St. John; and on the twenty-fifth anniversary of their wedding-day, the 27th February, 1906, the Kaiser and his Empress were handed the title deeds of the land on which the Stiftung was to be built. It was inaugurated in 1910, by Prince Eitel Fritz, ostensibly as a home for tired deaconesses and other missionaries, though ordinary travellers might stay there as well. It was more expensive than the other hospices, as well it might be, for it was much grander. The good missionaries were to be restored to health and vigour, apparently, by being housed in a Wagnerian *schloss*, heavy, elaborate, and allegorical, with a pompous *porte-cochère* (it is the draughtiest spot in Palestine) for them to go in and out by, a more than baronial hall for them to eat in, and a Valhalla of a drawing-room for them to sit in. Nobody believed that all this was for the deaconesses and missionaries, least of all the German propst, who, to show his disapproval of the whole plan, resigned rather than be connected with it. Most people thought that the Kaiser intended to live there himself, when "The Day" dawned. Was he not represented, in the garb of a Byzantine emperor but with his own moustaches, on the ceiling of the chapel, and had not a graven image of himself, as a Crusader this time, together with another of the Kaiserin, holding a model of the palace in her hand, been set up in the courtyard? But The Day never came, and even the staff of deaconesses, under Sister Theodora Barthausen, daughter of the highest lay officer of the Lutheran Church, never took full possession of the building. In 1911, the year after it had been opened, a great storm blew the roof off. Repairs took over two years; and the day of formal opening was fixed for the 1st August, 1914. The outbreak of the First War prevented it. At the end of the war, the German owners of the Stiftung were penniless; so being the most royally conceived building in Palestine, it naturally became the first Government House. It would probably have remained Government House had it not been badly damaged by the earthquake of 1927, during which a stone from the bell-tower crashed through the chapel roof, damaging the Kaiser's toe, and another fell right on to the pillow of Lord Plumer's bed. He fortunately was in England at the time. There was a long dispute as to who should pay for the repairs. This finally went to the Hague Court, which decided that the Palestine Government was responsible. Slowly, the building was put to rights again; but it remained unused for years. Meanwhile Sister Theodora, who had been trained at the famous Kaiserwerth Institution which still venerated the memory of Florence Nightingale, was directing the German Deaconesses' Hospital in Jerusalem. She wished to move the hospital up to the Stiftung, and arrangements were made for her to do so. The new hospital was to have been opened in September, 1939. Once again a German war frustrated German plans. During the Second War, the building was used as a military hospital. At the end of this war, too, the question arose, what was to be done with German property, including religious property, which had been sequestrated? It was finally decided that this particular building, since it had been ostensibly built for Lutheran uses, should be placed under the direction of the Lutheran World Federation, which had been formed in 1946, to unite Lutherans, not only in Germany and Scandinavia, but in America too. Its headquarters in Jerusalem are at the Church of the Redeemer, in the Old City, the church the Kaiser opened in 1898; there live the German Propst, Herr Doering, and his energetic helper and director of the charitable work of the Federation, Dr.

Moll, an American citizen of Australian origin who first came to Jerusalem as a soldier in 1917. To start with, the hospital was operated jointly by the Red Cross and the Lutheran World Federation, but since 1st May, 1950, it has been managed by the Lutheran World Federation alone, with help given by U.N.R.W.A. The hospital has 350 beds. U.N.R.W.A. provides a subvention of $14,000 a month and 450 "hospital" rations, the additional hundred being for the staff.

Thus the great Stiftung, designed for the glory of one western empire, and long the home of the representatives of another, has now become a hospital for the poor and needy of Palestine, a hospital staffed entirely by Palestinians. In this respect it is, I believe, the first of its kind. At its head is a very remarkable man, Dr. Tawfiq Canaan. Not only is he a skilful and beloved physician, who has for many years been the friend and healer of many citizens of all creeds and races, but he is also a scholar of unique attainments. Dr. Canaan realized that the impact of the West on Palestine was bound in time to abolish old customs and change old beliefs. He also realized that he, as an Arab and a doctor, had opportunities to observe and to record these customs and beliefs which no one else could enjoy. He therefore set himself to note down everything that he thought would be of interest to the student of folklore and psychology. Much of what he gleaned is preserved in the pages of the Journal of the Palestine Oriental Society, one of the best products of the Mandatory régime, for the Society united scholars of many nations and confessions, from both East and West. It perished with the Mandate. Dr. Canaan has also published a book, *The Arab House*, which describes the methods and materials used in its construction, its various types and designs and the uses of its various parts. The songs, proverbs, charms, talismans associated with birth, sickness, marriage, death, seed-time and harvest—all of these Dr. Canaan had written down and filed among his records. It was his hope that when he retired, he could devote himself to his studies, and give to the world a definitive work on the folklore of the Holy Land. In 1948, his house, which is now on the other side of the line, was looted, his possessions, including his beloved records, were scattered or burnt, and he and his family became refugees. But he is still the same Dr. Canaan; and to see him directing the hospital, full of the same affection for his fellow-creatures, with the same welcoming smile, and the same quick interest in mankind and its ways, you would never suspect that he had suffered tribulation and disappointment.

With him is another great physician, Dr. Kalbian. The rest of the staff are of a younger generation, but with the same standards, and the same sense of being devoted to the welfare of their countrymen. What an effect this attitude has on their countrymen, I shall tell in due place.

Tuberculosis has greatly afflicted the refugees. The conditions under which they live, the cold, the damp, and the insufficiency of food, have weakened their resistance to it. A tuberculosis sanatorium was needed as much as any single form of succour. Such a hospital has been provided by the energy and munificence of one veteran American missionary. Dr. Lambie ministered for many years to the poor and sick in Abyssinia; during the war, he helped the Bishop with St. Luke's Hospital, Hebron. He is well over sixty. But he and his wife decided that they still had work to do in the Holy Land. Ten miles south of Bethlehem, lie the spring and reservoir of 'Arroub, the head of an aqueduct which of old fed Solomon's Pools and so contributed to Jerusalem's water supply. By the reservoir has been established a Government Agricultural Station and, more recently, a refugee camp. It is here, by the side of the road to Hebron, that Dr. Lambie has built his hospital. It accommodates sixty patients. Attached to the hospital are a clinic, and houses for Dr. and Mrs. Lambie and their staff. This foundation is a memorial to the devotion and ability of two American Christians. They called it the Berachah Tuberculosis Sanatorium because it stands in the ancient valley of Berachah, "the valley of blessing" of 2 Chronicles xx. 26. It is well named.

Camps, schools, clinics, hospitals—such is the outline of the work which U.N.R.W.A. is performing, but these bare words give no idea of what their contribution is to the maintenance of all these hundreds of thousands of sufferers. For in addition to their own official activities, they give help wherever they can to all those who are working for the good of the refugees. In the Old City alone they assist thirty institutions, by giving them rations in bulk, which are distributed as cooked food. Christian benevolence is helping, too. Down by the old Serai, in the Old City, there is a little "tekya" or hospice, and in this hospice, itself a fine example of Mameluke architecture, is a soup kitchen. It is the oldest of its kind in Jerusalem. It was founded by the famous Roxelana, the Russian slave who became the wife of Suleiman the Magnificent. When she gave birth to a son, the future Sultan Selim II, she was awarded the honorific title "Khasseki Sultan," or "Sultan's favourite." She established a *waqf* or religious endowment in Jerusalem, like the one she had founded in Constantinople. It is still called the "Khasseki-Sultan waqf." This waqf was originally very rich, and its income before the war amounted to £12,000 a year. Now it has but a few shops left. Originally, it was a sort of U.N.R.W.A. in itself. Not long ago, I was calling on my old friend Sheikh Ya'qub al-Bukhari, who lives in the Nakshabandi hospice on the southern side of the *"Ecce Homo"* arch, under the shadow of the Antonia minaret. It is an abode of "calm and deep peace," and his diwan is surmounted by one of the most graceful saucer domes still standing in Jerusalem. We were talking of old times and new. (He is now a venerable and benign sheikh, but time was when he was strikingly handsome and wore a smart Turkish uniform. In 1917 he was in the Turkish military postal department of Jerusalem. On the approach of the British, he took a hammer, smashed the telegraph apparatus, went home, changed from his uniform into his ecclesiastical robes, and resumed his life of good works and contemplation. Only the photographs on the wall of his study tell of his military exploits, unless you ask for the story, which Sheikh Ya'qub will tell you with a quiet twinkle in his merry eye.) On this occasion, as we were discussing refugees and relief, Sheikh Ya'qub went and brought a small manuscript notebook, entitled "The Blessed Register, if God will, Exalted be He, containing the distribution of bread to those who are entitled to it from the Waqf of Khasseki-Sultan, may God make light her grave and multiply her benevolence." It is dated 1222, Hegira, which corresponds to A.D. 1807. The little book contains the exact particulars of all those who were entitled to their daily dole. First come thirteen "cloisters," or distribution centres as we should call them now. The "tekya" received twenty-four *rottles*, which is 162 lb., every day. Then come the names of 353 families in Jerusalem, who between them received 11,982 loaves. The allotment of each family is meticulously given, even down to half a loaf in certain cases. The total daily award weighed 1,721 pounds. The loaves, as can be seen from these figures, must have been very small. The daily allocation to one member of the Ja'uni family, for instance, was twenty-seven-and-a-half of them.

Besides this distribution of bread, at the "tekya" itself you could also get soup. You still can. And it is still brewed in vast copper cauldrons. Some of these enormous vessels, the size of a good bath, are preserved in the museum of the Haram esh Sherif. Those now in use must be of a respectable antiquity. To benefit from this ancient endowment, you do not need a card, nor do you have to register, nor go through any other formality. You simply take your cup or can, and go along to the hospice at noon, and you will be fed. About 600 people are thus helped every day. And it is pleasant to record that it is the Lutheran World Federation that is making it possible for its august Moslem predecessor to maintain her good work.

Last in the list of those who are helping to relieve the distress of the refugees come the volunteers. These include persons and organizations both of the country and from outside it.

When account is taken of the strain on the individual Arab, and the efforts which he is making to help his family, of which something has been said above, it might be expected that little energy or money would be available for corporate efforts; for it must always be borne in mind that the committee system, however efficient it may or may not be, is too impersonal and indirect to appeal to the Arab mind and heart. Nevertheless, there are quite a number of organizations which work for the refugees. The Red Crescent, for instance, which is the Islamic counterpart of the Red Cross, through its various local associations, is active. The ladies form sewing parties and hold bazaars, just like their western sisters. These have a double virtue, because the garments go to clothe the needy, and the money to such good objects as maternity homes.

Next come the special foundations. Here in Jerusalem, we have three: the Dar et Tifl ("Baby Home"), Dar al Awlad ("Boys' Home") and Rawdat al Zuhur ("Flower Garden"). Dar et Tifl and Dar al Awlad are both orphanages. The former maintains one hundred and sixty orphan boys and girls between the ages of four and fifteen. Its chairman is Anwar al-Khatib, of whom mention has already been made. The home was originally started in 1948, in two rooms in the Old City, to house fifty little survivors of the massacre of Deir Yassin. But there were unfortunately many other orphans; so the first makeshift quarters were soon abandoned for a large house which accommodated one hundred and twenty-five, a number which has now been increased to one hundred and sixty. The presiding spirit of the home is Miss Hind Husseini, a Moslem lady of Jerusalem, and a well-known social worker and educator. The orphanage has no endowment. It is supported by many within and without the country. King Ibn Saud gives an annual grant, so does the International Christian Committee, of which more will be said below. Here, too, U.N.R.W.A. shows its good sense and breadth of vision, by providing much of the food for the children, and meeting a quarter of the expenditure as well. From time to time other people help, too. Women's organizations in Dhahran, in the Persian Gulf, and Jedda, in Saudi-Arabia, among them. The aim of this institution is "to shelter and educate refugee children" and its hope is "to provide good future citizens who will help in reconstructing their community."

Dar al Awlad gives a home and education to sixty-six little boys. The foundress and moving spirit of the place is Mrs. George Antonius, in whose house the children live, and in whose garden they play. Mrs. Antonius is one of the four brilliant daughters of the late Nimr Pasha, the son of Lebanon who became the founder of the first great Egyptian daily newspaper, the "Mokattam." Her beautiful house on Mount Scopus used to be a centre of all that was kind and cultivated in East and West. The house is gone now; and so are all, or nearly all, of the bright and strong spirits who illuminated it. But in her little house above the Wadi al Joz, Mrs. Antonius is still the same as ever, still the warm-hearted, candid counsellor and friend she always was. How fortunate are the little boys of Dar al Awlad to come within the orbit of such a star.

The institution called Rawdat al Zuhur is administered by Miss Elizabeth Nasir, a member of a Christian family from Bir Zeit, north of Ramallah, who have long been honoured for their pioneer work in educating their fellow-Palestinians. It is a school, or club, if you like, of thirty little girls who are taken, literally, from the streets. Nothing is sadder than to see a little child become old before it has known what it is to be young, to be hardened and battered into a travesty of maturity, to acquire the whine, the impudent humility of the professional beggar, at an age when it should be learning the pleasures of affection. Alas! our streets are acquainted with such children now. But there would be thirty more of them were it not for Miss Nasir, and her garden. The children are cared for and brought up as children should be. They live in little groups, each named after its own flower. This home, too, is maintained by the International Christian Committee. For the very small children, there is the Arab Ladies Union infant welfare centre, which deals with over 5,000 children a month.

One of the most remarkable, and most successful, attempts to supply practical relief to the refugees was also one of the earliest. And it was started not by a society but by one man, Musa 'Alami. Musa 'Alami was one of the first Palestinians to go to Cambridge, where he read law. He then joined the Legal Department of the Mandatory Government, and later became private secretary to the High Commissioner. But he was not happy as a government officer, and resigned. Musa is a man of deep humanity, unalloyed patriotism and uncompromising honesty. He felt the sorrow and humiliation of his people intensely, and has given expression to his thoughts in a telling book. But he wanted to do something to restore the situation, and to point the way to others. He therefore organized a little group of friends, who put together a sum of money to buy some land near Jericho.

In antiquity, Jericho was proverbial for its fertility. It was a favourite resort of Herod the Great. Josephus and Galen praise it as a paradise, and the sole source of balsam. This happy state lasted almost to the end of the Middle Ages, after which a decline set in. At the beginning of the last century, Jericho had dwindled to a small and dirty village, of not more than three hundred lazy and unruly inhabitants, a mixture of Negroes and Bedouins. It is described with repugnance both by Mr. Nicolayson, who was there in 1835, rescuing Christopher Costigan, and by Mr. Finn, who was there in 1847, rescuing Lieutenant Molyneux, of H.M.S. *Spartan*. (Both these unfortunate young men had tried to sail down the Jordan, and to explore the Dead Sea. Both died of their exertions; and it remained for Lieutenant Lynch, of the United States Navy, in 1848, to succeed where they had failed.) But in the 'eighties the town began to recover. This was due primarily, so Laurence Oliphant tells us, to the enterprise of the Russians, who built a number of little stone houses set in gardens, round about the central hospice which the Russian Government had built for the use of the thousands of pilgrims who trudged from Jerusalem down to the River Jordan and back. In those days there was no carriage road. It was being contemplated in 1885, when Oliphant was writing, as was also the restoration of the Khan al Ahmar, the "Red Inn" or "Inn of the Good Samaritan," which in our own day has been once more relegated to unimportance by the coming of the motor-car. This first road was what is now called the "old road," down the Wadi Kelt, the new southern one having been constructed for the Kaiser's

visit, as we have seen. Then a bridge was built across the Jordan, on
the site of the present Allenby Bridge. Jericho quickly developed,
until by the end of the Turkish régime it had become a pleasant
and prosperous village. Under the Mandate, its irrigation was greatly
improved, and the area under cultivation steadily and widely
increased. But this increase, be it noted, depended wholly on water
from the springs in the Wadi Qilt (which I think takes its name from
the Latin *vallis cultis*, or "cultivated valley," just as the town of Salt
does from *saltus*, or wood; for it is the only such valley in all the
wilderness of Judæa) and other fountains in the vicinity of Jericho.
The most famous is Elisha's fountain, 'Ain es-Sultan, or the Sultan's
spring, at the foot of the mound of Old Jericho. Oliphant counted
nine different aqueducts, many of which have now been restored to
use. Pretty well every inch of land that can be watered with surface
water has for some time been under the plough. Musa 'Alami
realized that to bring new land into bearing, it would be necessary
to raise water from below the earth's surface. Now the experts had
said that this was impossible. They had written a report to prove it,
and had drawn a line on a plan to show that a little beyond the eastern
confines of Jericho, there was no water to be had whatsoever. Disre-
garding these pessimists, Musa 'Alami acquired 2,000 acres of desert
land, and started to sink wells. He found water at an average depth
of 40 metres. He has now proved thirty wells, of which ten have
been supplied with pumps and are providing water. The result
has been that in one of the most desolate and arid, but potentially
productive spots, on earth, a new oasis has been created, and 500
of his 2,000 acres are already under cultivation. As you drive along
the tree-lined avenues, and see the grain crops and banana groves
shining in the breeze, you can hardly believe that it has all been
done in three years. On this Aladdin's farm Musa 'Alami has built
an industrial school. It is a "Boys' Village" where over eighty
refugee children are being taught the mysteries of agriculture, and
of trades such as plumbing and carpentry. The village has its own
electric plant, and by night as by day attracts the eye of the traveller
from afar. Many of these children when they first came to the
village did not even know how to sleep on a bed, such neglected
waifs they were. Now, they are happy, normal schoolboys, and
come up to greet you with a frank and confident smile. Besides
training the boys, the farm employs between three and five hundred
refugees as cultivators, according to the season.

The refugees have also many friends who come from other countries. Many of them have been at work in Palestine for many years. The oldest is the American Colony Clinic. The history of the American Colony, and of its charitable foundations, has been vividly told by one of the daughters of its founder, Mrs. Bertha Spafford Vester. Mrs. Vester recently celebrated her seventy-fifth birthday here in Jerusalem. For more than seventy-three years, Jerusalem has been her home. In the house which the Spafford family first occupied just inside the Damascus Gate, General Gordon would come and visit them, during the year he spent in Palestine in 1883. That house is now once more the Spafford Baby Home, the only children's hospital in Jerusalem. It is maintained, as it has been for many years, by American friends of Mrs. Vester. I say "once more," for until recently, Mrs. Vester had lent it to the Order of St. John as a temporary ophthalmic hospital, to bridge the inter-regnum between the loss of the old hospital and the making ready of Watson House. The restored Baby Home now has fifty beds, and a staff of eight to look after the little occupants. Three hundred and fifty babies are registered "out-patients" in the clinic.

The American Colony itself also maintains a clinic. It is in a house just opposite the main buildings, on the very edge of no-man's-land. It suffered during the fighting, so that the main dining-room of the Colony hostel became for a time the casualty clearing station. More than seventeen thousand casualties were treated there during the sad months following May, 1948. Now, the old clinic is back in com-mission. The other day, I was motoring a visitor down past the American Colony. "What is this crowd doing?" he said. "Is it a demonstration?" It was the crowd of patients waiting outside the American Colony clinic. They had come from far and near, and they had spread up and down the footpath and out into the roadway. Such is the reputation of this centre of healing.

Which brings us to the Christian Church and its ministrations, of which the American Colony is a shining emblem. It is not necessary to say much of them in a review of this sort, because they should be taken as a matter of course. Just as the Jews, in the day of their affliction in Europe, turned to the Church as their chief source of succour, so now the Arabs do the same. I have already mentioned some of the institutions and people who benefit by Christian aid: there are many others. The majority of those who are receiving help are Moslems—naturally, since the majority of the inhabitants of Palestine is Moslem. But the Christian refugees have been cared for, too. In one cardinal respect, the Christians are better off than their Moslem neighbours: not one of them is in a refugee camp. Man for man, the Christian community was richer than the Moslem. Being far smaller, only about one-tenth of the population, it had always formed a self-conscious minority, which had been ahead of the majority in benefiting by the schools established by fellow-Christians from abroad. More Christians, proportionately, had been officers of the Mandatory Government, more had become agents of big foreign firms, or had founded their own firms. So far as urban property is concerned therefore, the loss of the Christians in Jerusalem, Jaffa and Haifa has been proportionately greater. This fact has no doubt coloured their attitude to the refugee problem in general; it is only human that many of them should see it less in terms not of a land alienated than of property not compensated for. In the enterprise and resolution with which they have rebuilt their fortunes, either in Jordan, or among their co-religionists of the Lebanon, or in lands beyond the sea (especially the republics of South America) the Christians have shown themselves the equals of their Moslem brothers.

The Christian communities have been engaged in charitable works for many years; so that when they were confronted with the refugee problem, what was needed was expansion rather than innovation. The Latin Church assisted by the Pontifical Mission, the official Roman Catholic Relief Organization, feeds nearly 7,000 people daily in Jerusalem; and in its various properties it houses over 500 refugee families. Other churches, including the Greek Orthodox and the Copts, have feeding centres. The Anglican Church in Jerusalem represents not only the Church of England, but the Anglican Communion throughout the whole world. It can claim, just as the Latin Church can, to be œcumenical. Its support comes from England, Scotland, Ireland, every Dominion and most Colonies. Above all, it comes from the United States of America, where the Protestant Episcopal Church (as it is there called) has responded to the call of the needy with characteristically American generosity.

The Anglican Church has its headquarters at St. George's Close, which is outside the city, on the ancient road to the north. In that particular area there was less urgent need for a feeding-centre than elsewhere. In the Old City, as we have seen, centres were opened by institutions which are established there. So the Anglican Church started a feeding centre in Bethany, where it had for many years owned a house. This centre gradually expanded. It now supplies 400 meals a day, collected at noon by the children, who take home to their mothers the shares to which each family is entitled. Milk is also distributed to little children, and in the winter blankets and warm clothing to those who are in greatest need of them. Nearly all the food for the kitchen, as well as the milk powder, comes from America. The clothing comes from both England and America. Bethany is not a big village, and yet, in addition to its ordinary inhabitants, it now has 995 refugees living there. Its sister village of Abu Dis has 1,677. In neither village have more than a handful of new houses been built in the last four years, and those not for refugees. It is clear, therefore, that these 2,692 extra souls must live either in caves or in ruins. They draw rations from U.N.R.W.A.; but many of them are in bodily need, particularly of clothing. So that both they, and the impoverished ordinary inhabitants of Bethany, are glad of the Church's help.

This description, brief though it is, of what is being done to alleviate distress, is already long. I am glad that it is, for at least it shows that man's humanity to man is still a force in this wicked world. Before I close it, I want to mention just two aspects of the Christian contribution. First, there are two new agencies in the field. I have already mentioned the Lutheran World Federation. It was a particular providence that ordained that this great union of Christians should be created just at the time when its help was so urgently needed. Among the communities not in obedience to Rome, it now takes the lead in charitable work in the Holy Land. The second agency is the Mennonites. Not many English people know of the Mennonites. They originated at Zurich in 1525, their founder being Menno Simons. They are a peaceful and practical community, having something in common with the Quakers. They established a settlement in Germantown in Pennsylvania in 1883. It is from the American community that the Mennonites now serving in Palestine are drawn. They are doing wonderful work.

The second aspect of the current Christian work for the afflicted and distressed is its unity. There exists in Beirut a body called the Co-ordinating Committee, on which all communities of the Church, from Rome to Germantown, are represented. They plan the work between them, for the best interests of those whom they serve. In Jordan, the regional co-ordinating agency is the International Christian Committee. This committee maintains "in the field" two relief teams, one at Nablus which is directed by an Anglican Scotswoman with an Arab assistant, the other at Hebron, which is composed of two young Mennonite twin sisters. Both teams work principally in the frontier villages, maintaining feeding centres, distributing clothing, directing schools for children and grown-ups, and organizing vocational training. They are to be found wherever

> "Hopeless Anguish pours his groan
> And lonely Want retires to die."

The committee also assists a number of institutions in Jerusalem. And it provides bursaries for many boys and girls, in schools of many denominations, who would otherwise have to continue uneducated. Above all, by its constitution, it gives help where it finds that help is needed, and never because the needy man or woman or child is of this or that faith.

Chapter Six

The harvest is past, the summer is ended, and we are not saved. . . . Is there no balm in Gilead?

JEREMIAH viii. 20, 22.

WE now have to face the question why, after five years, has no real progress been made towards settlement of the refugees? For five years, they have lived the life of the uprooted, lodging in caves and ruins, or herded in the collective squalor of tented camps. U.N.R.W.A., it is known, has made repeated efforts to induce them to move, to inhabit settlements specially built for them with comfortable houses, with the prospect of occupation and eventual independence. And always they have refused. Why?

The answer to this question is the crux, the turning-point, of the whole refugee problem. It is essential that we should get the right answer, and the full answer. First of all, before we can do that, we must decide from what source we are to seek it. Are we to ask the camps, to address a general enquiry to the group which gathers round us as we enter one? Are we to ask the "leaders," the politicians? Or are we to ask the individual refugee, away from his fellows, away from the group with its special pressure and psychology, like Nicodemus, by night?

For a question of such importance, it will be best to try all three, and then to collate and compare the answers.

In the camps, even if you talk Arabic, you are conscious of being in a hostile, embittered atmosphere, among people who have a grudge against life and society. Nothing, they feel, has been done for them, or is likely to be. Therefore, since they can have no positive satisfaction of happiness, let them at least have the negative pleasure of discomfiting others. It is exactly the attitude which Milton ascribes to the fallen Satan. It may seem unreasonable. It is. But it exists. This is not the first time I have met it. I was once connected with a leper hospital. It was the most depressing institution to visit, and that not primarily or principally by reason of the awful condition of the patients' bodies. For that can be overcome where the spirit is in the ascendant; and I have been in another leper settlement where proof of it was daily given. It was the spiritual decay of these men and women that made their company so terrible. They felt that, for no crime of their own, they were being treated as criminals, locked away from their families and fellows, and condemned to a hell on earth, a death in life. This had been done, not by an act of God, but by the calculated doom of their fellow-citizens. It was this that they could not forgive. And so they made life as difficult as possible for those who had to look after them. They were given little gardens, and refused to work them. They broke every window in the place as often as they dared. They kept the whole enclosure as filthy and untidy as they could. They shouted and they howled. They did everything in their power to defy and to disturb discipline.

The spiritual condition of the camps is much the same. Those who inhabit them feel that they, too, are victims, not criminals, that they have lost their homes and lands not through their own fault, but by the knavery or folly of others. This is the plain, unpleasant truth. As usual, of course, those who do not wish to probe into causes, lest their remedy prove bitter, will talk of "agitators" and "communists." It is true that agitators and communists are busy in these camps; they are their natural constituency; but to suppose that they originate the feelings which they only exploit is to suppose that ambergris is the source of the scent it only enhances. To talk of agitators is merely an incantation, a flattering unction. The real, basic feeling in the minds and hearts of these men and women is that they have been betrayed. And so they ask for nothing less than a complete restitution, a return to the very homes and acres from which they have been expelled. Is this unreasonable? Of course it is. But all our strongest impulses and feelings are unreasonable. These people are possessed by a longing for revenge, or, if you like, for justice, which as Bacon says, is but civilized revenge. The "psychology of the group," which is wholly irrational, depending on the reaction to external stimuli to the almost total exclusion of internal ratiocination, reinforces this feeling, this thirst. That is why the refugees will tell you that they want only to return. In a world where all else has dissolved, that proud dream alone remains real. And, to the Arab of Palestine, it is the strongest possible reality. For to him, the land is life. It does not belong to him: he belongs to it. The relation of land and peasant is throughout the world a mystical, god-hallowed relation. It is as strong in Palestine as it is or ever was anywhere. I have cited Naboth as a type of Palestine peasant. Read his story again, in I Kings xxi. "And Ahab spake unto Naboth, saying, Give me thy vineyard, that I may have it for a garden of herbs, because it is near unto my house: and I will give thee for it a better vineyard than it; or, if it seem good to thee, I will give thee the worth of it in money. And Naboth said unto Ahab, The Lord forbid it me, that I should give the inheritance of my fathers unto thee." There you have it—the lust for the other man's land, because it is near one's boundary, the excuse that it is to be put under better, more intensive cultivation, the claim that somewhere else will do for Naboth just as well—it is still the same story. The only difference is in Ahab's favour, for he did at least offer to pay for what he took. "Naboth's vineyard" has become accepted by the English-speaking world as a byword for unlawful possession—everywhere except in Naboth's own country. Naboth was unreasonable. The refugees are just as unreasonable.

The next class to be approached in our investigation are the "leaders." By "leaders," I do not mean the Jordan Government. Their attitude has already been mentioned, and I shall have cause gratefully to recur to it. I mean those who try to engage the support and suffrages of their fellow-countrymen. In general, the politicians of the Levant have a bad reputation in England. But we should remember that the reputation of English politicians in the Levant is just as bad. In England we are apt to despise the Near-Eastern politician, to call him a "mere townee," "unrepresentative," and to say that we would rather do business with the old tribal, feudal, "unspoilt" spokesmen. It is true that we should prefer to, because we do not like, with our conservative instincts, either to deal with what is new in other countries, or to admit that it exists in our own. This attitude exasperates our American friends, who are apt in consequence to talk to every Englishman they meet abroad as though he were Lord North; it also antagonizes the Near-Eastern politicians.

It is no good saying that they are "unrepresentative townees." To do so implies that English politicians are all country-bred, public-spirited gentlefolk, who conduct politics solely for the good of their country. Even before 1832 this was only partly true. Since the Reform Act, politics in England has become increasingly a profession, and increasingly lucrative to those who engage in it, who themselves have been drawn increasingly from the towns and from

G

among those to whom lucre is a necessity of material existence. It is not for the English, therefore, to sneer at townees in other lands. If, instead of so doing, we ask their views on the refugee problem and the prospects of settlement, we shall find that they, too, insist on return as the only possible solution. But they do not mean the word in the same sense as the camp-dwellers. Few of the politicians have any intrinsic connection with the land. They are mostly lawyers or men of property. They know quite well that any attempt at a complete and corporal return is now out of the question. What they are out for is compensation: they would accept Ahab's proposition. But they feel that Ahab is not going to make it, unless he is compelled to. If the refugees are settled, the claim of the property-owners will be forgotten, they say. So meanwhile, the refugees must be kept in their camps, and the problem must be perpetuated. It is the gambit of the importunate widow, a Palestinian whose methods succeeded. Callous—thus to exploit human misery? Yes, it is, from our point of view. But from the point of view of the leaders, it is hypocrisy in us to call it so. To them, their policy is like calling "one club" at bridge when you hold no club in your hand—a recognized convention in a game of which the rules are known and established. They, also, think of themselves and their country as having been betrayed. To accept settlement would be to condone the crime, and at the same time to acquiesce in their own impoverishment.

But if you ask the individual refugee, what answer do you get? First of all, you will get precisely the same one, that only a return will satisfy him. But there is an important difference in the way in which he states his case: being but one man, he puts it as a wish, not as a condition or a demand. But he feels it just as deeply. He is still Naboth. I had two instances of this recently. The first was at Jerash, beyond Jordan, the most vibrant relic of the Decapolis, and of the life that was lived there long ago. It is now a village of Arabs and Circassians, set in the fertile uplands of Gilead. A group of us had gone at noon one day to the spring of Calirrhoas, which at that hour is the village club, where you meet to hear the news, to do a bit of washing and to have a swim. Among the crowd, I noticed one man who was clearly from the West Bank. I asked him where he came from. He named a village near Jaffa. He was at present living in a camp, and he had come over to Jerash to help in the harvest. He was working for three shillings a day, and he would be employed for a month at the outside. But he would thus earn a little ready cash. I asked him where he thought he would be living in the future. His whole attitude changed. "Only in my own village," he replied shortly. He would say no more: he was tired of hearing alternatives, and was determined to accept none, nor even to hear them discussed. The second case also occurred east of the Jordan, but this time it was in 'Amman. The speaker was a man from the town of Jaffa. He was now employed at good wages in a kind household, where he was generously treated. When he had told me where he had come from, and how he had found his present employment, I said to him, "You are very fortunate to be here, earning such good pay, and with such good people." "True," he answered, "but not all the land in 'Amman is worth my own home." That, you will find, is the first answer you will get from them all. It is the expression of one of man's strongest and oldest instincts. Because it is used by the leaders for their own ends, it does not thereby cease to exist. We must accept it as the first factor with which we have to reckon in any attempt to find a solution.

It is against this stream of longing that any plan for settlement has to contend.

If, nevertheless, the scheme put forward were in itself sufficiently attractive, would it not, by its practical advantages, overcome the emotional opposition? Who wants to go on suffering? Why not, after all, settle down in comfort?

This was the argument behind the scheme for settling some scores of thousands of refugees in Syria. It sounds reasonable enough to the Western ear. But by no means to the Eastern refugee or citizen. To the refugee, it was simply another trick to lure the Arabs further and further from their homes, to leave more and more of a vacuum for others to fill. To the citizens of Syria, and to the Arabs in general, it was a Western trick to get a firmer hold on their country.

The sad truth is that the West is deeply resented and mistrusted by the Levant. The "West" used to mean England and France, but it now means the United States of America as well. If anything America is a little more disliked than England. It is hard to say, because naturally Englishmen hear the worst of America and Americans the worst of England. Both countries are now regarded as enemies for what they have done in the past, and suspected for any move that they may intend to make in the future. As these two countries are regarded as being the chief springs of the United

Nations, the United Nations comes in for the united suspicion that attaches to each of the two countries separately.

This will grieve many Americans and Englishmen. They will be shocked that people with whom they have such close relationships, and who have benefited so much and so long from American and British education should be so resentful. Strange, they will say, that men who have been educated at St. George's School, and have taken their degrees at the American University of Beirut should hold such views. "Ingratitude" is a word often heard in such circles; so often, indeed, that outside them it has come to be a technical term for one who puts the interests of his own people before those of Britain or America.

It is hard for Englishmen to reconcile themselves to this attitude on the part of foreigners towards an English government. When Lord Byron exhorted the Greeks

"Trust not for freedom to the Franks,
They have a king who buys and sells"

it never occurred to any Englishman that such an objection could apply to his own government. But unfortunately foreigners think differently. What to us are sensible and human questions, such as "But are they fit to govern themselves?" are in their eyes only devices for staying a bit longer in countries that would like to get rid of us. "Partnership," which to us is a new and salutary political conception, is to them cant: any child (it seems to them) who has ever played musical chairs knows that upon the one chair which alone confers the prize, there is room for only one sitter. Our belief in compromise, our belief that we can be liberal at home and conservative abroad at the same time, puzzles foreigners. They do not see the beauty of the little Whipsnade that every Englishman carries in his heart. They prefer their own natural surroundings. And yet, to the individual foreigner, the Arab is so kind, so welcoming.

Newcomers to the Levant are sometimes puzzled by the apparent inconsistency with which an Arab will loose off a violent tirade against the governments of Britain or France or America, spoken in excellent English or French, and will then end with a cordial invitation to his home, or a request for employment in an oil company. An Englishwoman who had for many years been a schoolmistress in an Arab capital told me that one morning she was walking along the street when towards her came a procession of schoolgirls carrying banners invoking God's vengeance on Britain, and raising their voices in denunciation of her country. Some of her own pupils, she noticed, were among them. Not wishing to be embarrassed, or to embarrass, she looked in the other direction as the procession went by. That evening, one of her pupils came to her with a hurt expression. "What have I done to offend you, Miss X," she said, "that you turned away from me when I greeted you during the procession this morning? Why did you thus humiliate me?"

The truth is that the Arabs, like many other sensible people, draw a clear distinction between peoples and their governments. In England, the distinction has been blurred until recently, because we were so well governed, so unobtrusively, so cheaply, so modestly and justly, above all so little, that we had forgotten how tiresome, costly and predatory governments can be. We are learning now. But the East has always known it. To them, a government has always been a natural enemy. It still is, and the stronger it is the more hostility it will arouse. When that government is foreign, you add another powerful factor of dislike. Even in England this feeling is to be found. To some Englishmen, the presence of American troops in Britain, and the transformation of Grosvenor Square into a semblance of the Forty-Ninth State, gives satisfaction, personal and historical. But by no means all Britons feel the same. What then must be the feelings of people in whose countries the foreign troops are far more powerful and obtrusive? No Briton would ever suspect that American troops stationed in Britain might influence internal British politics. No Arab would ever suspect that British troops stationed in his country were there for any other purpose. As governments, they are tired of us, they resent us, they want us to go. And so any scheme which can be interpreted as keeping us about in their lands, even one so typically subtle (they would say) as wanting to help the refugees, is bound to be met with suspicious hostility.

This is particularly true at the present time. Many of those who are still the leaders of their countries in the Arab world, have in their own lives witnessed the transition from subjection to Turkey, through a period of mandate, into national sovereignty. After the First War, Egypt, Iraq, the Yemen and Saudi-Arabia emerged as states: during and after the second, they were joined by four more,

Syria, the Lebanon, Jordan and Libya. This success has been astonishing, so much so that those who have experienced it want it to be
complete in every respect. By an ironical paradox, it was primarily
due to Britain that every one of these states became independent;
and it was in British and American institutions that most of the
leaders of the new states received their education, above all in the
American University of Beirut. This institution must be unique in
the world, a university established in a foreign country with no
object other than to promote the welfare of the inhabitants of that
country and its neighbours. For ninety years the American university
has done just that. When it was founded, oil was unheard of, and
so were airfields and bases. It had no political aims, overt or covert.
It has trained three generations of Arabs in a liberal tradition, and a
tradition of doing things and managing affairs for themselves. For
these men, it is doubly puzzling to look east into Asia, and to see
country after country achieving complete independence, to look
west and to see countries like—but I had better mention no names
—as members of the United Nations, and then to look inwards,
and to see themselves classed as "under-developed" and subjects
for this and that kind of foreign "aid." The whole mandatory
system was distasteful to the Arabs from the first. We held it to
be the beginning of a new and better system. To them it was but a
design for perpetuating a bad old one, for continuing "colonization"
under another name. The resultant malaise is political. It is a fallacy
of the West, probably its besetting fallacy, that you can cure political
ills with economic remedies. Britain has tried it again and again,
always unsuccessfully; and now America is following her bad
example.

At the root of the refugee problem therefore we find this
antagonism to the West. It is founded on the belief that it was the
West, more specifically Britain and America, that brought the
refugees to their present pass, and it results in deep suspicion of any
steps they may propose to get them out of it.

As for the share of Britain and America in creating the refugee
problem, there may be some superficial argument. But certain
contentions are hard to deny. First, Great Britain had accepted the
Mandate from the League as a trust. It had been formally conferred,
and willingly received. It should have been formally handed back
to the United Nations, or on to the power designated by the United
Nations to succeed in the administration of the country. To say

that Britain could not adopt any solution that was not agreeable
to both sides was hypocrisy. No solution ever has been acceptable
to both sides, no solution ever will be, and no one should have
known that simple fact from hard experience better than Great
Britain—it would be as reasonable and as brave for a judge to say
that he could not deliver any judgment that was not acceptable to
both the litigants before him. And then to slink off, leaving chaos
behind: it is a humiliation which stings to this day, and always must.
It is impossible to justify, or to palliate.

The Americans are blamed for what came next. The creation of
Israel was their work, say the Arabs. And its creation was only
partly due to idealistic motives. It was largely actuated by a desire
to win the votes of certain states for a certain party in the 1948
presidential election. Once Israel was in being, it was kept in being
by American money, and then, when the fighting broke out,
by American arms, some of them in the hands of American citizens.
Finally, when the truce came to be drawn up, it was Britain and
America together that allowed the line to be drawn that has
produced the present plight of the sixty-three frontier villages.

I do not say that all this is true, nor that Britain and America
were as knowingly guilty as some people make out. But what is
believed is what counts. And what is believed is what I have written
above. There is, of course, an answer. You can say, "In the first place,
look what we have done for the Arabs at large, the states we have
helped you to create. And besides, did you not for three years do all
in your power to try to *make* us leave your country?" But that is
not really a very dignified or honest way for a trustee to defend
himself to a ward. In this case as in others, if we say that we have no
sin, we deceive ourselves.

To sum up the situation, projects for permanent settlement are
obstructed by three obstacles:

First, the longing to return on the part of the great majority of
refugees;

Secondly, a demand for compensation for property, particularly
on the part of urban and professional men;

Thirdly, a fundamental distrust of the West, based on their past
actions, particularly the creation of the state of Israel; and a con-
sequent suspicion of their present plans, as designed to perpetuate
exploitation.

This triple problem is in its essence political, and must be solved by political action. Until that has been done, and by done, I mean resolved upon and enforced, there is little hope for the success of any national or international schemes for settling the refugees. The situation has been made worse by the number of resolutions which the United Nations has taken, such as that for the partition of Palestine, and for the internationalization of the Holy City, and has wholly failed to enforce. We do not start from scratch, but with a very heavy handicap. Nevertheless, we have a starting point, a precarious ledge, as it were, from which to begin the long climb. That is the tripartite declaration of America, Britain and France, made in 1950, that they will not allow the present frontier between Israel and her Arab neighbours to be altered by force from either side.

Is it possible to make any advance from so slender a base?

Let us take the first obstacle first—this longing for return. From what I have said above, and I have tried to report fairly, it will, I think, be clear that return is no longer thought of as primarily a physical act. It has acquired a psychological overtone, has become a concept rather than a fact. It should perhaps be written "Return." Once any act or fact has been thus invested with immaterial significance, it achieves an independent existence, and no longer depends on the performance of men for its continuance. It becomes a guiding beacon. Men try to approach it, as far as they can; but their failure to reach it wholly and personally does not invalidate or extinguish it. Take, for example, the idea of "Independence," which is a goal of many and achieved by few, and you will see what I mean. "Return" is in the same category. In fact, it has now acquired for the Arabs exactly the essence and force which it formerly had, and still largely has, for the Jews.

Gentiles do not always realize how ancient and powerful is the longing of the Jews for Jerusalem. In the Old Testament we read again and again of the attachment of the Jews to their Holy City, and, particularly in the Psalms, of the rapture which it excited. But it is easy to overlook the later manifestations of the spirit. In the Book of Wisdom, which was written about 100 B.C., you already (xii. 7) find the prayer "that the land which thou esteemedst above all other might receive a worthy colony of God's children." As the centuries passed, this longing became enshrined in the liturgy of *Seder*, the service which takes place on the first night of the Feast of the Passover, as the family and its friends sit at table. Seder is a beautiful ceremony. It rehearses, with special explanations for the children, the story of God's deliverance of Israel from the house of bondage, and the mercy which He continually showed them. After thanksgiving, it ends with the words, "Next year in Jerusalem." This sentence has been recited by thousands of Jews for hundreds of years. It is a kind of talisman. They know, most of them, that it is quite outside the bounds of possibility that they will eat the Passover "next year in Jerusalem"; but to omit that final ejaculation would be unthinkable. Equally unthinkable was any plan that would have established a Jewish community in any country other than Palestine, say Kenya or Cyrenaica. But not even now, with the establishment of Israel, can the majority of Jews look forward to being "next year in Jerusalem." Under the Mandate some thousands could. Now, as we have seen, even those who can approach the Holy City through Israel are confined to the modern western suburb. But that serves as a surrogate for Historic Jerusalem.

May not the same principle be applied to the Arab refugees? Clearly, a physical return of all of them to their former homes is not now possible. Those homes are occupied by others, who cannot be dislodged from them. Moreover, even if a complete physical return were possible, how many Arabs would care to live in Israel, under an Israeli government? Ask those who do. But what can be done is, first, to permit the reunion of separated families either within or without the territory of Israel, as the united family may desire. This is no more than common humanity. Secondly, the iniquity of the frontier line must be remedied, so as to restore their means of livelihood, that is to say their former lands in their entirety, to the sixty-three frontier villages. Thirdly, a resolute effort must be made to place as many refugees as possible as close to their former homes as possible; to fill up the west bank of the Jordan, in fact, with as close a settlement as possible. Just how many new dwellers can be accommodated no one knows. So many estimates have been made in days gone by, all of which have proved wrong, that the only method of ascertaining the capacity of the area is by actual experiment on the spot. When it has been shown that the West Bank has its full share of inhabitants, and that no more can be settled there, then the same process may be attempted on the East Bank. It becomes simply a logical and organic extension of a settlement which has been begun as near to the centre as possible: it is like blood, moving out from the heart to the limbs. Finally, the residue who find no habitation within the territory of Jordan might be enabled to seek it even further afield. But that must be the last stage of the process, not the first.

We now come to the second obstacle, the question of compensation. I call it the second, because its importance required us to consider it separately. But in fact it is an extension of the first. Here, there is nothing psychological or ideal. There can be no sublimation nor surrogate. Hard cash, and plenty of it, is the only just solution. But where can it come from? Israel is at its wits' end to find money to pay its workers' salaries, even. Its currency is as a tottering wall and a broken hedge; it is living, largely on American alms, from hand to mouth. It is quite beyond its capacity to find money to pay this debt of honour. What then can be done? This being an economic question, it is fitting that we should turn to the London *Economist* for an answer. In a recent issue, an anonymous but obviously acute and well-informed writer makes a practical suggestion: why not capitalize several years' current expenditure by U.N.R.W.A. on relief, and use the sum to provide compensation for Arab property? This is by far the most practical and promising suggestion that has yet been made.

Finally, there is the third obstacle, the distrust of the West. This cannot be cured easily or soon. If practical measures such as those I have mentioned are taken, a beginning will have been made. In time, they might lead to peace. It is against this background that any proposals for the "Internationalization" of Jerusalem must be examined. Like "Partnership" or "Federation" "Internationalization" has become a catchword. What would it mean in practice? That Jerusalem may be restored to unity with itself is devoutly to be wished. But the restoration of Jerusalem must be part of the restoration of Palestine, not a substitute for it. Any attempt to restore Jerusalem apart from a just and general settlement of the whole problem would do far more harm than good, and that for two reasons. First, it would flatter the nations of the world that they had achieved something praiseworthy and had solved a problem, when in fact they had not, and so could forget Palestine with an easy conscience. Secondly, the mere creation of a Jerusalem separate from a still hostile Israel and Jordan would only substitute two frontiers for one, and add further complications to the already contorted conditions of customs, currency and passport regulations.

The "international zone," like other international zones, would become an Adullam for adventurers and racketeers, and the last state of our still Holy City would be worse than the first. And why "internationalize" Jerusalem, and not Galilee—Nazareth and Capernaum? Far more important than the "internationalization" of Jerusalem, is the restoration of international intercourse between Jordan and the Mediterranean. This is essential to peace. Let those who wish to experiment in "internationalization" begin with the Ports of Haifa and Jaffa, and the road and railway to Gaza and Egypt.

Until the balance of justice athwart the frontier is adjusted, it is as foolish to expect tranquillity, either in Jerusalem or in Palestine as a whole, as it is to try to open a lock gate before equalizing the water level on either side of it. The day for expedients, for make-believe and "getting by" is over. We, by which I mean America and Britain, must seek justice, we must do justice, and we must make it clear that justice is being done. One day, perhaps, we may be liked for doing it; but that is a secondary consideration.

Some idea of the Zionist view of the problem may be gathered from the following statement which I give in its entirety, as published in the *Jerusalem Post* of 3rd July, 1953.

"The Government signed an agreement with the Jewish National Fund this week for the sale of two million dunums, mostly abandoned land, it was announced yesterday.

The agreement was concluded in accordance with Government decisions in 1949 and in 1951 regarding the sale of abandoned land to the Jewish National Fund and the Development Authority Law which specifically authorizes the Jewish National Fund as the principal body to purchase abandoned Arab land.

The land in question is in all sectors of the country and is mostly agricultural. About 400 new settlements have in the meantime been established on it by the Jewish Agency.

The Minister of Finance, Mr. Levi Eshkol, and Mr. A. Akaviah, director of the Development Authority, signed for the Government. Mr. J. Weitz and Mr. S. Ussishkin signed for the Jewish National Fund.

After the mass flight of the Arabs the Government took over the custody of their holdings. In order to normalize the land situation, abandoned land is being transferred to the Jewish National Fund in a series of land transactions.

The significance of the latest land transaction may be measured from the fact that the entire area of Israel is a little over 20 million dunums, of which only 5 million dunums are under cultivation."

This is not a political book, and I hope it is not a controversial one. My apology for what I have written in this chapter is that without it, it would be hard to understand the account of the experiment which I hope to describe in the next.

Chapter Seven

So built we the wall . . . for the people had a mind to work.
NEHEMIAH iv. 6.

AS soon as the fighting began in 1948, indeed even before it broke out, the river of refugees began to flow eastwards. Bethany, being so near Jerusalem, was one of the first villages to receive its tide. It is a small village, of not more than two thousand inhabitants in normal times; it has but little land, and that rocky and not rich. Most of its people used to get their living by working in Jerusalem, or by emigrating to other cities and lands. The village straggles in a horseshoe, on either side of the modern motor-road to Jericho, which here crosses the south-eastern slope of the Mount of Olives, or roughly the 2,000 foot contour, before plunging down into the wilderness of Judea. It is an outpost, "the strip of herbage" "which just divides the desert from the sown." There has been a village here for more than two thousand years. It is the Ananiah of Nehemiah xi, 32. Only a few months ago, seals of the fifth century B.C. came to light, and several Byzantine tombs. But the abiding interest of Bethany is that it was the home of Lazarus, and Martha and Mary. The association of Martha and Mary as sisters' names may have been common at that time and place. I was looking recently at an ossuary of the first century A.D., taken by the priest who showed it to me from a cemetery on the Mount of Olives, which bore the names Martha and Mary scratched on both sides of it in Aramaic, Our Lord's vernacular tongue.

The only glimpses we have of Our Lord at home, as a member of a family, and not as a wanderer and a teacher, come from Bethany. The picture is startlingly of our own times—the two contrasting sisters, with Martha so apparently up-to-date and go-ahead, and Mary so old-fashioned. Martha to-day would be chairman of at least ten committees, would wear a uniform whenever she could find an excuse for doing so, and would end up as "Dame Martha." Mary, having been neglected and disregarded for thirty years, would now be appreciated by more and more people, ordinary and extraordinary, who would find in her an interpreter of truths which they had long thought foolishness, but which she was beginning to make them comprehend.

The house of this family stood in the middle of the village. The Empress Helena built a church upon the site. It was twice thrown down and twice rebuilt. Then came the Crusaders. Mr. Runciman, in the second volume of his great and vivid history of the Crusades, has described how in 1143 Queen Melisende founded a nunnery in Bethany, and how her sister Princess Yvette became the Abbess of it. It was a rich foundation, endowed with those same estates in and near Jericho which nearly 1,200 years earlier Cleopatra had coveted and filched from Herod. The convent was protected by a great tower. Its ruins still dominate the modern village. Just below, in the middle of the horseshoe as it were, the good Franciscans are now completing a beautiful little church, which stands on the site of the earlier ones, and will reveal and preserve what is left of them. The village stretches away on either side along the road. There are a few modern houses. One of the first of them, consisting of but a single room, was built by an Englishwoman who used to walk into Jerusalem every day to meet Messiah. She always kept a teapot and two cups handy, because, she said, he would be tired after his long journey. Another Englishwoman built a larger house up behind the village just below the spur that divides it from Bethphage. It is a good solid house of two storeys. It stands in a little grove of olive trees. From it, you see not only Bethany, but the whole sweep of the wilderness, and Moab and Ammon beyond. This house was bequeathed to the Anglican bishopric. At one time it housed a school, and then for some years it was let as a dwelling-house.

There are two convents in Bethany, both at its eastern extremity. One is Greek. It stands by itself, and keeps itself to itself. Until recently it was a picturesque addition to the landscape, because its little dome was painted a jolly shade of blue. But it has now been daubed with aluminium, which makes it look garish and incongruous. The other convent used to be Russian, a hospice for the pilgrims on their way to the Dead Sea. It is now administered as a little school by a Scotswoman, who (like her friend who is the Abbess of Gethsemane) came to Palestine between the two wars, and found in the Russian Orthodox Church her true vocation and mission.

The indigenous inhabitants of Bethany are all Moslems.

When the refugees started arriving, the Bishop and Mrs. Stewart were at hand to help them. They had never left their post. The Close was often under fire. A shell hit the cathedral and destroyed the pulpit. Many of the windows were damaged. Another shell hit the Bishop's garage fair and square, demolished his car, and blew in the windows of the kitchen in which Mrs. Stewart was busy at the time. But the Bishop and Mrs. Stewart stayed on. Busy and harassed as they were by the many cares that came upon them in Jerusalem, they found the time and means to open the Bethany relief centre in the Bishop's house there.

Fortunately, they found a ready and reliable ally in one of the leading citizens of Bethany. Mahmud Abu Rish is one of a large family of brothers, who own property and houses in the village. How long the family has been settled there I do not know, but they are mentioned with gratitude by one of the early British excavators more than seventy years ago. The name means "Father of feathers," an allusion to the wavy hair that seems to distinguish all the family, young and old. Of the present generation, one brother was killed in the fighting, one is in Haiti, one works for U.N.R.W.A., one for the American Embassy in Amman, and another for an American news magazine in Beirut. Mahmud and two of his brothers live in Bethany. They look after the family property, which includes the neatest and most attractive coffee-house between Jerusalem and 'Amman. It has a garden with lavender hedges and jasmine-covered arbours; it is the social heart of Bethany. Mahmud looks like a genial and intelligent footballer, with twinkling blue eyes set in a rubicund face. He is short and stocky, but very agile in movement. And he knows all the tackles.

Since Mahmud and his wife live in the upper storey of the Bishop's house, it is natural enough that they should be in charge of the feeding-centre on the ground floor. It is also very fortunate. For better managers you could not find. As the centre became organized, lists were made of all those who came to it, where they lived, how many there were in the family, and what clothing and blankets they had been given. These lists were compiled and kept up-to-date by Mrs. Stewart herself, who would always find time for at least one visit a week to the Bethany house. When it was possible, Mrs. Stewart liked also to visit the people's homes, if that good word can be applied to the travesties of it in which they were mostly to be found. As I have already said, Bethany was badly hit by the earthquake in 1927, and many of its houses were ruined. It was to these ruins that the refugees fled, to them and to caves near-by. You might think that a cave was at least not liable to collapse. But not all caves have even that advantage. In the winter, therefore, it became necessary not only to feed and clothe these poor people, but to rent other accommodation for them if, as happened in the winter of 1951-2, their ruins or caves were threatened with dissolution by particularly heavy and prolonged rains.

Gradually Mrs. Stewart visited more and more of her refugee friends. Some of them lived in the neighbouring village of Abu Dis, others far away in tents. For they had come from many different parts of Palestine. The majority were from villages to the west of Jerusalem; but some came from the Beersheba district, who, being Bedu, kept to the open. They prefer to live in the freedom of a tent, however poor and patched, than to enter what to them is the captivity of a camp. In May, 1952, just before the Bishop was due to go to England for his annual round of business and meetings, Mrs. Stewart went to see a group of refugees who had been coming to the Bethany centre for some time. The group consisted of twenty-one families who had previously lived at Deir Rafat, a little village to the south-west of Jerusalem just in the foothills above the plain of Sharon, near the ancient valley of Sorek in the Samson country. The village had originally been called just Rafat, but under the Mandate, as communications improved and increased, it became necessary to distinguish this Rafat from another Rafat near Jerusalem, because their letters were always getting mixed up. So the prefix "Deir" was added, meaning "Convent," from a convent which the Latin Patriarchate of Jerusalem owned there. It was really a farm, established on land bought by the Patriarchate about seventy years ago, to provide food for the seminary in Jerusalem. The total holding of the village was 3,000 acres, of which the Patriarchate owned three-quarters, and the villagers the rest. It was a typical foothill village, moderately well off, neither very rich nor very poor. You can gauge its standard of living from the fact that there were in the village one motor truck, one bicycle and one sewing machine, but no more. A sixth of the village lands was rocky and rough, used only for grazing. A twelfth consisted of orchards, and the rest, that is to say, three-quarters, was arable.

There were three hundred families in the village, or rather I should say houses, for family is a misleading word in a society where near everyone is related to everyone else. Deir Rafat had two main divisions, or *hamoulehs* as they are called, between

(H. Neame)

The cave in which eleven families lived for four years.

(H. Neame)

The road between Rafat-al-Zayyim and Bethany. The Mount of Olives is on the right.

PAGE 117 (D. Baly)

The site of Rafat-al-Zayyim.

PAGE 126 (D. Baly)

Mrs. Stewart lays the first stone of the first house. Mahmud Abu Rish behind.

which the village was about equally distributed. One was descended from an ancestor who came from "Tripoli of the West," which is Tripoli in Libya, and the other from a soldier or soldiers who had come from Egypt with Ibrahim Pasha in 1831. It is to this latter hamouleh that our group belongs. As their ultimate, or "totem" ancestor, they claim Kuleib, a pre-Islamic Arab hero.

The villagers cultivated much of the Patriarchate land on a *métayage* agreement. They were also able to hire the Patriarchate tractor to plough their own lands. The rent was one piastre ($2\frac{1}{2}d$.) per centimetre of depth ploughed per dunum (a quarter of an acre). The Kuleib hamouleh were industrious. By 1939, they had saved up enough money to buy another 500 acres from the lands of a neighbouring village.

When the villagers fled, they became separated and scattered. Where the Tripoli hamouleh went, the others do not know. The Kuleib section were divided into four. A few went to Ramleh, where they still are. Others, to Bethlehem, 'Amman and Jericho, where they were gradually taken on to the ration strength of U.N.R.W.A. and most of them installed in camps. One little group of twenty-one families rallied round the mukhtar, or headman. The mukhtar's full name is Abdulaziz al Abd Khalil Ibrahim Musellam Kuleib, but he is generally called, according to Arab custom, Abu Musa, "Father of Musa," Musa being the name of his eldest son. All the other families of the group are related to him in closer or looser degree. They managed to bring away with them a few of their sheep and goats. Animals require daily care: they must be led to their grazing grounds and watered. Also they are easily stolen, so that to have come away without them would have been to lose them. But the rest of their property the villagers left in their village. They did not worry about it, because they were certain that they would soon be home again—in a fortnight's time, a month's: it would not be longer, their leaders assured them. The mukhtar had acted as a sort of bailiff to the Convent, and so he left his property there. You can get some idea of his circumstances from the list of what he says he stored there. Besides his clothes and the modest furniture of his two-roomed house, he had twelve beds with their bedding and pillows. His stores and provisions consisted of six tons of wheat, one ton of barley, three-quarters of a ton of lentils, over half a ton of onions, two hundred pounds of *lebani*—the dried crudded milk or *yoghurt* which is a staple and very wholesome relish. This was his year's supply. He also had one hundred pounds of *samen*, or clarified butter, which he intended to sell, together with nearly four hundred pounds of sheep's wool. All this he lost. The rats and mice and weevils made an end of the provisions. For the remainder, the Convent, out of the kindness of their hearts, paid him the equivalent of £15 sterling last year. The mukhtar's case is typical of thousands, only that he did receive a little compensation, and very few of the others did.

The little party journeyed east, so as to be within the protection of the Arab lines. But, as month succeeded month, there was still no news nor sign of the return. Meanwhile, how were they to live? They heard tell that on the very fringe of the eastern skirt of the Mount of Olives, there were some caves. The prospect of finding grazing for their animals, however scant it might be, in the wilderness of Judæa, led them to go thither and camp in these caves, on the very edge of the desert. The caves are three in number. The largest is roughly oval in shape, its longer axis being about the length of a cricket-pitch, and the shorter half as long. It is nowhere higher than ten feet, and in many parts much less. The second cave is circular, with a diameter of about six yards. You have to stoop to get into it. The third is but a recess in the rock face, about the size of a third-class railway carriage. The two larger caves have narrow openings, facing south. It is this southern aspect which makes them habitable. For the surrounding area is bare rock, swept by the north-west wind. Even in summer, this prevailing wind can be chilling; in winter, laden with rain, or sometimes with snow or hail, it is as bitter as death. These caves, like all caves in Palestine large enough to admit more than one animal, have from time immemorial been used as sheepfolds and goatpens. The walls and ceiling are blackened by centuries of smoke, the floor thick with accumulated dung. No sun, and but little fresh air, ever penetrate them. Fleas and ticks abound. The smell is strong and foul.

When Mrs. Stewart visited the Deir Rafat group, she found the twenty-one families living in these three caves. The largest, and it is, as you have seen, by no means big, housed fourteen of them. All of them, by that time, were on the ration strength of U.N.R.W.A., so were kept from starvation. They were also receiving blankets and a little clothing from the Bethany centre. But this help could not alter the overcrowding and the discomfort. You must be wondering how fourteen families can live in one cave, even if they are all friends and relations. Each family made a sort of perch for itself. Some found a natural shelf of rock at the side of the cave, but most had to build them out of stones and earth. On this little ledge, man and wife would place such rags as they had, and that became their home: there they would sleep, beget, give birth and die. Any little bits of property, such as a cooking-pot, or a broken lamp, or an empty tin, would be placed as close as possible to the ledge; bits of clothing, if there were such things, and an occasional sack of food, or a precious little bag of rough tobacco leaf, would be hung from lines overhead. Thus, herded in the dim, dream-like penumbra of this dirty cavern, these men and women passed their days. They had nothing to do. Hope deferred was making their hearts very sick. They were still living honestly, they were still gentle and courteous. But the sap seemed to be falling back, the tree withering. The men and women were sallow, the children grey-faced. When it was fine, the sheep and goats stayed outside in a pen made of rough stones. But when it was cold or wet, they, too, had to share the cave with their masters.

Mrs. Stewart decided that these people, if they were to survive, must be moved out of the caves. But where were they to go? As it turned out, it was their very remoteness which was their salvation.

Before leaving for England, it was not possible to do anything; but as soon as the Bishop and Mrs. Stewart came back, in August, they went out to see how the cave-dwellers were faring. They found them no better off. They could see only one solution, and that was to get them out of the caves and into houses. It seems, when you read it, to be the natural and obvious solution. But if you recall what was said in the last chapter about the necessity of the "return," and the way in which certain people were exploiting it for their own ends, you will understand that to talk of houses was represented by such folk as "treachery," and those who wanted to build them as traitors. That is why so far no houses had been built to replace the tents of the camps, except, ridiculously enough, by the refugees themselves, who in some cases had put together shacks from tins and mud and stones, without any concerted plan, or proper design, and had thus transformed a canvas slum into a more permanent one.

In fact, in August, 1952, only thirteen families had been placed by U.N.R.W.A. in permanent dwellings in Jordan, in such a manner as to justify the word "settlement" being used of them. That was at Beit Qad, near Jenin, where each family had been given a house which had cost £250 to build, and an allotment of 25 acres of land. These families are now self-supporting. Since that time, the Agency has settled another thirty-four families at a place called Merj Naja', in the Jordan valley below Beisan. Each family has 6 acres of irrigated land. This settlement, too, is now independent.

In August, 1952, no other village had been either built or designed, either far away from Jerusalem, as these two settlements are, or nearer to it. To build a new village so near to the City was therefore an innovation. Yet the plan had one aspect which should tell in its favour. It was not intended to move the families to another district; the idea was simply to obtain some land immediately adjacent to the caves, and there to put up the houses. The proximity of the new to the old had two advantages. First, it was hardly really a removal at all; secondly, the presence of the former foul habitations so near to the intended new ones made it hard (though not, as we shall see, impossible) for anyone to decry the scheme on grounds of public interest.

Mahmud Abu Rish supported the idea. So it was decided to put it to the mukhtar. Abu Musa is an intelligent man. He is about forty-five years old and five foot six high. He has a face tanned by sun and wind, keen grey eyes, and a gentle, thoughtful cast of feature. His face is often lighted by a smile of humanity and sympathy. I have never known him to be angry, nor to say a bitter word against anyone. Even when he was telling me the story of the flight from Rafat, he uttered no blame, either of his compatriots or of others. He has suffered too much to be resentful. He is looked up to by his people, who never question either his wisdom or his authority.

The plan as put to him was that he and his folk should build their own homes. That was the essence of the scheme. What you make for yourself, you value far more and take more to heart than what is built for you by others, to whom you are a "unit." The Bishop would acquire the land, and would also provide the skilled labour, such as quarrymen and masons. Abu Musa and his people made up their minds at once: they would accept. The mere occupation would be welcome to them after four years of idleness. But they would need instruction, because they had no experience of anything except farming.

That point being settled, the next thing was to set about acquiring the land. The area in which the caves are situated is on the edge of the lands belonging to the village on the Mount of Olives, which is called Al-Tur. From the village, the land drops away abruptly to the east, until, a mile away as the crow flies, it comes to a little plain or shallow valley, about three hundred yards across, and 600 feet below. Down to this valley runs the old Roman road from the Mount of Olives to Jericho. The valley and the road wind away to the north-east, and on the southern flank rises a little knoll, not more than a hundred feet high, a mere undulation in the landscape, which descends with many other such corrugations, first to sea level, and then, 1,300 feet below it, to the Dead Sea; so that the total drop which lies before your eyes as you stand on the Mount of Olives, is more than four thousand feet in fifteen miles. This first little fold or bottom is filled with earth, and can produce a scraggy crop. Beyond, there is only rock, with little pockets of earth, growing smaller and smaller and poorer and poorer.

You do not see the actual caves, because they are on the eastern side of the knoll. But you can see the rocky brow beyond them. It was there that it was hoped to obtain land for the houses. The knoll is covered with patches of thorn, and below it to the south-east is a sloping patch of half-calcined earth, which can just pass muster as a field. Here, you feel, if anywhere, nature and life must make their last stand against the stark, primordial matter of the world, or capitulate for ever to desolation and death. It is a fine place for building a village.

August was now far spent. The first heavy rains might be expected in December. That gave us three months for building. We should have to be quick. Mahmud seemed to be everywhere at once. His first object was to gain over the elders of Tur village. The inhabitants of the Mount of Olives are a tough lot. I remember that Ahmed Samih al-Khalidi once told me that you would always find the bad hats living not in a town itself, where they would be too near to the police for the general comfort, but on its outskirts, which accounted, he said, for the existence, and reputation, of, for instance, Saffuriyeh near Nazareth, Tireh near Haifa, and Lifta and Tur near Jerusalem. The people of Tur have lived on visitors and pilgrims for centuries. The Mount of Olives was venerated by Christians before any of the sacred sites of Jerusalem itself, and it was to the Mount of Olives that Jewish pilgrims also used to repair. Although the people of the village own land, they have not been in the habit of cultivating it themselves very extensively, until the

present distress has forced them to do so; it was easier to live off the
strangers. Mahmud's strategy was adroit. He knows the people of
Tur, they are his neighbours. He did not negotiate with them himself; they might, with decency, refuse to do business with him, as
being the representative of a stranger, and a Christian Bishop at that.
He sent Abu Musa: it would be much harder for the villagers of Tur
to say no to a poor brother Muslim, who only wanted to live, like
them, in a house. Even so, when Abu Musa went to see them, the
Turis were suspicious. They soon knew, of course, that the Bishop
was backing him. What did the Bishop want land for? Was he
going to build a church? Houses? For whom? All these questions
had to be debated at great length. Finally Abu Musa persuaded them
that all the Bishop wanted to do was to provide habitations for
him and his people. The owners of the land, finding that public
opinion was not opposed to their letting the Bishop have their
land, agreed to make it available. But, as a final display of caution,
they would not sell it: they only agreed to lease it for forty years.
On this condition an acre and a half was acquired. The deed does
not mention the Bishop. There are two reasons for this. The first
is a technical one. The laws of Jordan do not allow the purchase of
land by foreigners, unless special permission has been obtained from
the cabinet. This is a wise and justifiable precaution, to safeguard the
alienation of the nation's chief asset. This condition would not apply
to a lease; but it would if it were ever desired to convert the lease
into a sale. The second reason is more potent. The Bishop had no
wish to own the land. The whole aim of the scheme was to make the
people of Rafat independent, and to make them feel that once again
they were citizens with a stake in their land. This cannot be achieved
speedily. Restoration of any sort is a lengthy business. You can
create a refugee problem in a day; but it will take years to solve.
It is not to be thought of in terms of an annual report to an international body. And the first step is psychological, not financial.
It is fruitless to aim at showing, as your main achievement, a diminution in the ration strength for which you are responsible. In days
gone by, the Agency was apt to move along these lines. It saw any
scheme in terms of ration cards. That was one of the chief reasons
why it found it hard to get the schemes going; because the refugees
saw the schemes in terms of ration cards, too. And at any suggestion
that a ration card might be taken away, the scheme was dead, so far
as the refugees were concerned.

The Bishop was in a stronger position. He had no connection with the ration cards, and his action would not influence the continuance or withholding of rations. The word was never even mentioned. The first and principal aim was to make these men householders again. The Bishop felt that once they had their own homes, with their own children in them, the normal instincts of enterprise and self-preservation and family love would begin again their beneficent operation. From the very first, therefore, he was determined that the new houses should be the property of those who were to live in them. His eventual aim was that, when the occupants had become consolidated, as it were, in their spirits, the whole undertaking should be made into a co-operative society. But that was still in the future. The first step was the drawing up of the deed of lease.

Land tenure in Palestine is complicated. Many tenures are traditional, and much land is held by a village in common. The Mandatory Government set out to survey the whole land and to grant title deeds to all owners. It largely succeeded in doing this. But the Moslem law of inheritance does not proceed by primogeniture; it requires that property shall be divided, in accordance with precise rules, among all a man's heirs, male and female. Sometimes a co-heir or heiress can be bought out; but if you want to rent or buy a plot of land however small, you generally have to do either, in the case of undivided land, with the whole of the male inhabitants of the village, or, in the case of divided land, with the heirs of someone who died a long time ago, after begetting a large family. So, to obtain this acre and a half of land next the caves, Abu Musa had to gain the consent of several families. Finally, four men were authorized to sign for the owners, and Abu Musa took with him two of his relatives to sign with him. The document was executed on 25th August, 1952. It is quite simple. It provides that the party of the first part, the owners, will be pleased to give the plot of land to the party of the second part for forty years, for the purpose of erecting houses, and that at the end of that time, the land and the houses will return to the ownership of the party of the first part. The party of the first part also undertakes to deal with any claims that may be put in by any other pretended heirs or part-owners. The document bears four signatures, and six purple thumb-prints, the three extra names being those of witnesses. To it are affixed five crimson revenue stamps, of a shilling each, which for some strange reason show a picture of the well-known arch and colonnade of Palmyra, which is in Syria, not Jordan.

There is no mention of money, you observe. The sum which changed hands was £40. But it is not considered mannerly to mention it; customs have not changed since the days when Abraham bought the cave of Macpelah in Hebron, as we may read in the twenty-third chapter of Genesis. When this bargain was concluded, it was the best which could be obtained. The villagers could not be persuaded to sell outright. We had to build at once. The plan was, and is, to exchange the agreement for a deed of sale at some future date. Meanwhile, forty years gives us a useful breathing space. At a pound a year, it is not expensive.

Having seen our way open with the landowners, the next thing was to ask the blessing of the government. We called on the Mutaserrif of Jerusalem, Seyyid Hassan Katib. In Arabic, each grade of high official has its own particular prefix just as their Imperial predecessors had in the days of St. Jerome. In English, the one word "excellency" has to do service for the lot, which is a pity, because the nuances are worth preserving. The style attached to a mutaserrif is '*Atufat*, of which an English equivalent would be "His Benignity." The term fits Seyyid Hassan. He is well over six feet high, and has a dignified, rather reserved look, which sometimes borders on the melancholy. But at any opportunity of promoting the welfare of his people, his face lights up with happiness. Seyyid Hassan was for many years an officer in the Palestine Police, in the days of the Mandate. He has many English friends, has a natural liking for good administration, is candid and straightforward, and has no use for intrigue or hypocrisy. He is a personal friend of the Bishop. He at once gave the new scheme his blessing. His assistant, Seyyid 'Abdulqader Ja'uni, also made it clear that he would do everything he could to further our plans. Western readers may not at first grasp what a difference such official patronage makes; but the direct, administrative power of an Eastern government is far greater, and always has been, than that of a Western one, even a modern Western one. If the government is on your side, and known to be on your side, many doors will be opened to you that might otherwise remain shut.

The refugees had agreed, the landowners had agreed, the government had agreed. The only thing now necessary was to build the village. None of those concerned had ever built a village before,

We were not quite certain how you went about it, nor did we know what a number of different things can go to the making of even one house. This was just as well; or I doubt whether we should ever have faced the task. At first glance, the building of a house seems to involve no more than putting up the walls, fitting doors and windows, and covering the whole thing with a roof. You would be surprised how many other things have to be found, such as tiles and whitewash and clothes hooks, and numbers of knobs and handles for keeping things open or shut. We learned about them all in time.

Our first task was to plan the general lay-out of the village. By good fortune, for it certainly was not by any design of ours, the plot of land we had acquired lay just below the sky-line, so that we did not have to consider how we should affect it by our activities. The village was to lie in the hollow flank of the hill, rather like seats in a theatre. The first thing we decided, therefore, was that the main street should follow the contour of the hill. This meant that it would be shaped like a partly-drawn bow, and would not be a straight line. In making this alignment we were influenced not only by æsthetics: we had another deliberate aim. We wanted our little village to look as unlike a camp as possible, and as natural as it could, so that it should appear as though it were an organic growth, and not something alien applied from outside. In this, again, we were greatly helped by circumstance: nothing makes a building look more at home than being built of local stone, being literally of "the rock whence it is hewn, and from the hole of the pit whence it is digged." It is this quality that makes Cotswold villages, for instance, so living and welcoming. In Palestine, in the hills at least, it has for thousands of years been the custom to dig your stone from the site of your house. This saves you all expense of transport. More important, it makes the house a true child of its mother rock, so that a Palestine village, also, has that living, human, look which satisfies the eye and the heart at once. The shape of our bit of land meant that we could put five houses above the street, and then four below it, and then another two at the bottom of the wedge. That would give each house a little space round it for a garden, where the rock allowed, and it would also permit us to put the lower houses in the gaps between the upper ones, so that no house would have its view obstructed by its neighbour. You may think that views do not count to those who live in Palestine villages. I am not so sure; but

it was not only of them that we were thinking. The village was to be
visible, and conspicuous, both from the Mount of Olives, and also
from the Jericho road, the main road and artery of the kingdom.
Just as you leave Bethany, up on the north side of the road, there
stands the village. So it must be made to look as right as possible.

The siting of the individual houses was conditioned by two
considerations. First came the actual formation of the rock. It is
unequal, and there are little pockets of soil here and there. It is a
pity to cover soil with a house; it is also a waste of money, because
it means you have to dig down to find the rock for your foundations,
and so bury good building stone below the surface of the earth. If
you keep to the rock, you can build straight from scratch, as it
were. The second consideration is, again, to avoid the straight
military line. In the bright light of Palestine, you have to take into
account not only the mass of a building, but also its shadow. If you
have a rigid elevation, or a row of houses set in a straight unbroken
line, it is remarkable what an aggravation the equally rigid shadows
become; they more than double the hard effect. As I have said, the
formation of the rock itself largely solved the problem of the
individual sites; but we were careful to see that no two blocks were
on the same alignment—some stood back, others forward. Secondly,
between no two blocks was the lateral interval exactly the same;
thirdly, of no two blocks was the orientation exactly the same, so
that the light should fall on, and the shadow from, each one in a
personal and individual way.

Before the houses went up, we had to decide what style of house
we were going to build. As I have said, the Arab house, its nature,
materials and lay-out, has formed the subject of a full-dress study by
Dr. Tawfiq Canaan. Arab houses can be as elaborate as Western
houses. But in practice, village practice, they are very simple.
The villager is a farmer, and so he spends most of his time out of
doors. The Palestine climate favours outdoor life. From May till
November, no rain falls, except perhaps for a thunder shower or
two towards the end of the period. During the rest of the year, if the
season is an average one, the country will receive as much rain as
East Anglia does in a year, which is about twenty inches. But either
it is raining, or it is not. There are no dull, cloudy, undecided days.
It may rain all day, or perhaps for two or even three days on end;
but when the rain stops, out comes the sun. And out come the
people, too. The house becomes less of a dwelling than a store.

In it they keep things, and sleep. But they do not live in it. The ordinary house of a peasant consists of one room, with a verandah or stoep in front of it. It is on the verandah that most of the time is passed, especially by the women, who will sit there with the children, doing sewing or preparing food, while the men are away in the fields. Only when the rain comes, or the wind is too cold, or the sun too hot, do they go inside. Cooking used to be done in a little mud oven, in an enclosure at the back or side of the house. But nowadays the pressure stove has largely superseded this method. It is all for the good: the gathering of the fuel fell on the women. They would have to scour the countryside to bring back great loads of *netsh*, the local thorn with which pots have been made hot ever since the days of the Psalmist (Psalm lviii. 9). Or else they would send the children out to collect dung, which when dried makes a hot slow-burning fuel. The stove saves the women and children this drudgery. Further, in a model village you will find a communal oven, of which there will be more to say later.

The inside of the house strikes a Western visitor as bare. There are no chairs, no table. They are not necessary, and would only get in the way. You sit on the floor, on mats or rugs, which are far more comfortable, even for a Western body. The Arab will sit on the ground with the grace of a tulip. You do not see his feet or legs, only the upper part of his body, balanced and at ease. Like royalty, he does not lean back, or loll. His table is the floor, which, be it remembered, he keeps as we would a table. You take off your shoes when you enter his house, lest you bring in dust or mud from outside it. In a corner, or on a raised niche, will be found the bedding, rolled up by day. This consists of a mattress, which is spread on the floor mat. Above that is placed a *lihaf*, which is a thick, quilted coverlet, the heavier the better. In winter, blankets are needed as well, two or three of them. The rest of the furniture will consist of a chest, to keep clothes in, an oil lamp if you are well off, and a few odds and ends suspended from pegs in the wall and from the ceiling. It is a simple life. But it is a life that can be lived well. The land is the life-giver: the house is only the bond of union and continuity.

As we have seen, the mukhtar of Deir Rafat, the chief citizen of the village, had in his original house only two rooms for living in, though he had others for his animals and his stores. Single-roomed houses are the village unit. All around Bethany, you can see them— squat little buildings, with domed roofs, with a door and one or two little windows, set deep into the thick stone walls like the eyes in the face of an ascetic. These houses have greatly increased of late, in areas where formerly there were only houses of hair, as the Bedu call their tents. All over the slopes of the wilderness of Judæa, below the fortress-tomb of Herod the Great, you see them now, where a few years ago there was none. They are built in the traditional fashion, with the dome rising from groins, and covered with *huwwar*, the local whitish kaolin which, mixed with *tibn* or chopped straw, is used to seal a roof. (As in the days of Moses, if you skimp the straw, the work is spoiled.) To have built one such house for each of the twenty-two families would have been very expensive, more costly, in fact, than we could afford. We felt that there should be some cheaper way of achieving the same end. We asked U.N.R.W.A. for advice. As you might expect, U.N.R.W.A. had made some experiments in building, in order to house its schools and stores and watchmen and such. Near the Jerusalem airport they had a group of buildings; so out we went to have a look at them. There, among various types, all made of local hewn rock, we found what we wanted. It was a stout hut, four metres by three-and-a-half and three metres high. It had a door and a window. Why not, we reckoned, build two such rooms in one block, giving each room two windows instead of one? The houses would be cooler in summer, and warmer in winter, for having a common inner wall; and we should have to pay for one party wall only, as against two outer walls. In front of the two houses would run a continuous verandah. The mukhtar said this plan would do splendidly. To secure privacy, we would put the door of one of the houses round the corner, we said. We actually did so in one or two of the houses; but the mukhtar laughed at what he thought our prudery: if we knew the womenfolk of his village as well as he did, he said, we should not be so solicitous to spare their blushes.

There remained the question of what the roof was to be made of. Some ingenious spirit at U.N.R.W.A. had evolved a type of roof of which the basis was empty tar barrels, rolled flat, made up into sections like an L turned over to the right, and then riveted together. The result was astonishing. The flimsy tinplate of the barrels took on the strength of a girder; and on the flat surface so produced, it was quite safe for several men to walk at once. On this structural foundation, was placed a layer of huwwar, to keep off the sun, and to preserve the traditional aspect, with a thin coating of tar and finely-ground stone above it, and there was the house. Fortunately for us, U.N.R.W.A. had a number of these "barrel roofs" left over; and they generously gave them to us. The doors and the windows were to be made of wood. There is no point in a glass window. You only want to shut the window when it is raining, and a wooden shutter is much more solid and durable than a glass one. But timber is hard to come by in this treeless country. Here, we were able to fall back on our own resources. Kind friends in England send the Bishop a quantity of clothes for the refugees. These are all beautifully packed in stout wooden boxes by the Church Missionary Society in London, who act as clearing agents for all donors. These packing cases were to provide the doors and shutters for the entire village.

While we were working out these problems, the stone-cutters had been at work. Stone-cutting is a skilled profession. This was of advantage to us. You might have thought it would be the reverse, and that we should have preferred, if possible, to employ our unskilled villagers on it, and save the expense. This touches one of the main problems of helping refugees on a small scale or a large one. You have to be very careful lest, by helping the refugee, you make him a specially cared-for and privileged person; so that the people among whom he lives, who do not themselves benefit from your activities, come to resent him and, of course, you. This is as true of states as it is of individuals. When you set out to help refugees, you must also help the society in which they live. So we were very glad to be able to help the stone-cutters of Tur, and the masons of Bethany. Stone-cutting is done by piece rates. The quarryman undertakes to deliver stone on the site, cut to an agreed size, at so much a cubic metre. When we started work, it was two shillings, but we soon raised it to half a crown. The head quarryman supplies his own labour, and his own blasting powder. Our head quarryman is a fine-looking man from Tur. He is tall, with a grizzled beard, and has a face that might have graced an apostle. He has been hewing stone for many a year. The rock seems to have softened him. He has a gentle manner, and speaks with a rustic burr. He is assisted by three apprentices. The method of quarrying is this. The master chooses the rock he knows from experience is going to yield the best bulk of stone. He then—and he has to be an expert to do this—chooses the exact spot in which to sink the blasting charge. An apprentice then takes a long iron pole, with a sharpened end, and starts to sink it into the rock, by dint of working it up and down. The pole is about six feet long, and two inches across. The limestone rock soon yields to its blows, and a small bore-hole starts to appear. The blaster pours water into it so as to ease the working of the pole. When the requisite depth has been reached, usually about two or three feet, depending on the depth of the stratum, he tamps down a charge of black powder, and fits a fuse. Then he lights it, and shouts "*Bar-oo-ood*," which means gunpowder. Those who happen to hear him take cover—those who don't would not be near enough to matter anyhow—and bang goes the charge. A few bits of rock fly up into the air, and some small stones may travel a score of yards or so. But the clever blaster places his charge so that it will crack and splinter the rock without shattering it. And this is why, for this sort of rock, the old black powder is better than more energetic explosives. The old primitive method yields better results than an up-to-date drill and gelignite would do.

It is seldom necessary to go very deep, on these hill sides, because generally the rock is a comparatively thin stratum overlying earth. By removing it, the blaster not only produces building stone, but if he is lucky, he will expose a potential garden.

The deed of "gift" had been signed on the 25th August. By the 13th September enough rock had been quarried to enable us to lay the first stone. It was a simple ceremony. There were present the Bishop, Mrs. Stewart, Mahmud Abu Rish and his brother Musa, the elders of Tur, and the mukhtar and villagers of Rafat. Mrs. Stewart was to lay the stone, because the original idea of helping the villagers to build homes was hers. The stone was soon in place, and work began at once on the first three blocks.

As you can see from the pictures, the walls are very solidly built, and each door and window has a single big stone as its lintel. The actual fetching and carrying of the stones and the mortar was done by the villagers. U.N.R.W.A. readily supplied us with wheelbarrows, picks, shovels, and earth baskets. These baskets have been the traditional method of moving earth from one place to another since the days when the pyramids were built: only to-day, instead of being made of rope, they are made of old tyres. The villagers were men of all ages, mostly heads of families. Their children helped them. Among them was the local Albert Herring. He is a simple, mild-natured young bachelor. He is always good for a laugh, which he never resents. On the contrary, he recognizes with pride that his office in life is to add to its gaiety. You can see him laughing as he stands on a ladder, helping to build one of the houses. This picture is an enlargement of a small part of one taken by Lance-Bombardier Durrant. I said that if he would aim at Mohammed from the security of a window aperture, I would try to make him laugh at the psychological moment. The result was this picture, which, under the title "Man with a Glove" was later made into a Christmas card.

The mortar is made of lime, locally burned, and earth. The final pointing is of cement. The floors are mostly of cement, too; but it happened that a number of red tiles were being discarded from the Bishop's house, and so we were able to have the first few houses tiled. The method of making the roofs I have already described. In practice, when we came to fitting the iron plates in position, we had quite a lot of fun. As I have said, the locality is open to the winds of heaven, and even in autumn, the north-west wind blows quite strongly. An expanse of tin-plate, therefore, measuring four metres square, offers a tempting target to the breeze. The method of assembling the roofs was to rivet the plates into strips of the required length on the ground, and then to lift the strips to the roof, and there to rivet them together, so that they formed one single structure for each room. A joining strip, resting on the party wall, was the finishing touch. The huwwar was to be put on later; so that when the plates were first hoisted there was nothing to keep them in place but their own weight. I pointed this out to the villagers, and said that they must be sure to put some heavy stones on the roofs, or they would be blown away. "Your words on our heads," they said, "stones will be placed, if God will."

The next morning, I went out to the site. I was greeted with bland smiles. Everyone seemed working as usual, perhaps even a little more eagerly. By this time, we had started some of the houses below the street; and they were most anxious that I should see how they were getting on. They wanted me to examine their work in all its detail, and to hear how much, and how skilfully and how willingly each man had worked. It was touching to experience such enthusiasm, and such devotion to the common task and welfare. At length I said I must be going. "Then we will walk with you to the entrance," they said, "it is our duty." We set off, obliquely, on such a course that we should have got clear of the village without visiting the upper range of houses at all. "How are the first houses?"

I asked. "Well," they answered readily. "I will see them," I said.
"Dear brother, do not weary yourself, the hill is steep and it is
warm to-day." "May God pardon me," I answered, "I am your
servant." Thus mutually protesting, we approached the second
block of the upper row. It was bare to the sky. Its lovely roof lay
all twisted and bent on the ground about two metres away. I asked
the villagers how it had happened. They seemed quite bewildered,
as though they had only just noticed the iron lying there. "Perhaps,"
said one of quicker wit than the rest, "it was the wind?" "And did
I not warn you that the wind would damage the roofs?" "Ah! You
did: but how could I know that the wind would come at that
particular hour last night?" There, I had to admit, he had me. I was
put to silence. After looking at the roof and the house from which it
had been torn, I said, "This must be put back." "To-morrow," they
said, as we should say "At once!" "No," I said, "now." They
decided to humour me. Ladders were brought, and to the accompaniment of much generous advice, the roof was finally lifted up,
straightened out, and put back. Not much damage had been done.
Everyone was happy. "Now for the stones," I said. "*Stones?* But
indeed, he is right," they said to each other. It was a new idea,
and a good one. Soon they were all telling each other just what
rocks to bring, how to place them, and where; and so the roof
was anchored.

The "barrel-roofs" given us by U.N.R.W.A. were enough for
seven houses only. The Agency had no more, or they would certainly
have let us have them. Nor could we have any more made; for at
that time, the Public Works Department, the only provider of
empty tar-barrels, had none to sell. We must find some other
sources of supply. It is a good rule in the Levant, that when you are
at a loss where to turn for something, you turn to the Iraq Petroleum
Company, or I.P.C., as it is generally known. The I.P.C. interpret
the term "public service" very generously. If a distinguished scholar
wants transport to far places, the I.P.C. provides a car. If an eminent
novelist is in search of material, the I.P.C. looks after her. When you
cross the desert, the I.P.C. is your host at night. All this is "on the
side." In the countries where they operate, they never seem to miss
an opportunity of doing a kindness or a service to the people among
whom they work. In matters such as hospitals, social welfare,
housing and general amenity, they are exemplary pioneers. Knowing
the I.P.C., it seemed quite natural to ask them for roofing material

(R. Bird)

Building.

(R. Durrant)

"Man with a Glove."

(D. Baly)

Mrs. Stewart, with Sarah, the Mukhtar's wife; his sister, holding "'Eid"; and the Mukhtar.

(H. Neame)

PAGE 131

The village of Rafat-al-Zayyim complete—except for the oven, which now stands in the bottom left-hand corner, and the mosque, which is being built above the second block from the left.

(Elia)

PAGE 146

Panorama from the site of Al-Mansur looking north-east. The Russian Tower and Augusta Victoria Hospital are on the sky-line.

for our houses. I wrote to their 'Amman representative, Mr. Charles Littledale, asking him whether he had any old barrels suitable for making into roofs. He answered that he was sorry he had not; but added politely that he would bear my needs in mind. We started looking about us to see whether we could buy some corrugated iron. It was scarce and expensive, we found. Then one day, just as we were feeling nonplussed, a telephone message came from Mr. Littledale that "if we would send a lorry to Zerqa, he would fill it with corrugated iron." That is how we were enabled to put roofs on the other fifteen houses.

The iron, of course, needed support; it has not the girder-structure of the converted barrels. So we had to buy timber. It was of poor quality. When we had put up the roofs and the huwwar on top of them, and the rains came and wet the huwwar, these roofs began to sag. Stronger supports were called for. This time, it was the Director of Forests, Sayyid Ya'qub Salti, who came to the rescue. As I have said, he is a former pupil of mine, and was for many years a signals officer in the Arab Legion. I was surprised to find him, when I returned to Palestine last year, Director of Forests. "I wish I had changed to forestry fifteen years ago," he said. "I like working with nature, it is good to help things grow, isn't it?" He promised us any poplar poles we might need, and while we were on the subject, gave orders that we were also to be supplied with all the tree seedlings we wanted, from the Government nurseries at Nablus. Thus our final, "standard" form of roof was evolved. A stout poplar beam running transversally supports a framework of smaller beams of imported timber. On these is laid the corrugated iron, then comes the huwwar, and finally the top-dressing of tar.

The work on the little hill had not gone unnoticed. The people of Tur looked down from their eyrie, and saw that real houses were really springing up. Interest spread. At one time, it was being said in the town that the moving spirit behind the whole enterprise was none other than Mr. Victor Gollancz—an unforeseen and cheering compliment. So many people asked to see the site, and the houses, that the Bishop finally decided to have a little "At Home" as soon as the first families had moved in. This was fixed for the 29th October. The Mutasarrif was asked, and his assistant, the Commandant of Police and his deputy, British and American consular representatives, U.N.R.W.A. officers and other friends, both Arab and foreign. There is a rough motorable track to the western foot of

I

the hill; but the last half mile must be made on foot. Gradually the
little groups arrived, and started to explore the half-completed
village. Mahmud Abu Rish was there, and also his brother Musa,
whose assiduity as honorary clerk of the works had resulted in so
much being achieved in six weeks. Mahmud and I had walked
down to the foot of the hill to receive the Mutaserrif. Unfortunately,
he had been called away at the last moment to attend a state funeral,
and had been unable to get in touch with us. Finally we realized
that he was not coming, and walked back to the village. We
arrived just in time to see, and hear, someone addressing the Bishop
in loud and vigorous Arabic. It was one of the local deputies. He
was just finishing his speech as we came up. "We will never accept
these huts," he was saying, "we demand a Return, and nothing less
than a Return." Shouting which, he walked dramatically away, and
off over the hill. There was a hush among the villagers and the
guests, like that which falls on the assembly when the Uninvited
Fairy has cursed the poor little princess. The deputy had been invited,
but it was not expected that he would take the opportunity of
denouncing the Bishop on his own ground, as it were. The man's
behaviour had two distinct effects. First, the villagers were perturbed.
The terror of flouting "public opinion," of going against "the
leaders," of being branded as a "traitor," is very deep-rooted in this
country. So much so, that again and again I have known Palestinians
to follow a rogue of their own people to disaster rather than hearken
to the salutary counsel of a foreign friend. This weakness is by no
means confined to Palestine and its people: it is only that they have
had more opportunities in recent years of showing it. The villagers
were quick to say, therefore, that they would do nothing against
the wishes of "the national bodies," or the Government, and were
duly reported as having said so in the newspapers. Fortunately,
although the Mutaserrif was not there, the Commandant was.
Colonel Suleiman Subhi has a poker face. He waited till he was about
to leave. Then turning to the villagers he said, "Stay here; if you
have any trouble, let me know." So they stayed, and they had
no trouble. Meanwhile, people reflected that the deputy had not been
at all polite. They also remembered that he himself had three
houses. Of course, being a deputy and a patriot, he was entitled to
exercise his profession. Nevertheless, perhaps this time he had gone
a bit far. The Mutaserrif made no secret of his views. Without
informing us, he went out to the village as soon as he could, walked

round it with the villagers, told them it was a fine scheme and that
the Government gave it its full backing.

Personally, I regarded the incident less as a trial of strength than
as an inoculation. So many schemes had been mooted, some even
started, only to be struck down by the virus of "Return" agitation,
that it seemed healthy to have a mild attack of it, as a prophylactic
against severer bouts. The fact that the deputy had shown bad
manners had told in our favour; also, that the Bishop had shown
conspicuously good manners. He had made no reply. A French
friend who was present said: "No French bishop would have taken
that in silence!" Gradually the discussion dropped. The work went
ahead, and just before Christmas, all the houses were finished and
occupied.

The village had also been surrounded with a ring wall, with a
gate in it, as you see in the picture. This was provided partly by
our design and partly at the request of the villagers. We wanted to
keep out goats and other marauders, so that when we came to plant
the trees, they would have the best chance of survival. We also
thought that a wall looked well, and would make a frame for our
picture. It certainly does improve the look of the place, specially
from a distance. The villagers, without knowing our intention, also
asked for a wall. They did not want any "frontier incidents" between
them and the Elders of Tur. They were afraid that if there were no
wall, their children might wander on to the Turi crops, or otherwise
encroach on Turi lands. So the wall too was built with a will. The
Gate was a necessary adjunct of the wall, we thought. Here also, the
question of looks came in as well. But when the gate-posts began to
go up, down came the Elders of Tur, demanding explanations. The
village street, they said, was a right of way, which led to their
grazing land down below. We said we knew this, and that we had
no intention of blocking it. We only wanted to keep out animals,
not the children of Adam. Our gate would have on it only a latch,
and no lock or bolt whatsoever. They were satisfied, and returned
to their Mount.

There were still three other adjuncts of village life which had to
be found: a cistern, an oven and a mosque.

In a land where there are no streams at all, and very few springs,
where for more than half the year you cannot count on a drop of
rain, the storing of the water that the winter brings you is essential.
You cannot live without a cistern. Near the caves it happened that

there were three very ancient cisterns still in use, besides another which had been allowed to fall into ruin. It was from these three that the villagers had been drawing water for themselves and their flocks, and they had somehow scraped together the few pounds necessary to pay the yearly rent. They hoped still to go on using these cisterns; but in a dry season they might not be enough. Already, for the building operations, we had had to bring water from a cistern nearly a mile away, on donkey-back. Besides, if you have your own water-supply, you are in a stronger position to resist any attempt at forcing up the rent of the ones you hire. We therefore decided to dig a cistern in the south-west corner of the village.

Cistern-digging is a skilled calling. Like quarrying, it is carried on by teams or companies consisting of a master and his apprentices. Our cistern-digger undertook to make us a cistern of one hundred cubic metres capacity for the sum of one hundred pounds. It was interesting to see him start work. He had no plan, the whole operation was done by touch. The cistern is of the type known as "pear," because it is shaped like one. First comes the stalk, which is a perpendicular cylindrical shaft. This forms the mouth of the cistern, and is just wide enough for a man to go down, or a full swinging bucket to come up. It is carried down for a yard or so, according to the quality of the rock. The cistern-digger has chosen his site in an area which experience leads him to think will have a good sub-stratum of friable limestone. He does not want to widen his shaft out into the body of the "pear" until he has reached it. When he has, he goes down the shaft, and, again working solely by sight and touch, starts to hollow out the chamber of the well. The spoil is raised to the surface on a windlass worked by his assistant. It is like those wooden machines that people used to wind wool on, only lying on its side. To raise the bucket, you grasp the spokes with your hands, and also with your feet, and turn the contraption towards you.

When the cavity of the well has been finished, it must be cemented. The limestone is porous, and a cistern without cement is useless. The cement is made of small stones, lime and ashes. It is a traditional mixture, and very strong and water-tight. (In the Talmud (Aboth II, 8), a certain exemplary pupil is likened to "a well-plastered cistern: it loseth not a single drop.") When it has been applied, it must be left to dry. Then the walls of the cistern must be given a double coat of sand and Portland cement, each of which also must be allowed to dry. When finally the water is allowed to flow in, a cistern must not be filled to more than two-thirds of its capacity the first year, or the pressure of the water will be too much for the immature cement. The rains were late this last season. December was practically dry. This caused us a good deal of anxiety; but it turned out well for us, because it gave us a month of much needed building weather. It also meant that we were able to get our cistern dug and cemented and dried before the March rains. At first, when the water was allowed in, we thought that the cistern was leaking, because the level fell. Several solemn inquests were held, with plummets and measuring lines. We finally concluded that it was only the water sinking into the outer layer of the cement, that had caused the level to fall. Apparently we were right, because the level is now stationary. The cistern is not being used, but is being kept in reserve for when the hired cisterns are empty. You will naturally wonder what has been done to save the cistern from pollution. We consulted the U.N.R.W.A. health authorities as to whether we should instal latrines in the village or not. They said no: an untended latrine was worse than none at all; and as our village was such a small area in such a large expanse of open land, they thought it would be better to leave things as they were. But we have a rule that the whole space within the walls, including the catchment area of the cistern, is to be kept absolutely clean. No rubbish is to be thrown down, no animals, not even hens or rabbits, are to be kept there. Only the bees are admitted. The villagers appreciate the advantages of having a clean village, so they keep it beautifully. The livestock is relegated to the caves. When the houses were occupied, both they and the caves were thoroughly treated with D.D.T., so that both the villagers and their animals had a good start in their new way of life.

The next communal necessity is an oven. This is not perhaps a necessity; and there are villages that do not have one. But however individualistic the men may be, the women of the community dearly like to have a communal oven. This is partly because it saves them a household chore, and partly because, like the village well or cistern, it provides a meeting place and somewhere to gossip. So the women were insistent that an oven they must have. Building ovens is another skilled craft. The "ovener" must be prevailed upon to come and build one for you. Its size depends on the size of the village, but the plan is the same. It consists of a domed baking-chamber, shaped like an old-fashioned dish-cover, on top of a square platform. The platform is not solid. It is filled with a special mixture of flint and salt, so that when a fire is lighted in the chamber, the heat will be absorbed, and given out again to bake the bread. The platform is waist-high, just right for pushing the loaves in and drawing them out. It has a door which is shut while the baking is going on. Outside this door is a sort of vestibule, from which rises a chimney, to carry off the smoke while the oven is being fired. Outside the oven, the walls are extended backwards, like blinkers, to enclose a kneading table. The man who works the oven climbs over the kneading table and stands between it and the oven door. Our oven is to be oil-fired. The women are very pleased that at last it is finished. Every time we went to visit the village, they would greet us with cries of "where is our oven?" and from the ardour with which the men also commended the request, it was clear that the women had had a word, or perhaps two, with their mates.

Lastly, there is the mosque. When the Bishop paid a visit to the village at the New Year, the elders asked him whether they might build a room which would serve as a school during the week for the little children who were not yet big enough to walk into Bethany, and could also on Fridays and feasts and fasts be used as a mosque. The Bishop of course said yes. It would hardly become a bishop to build a godless village, particularly when the inhabitants had themselves asked for a House of God. Their ideas about Him might be different from those of the Bishop: but He was the same One and Only God. This decision of the Bishop had a deep effect. It was known and reported on all sides. It finally shut the mouths of those who still attributed to his kindness some sinister ulterior design. A site for the mosque was chosen just outside the north wall of the village. The stone is now being prepared for it, and after the harvest is over, and the men return to their homes, building will begin. It will be small, but it is to be as beautiful as we can make it. It will be seen from far away both to the north and to the south. Inside, it must be plain and austere as all mosques are; but we hope to adorn the *mihrab* or prayer-niche with a course of green marble, from a quarry near Amman, and to introduce a few tiles with suitable inscriptions over the doors and windows. Perhaps, too, we may be able to run to an *œuil-de-bœuf* over the mihrab. There is a model for it in one of the finest Islamic buildings still standing in the Old City.

When Ramadan came round this year, the old gentleman who

acts as Iman or prayer-leader of the village said he wanted an alarm-clock, so that he would know when to call the people to their prayers, particularly at night, when he could not tell the time by the sun. I found, by chance, a travelling clock I had, with an alarm attachment. I took it to him, and explained that it was not only very beautiful, and had fingers which glowed in the night-season, but that it also had a bulbul inside it. This gave much pious satisfaction. I was told later by some of the younger bloods of the village that the old man had put the clock, all set, into his pocket, and had then forgotten about it. When it went off, at two in the morning, he jumped up and roused the village with a call to prayer that sounded more profane than sacred.

I have mentioned trees. We planted about two hundred this season. Some are cypress, by the side of the street, some are Aleppo pines near the walls. Through the generosity of an English friend, we are now acquiring a considerable area outside the walls, to the north and east, and this also we intend to plant with forest trees. But it is the efforts of the villagers that have been so striking and so touching. As soon as they moved into their homes, they started making gardens. Every little pocket of earth was levelled and terraced. The chief agricultural authority is a twinkling old gnome whom we call "Al-Wazir"—the Minister. Fruit trees, olives, fig and apricot mysteriously appeared. Vines were planted, and many sorts of vegetables, tomatoes and marrows being the commonest. At last they are reunited with their beloved mother, Earth.

The rest of the story, so far as it has gone, is soon told.

There was one person whose opinion on what we had done I was very anxious to have, Sayyid Anwar Nuseibeh, the Minister of Development. I knew him to be a man of intelligence and energy, one who had absorbed the best that East and West could give him, and above all a sincere patriot. He had lost a foot during the fighting in 1948. At Cambridge, and afterwards in Jerusalem, he has been a champion tennis player; so that his injury was particularly hard on him. But he never by so much as a gesture allows anyone to suppose that he was in any way incapacitated by his misfortune. I did not therefore like to ask him to visit the village, because knowing Anwar, I knew he would at once accept; and I thought the last half mile over the rock might be too much for him. But one day as we were sitting together, he said that he wished to visit the village and when could we go? So we went one afternoon, he and Sir Patrick

Coghill of the Arab Legion and I. Anwar walked over the rock as though it were his normal stroll, and only on the way back did he let out that it was the first time he had tried such a terrain. As we came over the rise, and the village came into view, he stopped, took a long look at it, and then said: "That is what a Palestine village ought to look like." He said a good deal more that was encouraging both to the villagers and to us, during his visit; but it was his first impression that gave us the deepest satisfaction. It showed that we had fulfilled at least part of our aim. Later on, Anwar as Minister of Development started on the programme of village-building himself, to which I referred in chapter five. His successor is carrying on with the scheme. It is one of the most imaginative and constructive enterprises yet taken in hand by the Jordan Government. The villages are to be placed on the West Bank of the Jordan, and will be a solid proof of the Government's interest in those of its citizens who dwell there, for these villages will provide dwellings for refugees in their own homeland, if not in their own original homes.

On one of the gateposts of our village are carved in Arabic its name and the date of its foundation. It is to be called Rafat al Zayyim: Rafat for the original village, Al Zayyim because that is the name of the new site. It is the old in a new setting. The other gatepost bears a text from the Quran: "Enter ye in peace and faith."

Already the people are transformed. They are still technically refugees, they still draw rations. But they are citizens again. The natural spirit of enterprise has come back to them. Now that they have homes, their instinct and pride is to maintain them. Some of them have found seasonal occupation, such as the harvesting I mentioned just now. One of them goes round neighbouring villages selling coffee. Another carries on an apparently profitable trade as a huckster in Silwan. He is tall and rangy, and is known as "Al-Qaid," "The Leader," because he took part in the revolt against the English in 1936—or so he says: the villagers sometimes call him by a slightly altered version of his name, which has a considerably less honourable meaning. Mohammed, "Albert Herring," not to be outdone in martial prestige, recently appeared with a large leather belt, like a Sam Browne, across his chest. I could see he was longing to explain what it supported, so pretended not to notice. At last he could bear it no longer, and said, "Look, O brother, what I have here," and at the end of the belt, hidden by his jacket, showed me a holster. Inside was a revolver, carefully wrapped up in a grubby handkerchief. He unwrapped it with a grin of pride. "Is it loaded?" I asked him. "No," he said, "it is not loaded: no, I cannot afford bullets, but it is very beautiful."

Recently, the Mukhtar made a métayage agreement of the usual kind with a landowner near Jericho, to work eighty acres of irrigated land. It lies below the spring called Al-Nu'eimeh—the Little Mercy, on the estate which Cleopatra took from Herod, and which twelve hundred years later supported Princess Yvette's convent at Bethany. Already some of the land has been ploughed, and sesame has been sown. The rest is to be put under vegetables and wheat. The villagers take half the crop, and the owner half. The proprietor is a member of the Dajani family. He likes having these people to work his land for three reasons: first, they are good farmers, secondly, they are refugees, thirdly, he feels that if they are sponsored by the Bishop and Mahmud Abu Rish, they will be good tenants.

The children are already being sent to school in Bethany, the boys that is; when I asked whether any of the girls were going I was answered with laughter. The benefits of cleanliness are understood, and even, now, the advantages of a hospital. These took some time to appreciate. To start with, we arranged that a nurse who is a member of the Bishop's staff, Miss Regina Shiber, should go out to see the children, and specially to look after their eyes. Then the Crown Prince of the village was taken ill. He is a beautiful baby called 'Eid which means Feast, for he was born on the end-of-Ramadan feast day a year ago—the first boy to be born to the villagers since they left their old homes. Miss Shiber's treatment soon restored him to health. The villagers were impressed, but not convinced. The next thing that happened was that two little girls caught measles. We went to see them, and suggested a visit to the U.N.R.W.A. clinic. This idea was not approved, so we left what instructions we could, and told them to let Mahmud know if the children took a turn for the worse. Shortly afterwards, a blizzard struck Jerusalem. Snow and hail and wind and rain lashed us for three days. On the second day, we went out to see how things were. We had to walk all the way from Bethany this time, because the track was waterlogged. When we enquired after the poor little measles patients, we were told, casually, that one had died. The reason given for not letting us know that she had become worse was that it was very cold and they did not wish to trouble us. We could do no more that day, as to take any sick persons or young children out in the storm would have been to hasten their deaths. But the day after the end of the blizzard, we went to the village and carried off the other measles case, on the ground that home treatment had been a failure, and hospital treatment could at any rate be no worse. Under the care of Dr. Canaan and his helpers, the child recovered. The mukhtar looked crestfallen, I hope with shame, when I met him with the good news in the hospital grounds the next day. After that, the hospital became the thing: there were soon twelve measles cases there. They all recovered. The fame of the institution spread. There was a girl lying ill in a cave near Abu Dis. One day, Mrs. Stewart and Mahmud and I went with a car made into an ambulance, with a stretcher also and hot water bottles, because the car could not get within a furlong of the cave, to take the girl to hospital. We were met with a blank refusal. The girl looked to our unprofessional eyes as though she were in the last stages of consumption. She was clearly in great pain. There she lay wrapped in rags, with only the blankets which Mrs. Stewart had given her between her body and the damp earth. But neither she nor her mother would hear of her being moved. Defeated, we had to take the stretcher and the hot water bottles back. Suddenly, about a fortnight after the measles-pilgrimage, as Mrs. Stewart and I were walking back from the village to the car, up came two men from Abu Dis, imploring us to take the girl to hospital at once. In no time we had the stretcher and the bottles and the blankets ready, and sped out to the cave, lest the girl should change her mind again. But she didn't. Dr. Canaan took a special interest in the case, which wasn't consumption at all, but an affliction of the liver. He kept the girl in the hospital until she was completely cured—pressure on the beds generally makes it necessary to send patients out as soon as they can walk—and now she has gone back to Abu Dis, and to a house this time, to commend the virtues of modern medicine. The fact that the Augusta Victoria Hospital is run entirely by Arabs, and that a patient hears only her own language spoken in it, and is cared for by her own countrymen and women undoubtedly makes her feel more at home there than she would in a foreign hospital, however good.

Such is the story of Rafat al Zayyim.

The Feast at the end of Ramadan—the 'Eid al Fitr—began this

year on Friday the 12th June. On that afternoon Mahmud and I
went out to call on Rafat al Zayyim, as custom enjoins. When we
appeared on the horizon, the villagers came out in a procession to
meet us. First came the Mukhtar and Ahmed his brother, then the
Wazir and the Iman, "Al-Qaid," "Albert Herring" and the rest,
great and small. They were dressed in new cloaks, russet with gold
embroidery on the collars, newly washed white head-dresses, and
neat robes beneath. We shook hands all round, while the villagers
invoked God's blessing on the Bishop and Mrs. Stewart, who were
in England. We passed in through the gate and went up to the
Mukhtar's house, where, from a bashful distance, the women also
called out their welcome. We went in and sat down on the mattress
that had been placed over the floor mats. The men ranged themselves round the walls, and the younger folk gathered outside the
windows. Tea was brought, and sweets. The amber light of the
setting sun gilded the little houses and gardens below us, and threw
sapphire shadows over the wilderness to the east. We sat and talked
the time-hallowed village talk. We spoke of children, and crops, of
man and beast, of works and days. We felt the rhythm of life. It
was just ten months since Mrs. Stewart had laid the foundation stone
of the house in which we sat.

In time the trees will grow up, the villagers will acquire more
land to work. Given five or ten years of tranquillity (and what is
that in the history of their land and their people?) there is every
reason to expect that the men and women of Rafat will once again
be happy independent citizens, and their children after them.

Chapter Eight

Then the disciples, every man according to his ability, determined to send relief unto the brethren which dwelt in Judæa; which also they did.

ACTS xi. 29, 30.

SO far I have said nothing of how much this village cost, and how the money was found. As we have seen, much of the material was given, either directly as in the case of the roofs, or indirectly, as in that of the packing cases from which the doors and windows were made. Labour, too, was largely provided free, and tools and wheelbarrows had been lent by the Agency. Mahmud and his brother, in this enterprise, as in others for the benefit of their countrymen, willingly gave their services. We had no drawing-office, no planners, no administrative expenses. We were able to do the work as economically as it could be done. Still, there were expenses which had to be met with cash payments. There was the lease, the quarrying of the stone, the masons, the carpenter, the well-digger, the building of the ring-wall and the gates, and the mosque.

When as a child, I used to hear read the passage (Luke xiv. 28-30) asking, "Which of you intending to build a tower sitteth not down first, and counteth the cost, whether he have sufficient to finish it? Lest haply, after he hath laid the foundation, and is not able to finish it, all that behold it begin to mock him, saying, This man began to build and was not able to finish," I felt very smug and certain that I should never have been caught out so easily. I know better now. Even Sir Winston Churchill, a provident and far-sighted man if ever there was one, admits in his *Life of Marlborough* that building always seems to turn out more costly than you think it will. Ours did, and still does.

When we started, not one of those who were in charge of the operation had any experience of building. Nor had the villagers. Our first calculation, liberally salted with enthusiasm, led us to think that we could do the work for £500. This soon rose to £600.

The question was, where could we find it? As I have said, the
Bishop's relief work has been generously supported, particularly
from America. But that money is allocated for the daily needs of
the needy, for food and clothing. It would be possible to advance a
hundred pounds or two from that fund; and the Bishop did not
hesitate to do so. Faith, Hope and Love are not seldom better
counsellors than caution and economy. The work had to be done,
and it had to be started at once. Nevertheless, it was clear that this
was a wholly new departure, and must be paid for by "new money."
The Bishop therefore determined to make the time-honoured
appeal of the Briton. What Cæsar was to the Roman citizen, *The
Times* is to the British subject.

On the 15th October, *The Times* published the following
letter:

"Sir,—Four years ago, when the Arab refugee problem first
emerged, you published a letter of mine appealing for help for
more than a quarter of a million refugees. To-day the official
figure is more than three times that number. The problem is
unsolved, and the United Nations Agency, restricted by their
terms of reference, and never certain of future funds, have invited
the co-operation of voluntary bodies. May I, therefore, ask again
through you for help towards what the Church can do and is
doing?

"At this moment we are building near Bethany, for a total of
£600, with refugee labour and stone found on the site, simple
houses for a group of 21 families still living in five [*sic*] caves. In
another area, near 'Amman, we are building better houses, at a cost
of £320 each, for refugee families of an artisan or clerk type, whose
breadwinner has found work at a wage sufficient to enable him to
repay the cost of building over a period of, say, four years till the
house is his. Such pilot projects could be multiplied if we had the
funds.

"Housing, feeding, clothing, rehabilitation—Lynmouth has
shown what British charity can do near home. Our refugees
are much farther off—but there are far more of them. Gifts of
clothing and blankets should be addressed to the Church Missionary Society, Palestine Relief, 6 Salisbury Square, London, E.C.4;
and gifts of money to the Secretary, Jerusalem and the East
Mission, 12 Warwick Square, London, S.W.1. Cheques, money

orders, and postal orders should be made payable to the secretary, and should be crossed 'Bishop in Jerusalem, Relief Fund.'

Yours faithfully,

WESTON,

Bishop in Jerusalem

St. George's Close,
Jerusalem Old City.

The response was immediate and generous. In little more than a month, £1,500 had been contributed. In the circumstances which the Bishop recalls in his letter, this speaks well for the liberality of the people of Great Britain. It is also a testimony to the authority of *The Times*. The village, we reckoned, was paid for, two houses could be added to the housing estate at Zerqa, and there would be something over for expansion.

The Zerqa housing estate is but one of many enterprises organized and administered by a very remarkable lady, Miss Winifred Coate. Miss Coate started work with the Church Missionary Society in Cairo many years ago. She later became Principal of the Jerusalem Girls' College, which, throughout the period of the British administration of Palestine, was one of the finest schools in the whole Levant. By the end of the Mandate Miss Coate had retired; but when the refugees were in need of help, back she came to see what she could do. She knows the people, they know her; she is imaginative and sympathetic, and full of energy; she has a fund of humour which has proved the solvent of many an obstacle, human and inhuman. Zerqa is a bare dusty spot twelve miles north of 'Amman. It was a military cantonment and little else, until the refugees established a camp there. You could hardly find a more desolate and depressing place. That is why Miss Coate chose it to work in. Single-handed she has established a feeding centre, a maternity clinic, an embroidery school, a shop for the sale of local wicker-work and other crafts, a pottery and brick-works, and a farm. It is as an adjunct to all these, that Miss Coate has also hit on the idea of starting the housing estate which the Bishop mentions in his letter; and a very flourishing and useful concern it is.

As it turned out, the Bishop's first village finally cost just over £1,000, not counting the mosque, which will add about £100 to the total. Most people who visit it, think it must have cost far more.

Even at a thousand pounds, the price is not high. It is in fact very low. To house twenty-two families, and to supply the amenities of a village for them, £1,000 is not a high price to pay. (The Bishop mentions twenty-one families in his letter; and this was the number of the original cave-dwellers. But as the houses were built in blocks of two, there was of necessity an extra house, which was occupied by a Rafat villager who had been living in Silwan.)

As the village took shape, travellers from abroad would sometimes go out to visit it, and often they would leave a gift with the Bishop to advance the work. It was very small; but it was there. It was practical, and it seemed to be an improvement on the conditions in which the villagers had recently been living. Gradually we came to wonder whether it might not be possible to make this not an isolated experiment, but the beginning of a larger programme. We were not the only ones. Some of the refugees were also thinking in the same way.

This was encouraging. After all, the little group we had assisted to build their homes were, as I have said in the last chapter, a special case. They were isolated in space, they were all related and they were not being moved from one area to another, merely from caves to houses a few hundred yards away. But what would happen if it were proposed to build houses for refugees who were living, say, in Bethany or Abu Dis, and who came from different villages? Would they want to move into houses, and if they did, would they wish to live in houses near a village or a town? We decided to let the answer come from the refugees themselves. It was not long in coming. First, a group of villagers from Suba said they would like to have houses. Soon afterwards, a number from Qastel said the same, then some from Saris and finally a few (there are only a few living) from Deir Yassin. All these villages, to the west of Jerusalem near the road to Jaffa, are now in Israel. Applications came from so far afield as Hebron. We soon had the names of a hundred people who wanted houses, and then we closed the lists—we could not possibly build even one hundred houses this year, and we had no wish to raise hopes only to disappoint them. The procedure for those whom we did register was as follows. First, they must write to the Bishop saying that they wanted to live in houses, and that they were ready to help build them. We then placed their names on our list. What we wanted to make quite clear was that the initiative must come from them. The Bishop had no wish to compel refugees to occupy houses; he was merely ready to give practical help to those who wanted to make their own homes.

This point, as I have already indicated, is of the first importance from the political point of view. We reply, if any one accuses us of re-settlement, first, that we are not concerned with shaping the future, which is none of our business: we are anxious only that whatever the future may hold, as many refugees as wish to face it as healthy householders may be able to do so; and secondly, that we are merely helping refugees to help themselves. But even more important, I think, is the psychological bearing of the question. These people, through no fault of their own, have become dependents. They have lost their initiative, they have lost their spirit of enterprise. They have ceased in varying degrees to be individual citizens, and have become "units," "card-holders." I say in varying degrees, because the camp-dwellers are far worse off mentally than those outside. Not long ago, I visited one of the largest camps in the kingdom. It is in the Jordan valley. It houses 20,000 refugees. It is a town, not a camp. Its population is as large as that of Jerusalem a century ago. It is well-administered. It is barren and dusty, but it is clean. The camp director is an Arab. He has an excellent staff, which includes a Lebanese doctor, a British doctor, a Dutch welfare worker and a Mennonite volunteer assistant. The medical services at the disposal of the inhabitants are better, and nearer, than anything they have known before. There are schools for their children, there are feeding centres, and every sort of clinic, eye, tooth, maternity, and general, for both them and their children. There is a laundry and slaughter houses. But there is no spiritual response from the people. The inhabitants of this town do nothing for it. A few of them cultivate an acre or two which are irrigated by the pumps that provide the water-supply. But they do that for themselves. Not only do they do nothing for the town, but they actively oppose the town when, as such, it proposes to do anything for them. As I said, this particular camp is in the Jordan valley, in one of the hottest places on earth. It is absolutely barren. The heat and the glare are overpowering. The first thing that even a visitor longs for is shade. Yet when the camp authorities proposed to plant trees, the inhabitants prevented them. They said that trees would be a sign of settlement, and would mean that they were permanent dwellers, and not just migrants waiting to go home. To such miserable shifts can the combination of affliction and dependence reduce men. As

(Elia)

The Bishop lays the first stone of Al-Mansur. Abu 'Ali and Mahmud Abu Rish assist.
Musa Abu Rish is behind the Bishop.

(Elia)

The Bishop inspects the site.

(Elia)

Abu 'Ali (left) and Abu Musa exchange notes on 22nd April 1953, before the stone-
laying at Al-Mansur. Rafat-al-Zayyim is at one o'clock from Abu Musa's left
shoulder, just below horizon.

(R. Walmsley)

The Church of the Holy Sepulchre—roof. The larger dome on the left covers the Sepulchre, the smaller, on the right, the

(R. Walmsley)

Ascension Day on the Mount of Olives—one of Christendom's first shrines, with Bethphage, Bethany, the Wilderness and the Dead Sea

the Preacher said long ago (Ecclesiastes vii. 7), "Surely, oppression maketh a wise man mad; and a gift destroyeth the heart."

But even if you remove the feeling of oppression, you have still to reckon with the gift. I also visited recently a village created by U.N.R.W.A. There are in it thirty-two families who formerly lived in camps. The little houses are a joy to behold. Their design is good, a clever adaptation of traditional style, executed in traditional materials, stone and mud brick, and also in modern concrete, some with domes and some with flat roofs. There is nothing monotonous about the village, nothing mass-produced. Below it, there is a copious well, which is producing 270 cubic metres of water an hour. This is enough to irrigate a substantial holding—six acres—for each villager; and the water is distributed through concrete flumes. You would say that such a village would be a model of cleanliness and happiness. But it is not. The pretty houses are ill-kept. The yards are messy and the houses are in many cases used simply as stores for vegetables and roots. Why is this? I think there are two reasons. The first is that although there is plenty of water available, and only a matter of yards from the houses, it has not yet been laid on to the houses themselves. This needs only the installation of an auxiliary pump, and a reservoir on the hillside above the houses—quite a simple operation. If each house had water, every householder would become a gardener. He would perforce take an interest in his garden, because he would benefit by its cultivation, and the neglected yards would become neat and verdant. The second reason is that the houses were built by the Agency, and not by those who dwell in them. They were alien gifts. The villagers had no personal interest in their homes, into which they were simply drafted. They felt themselves "inmates," not owners. Many of the original dwellers were so listless and uninterested that they left, to be replaced by others.

What we can give those whom we try to help is far less materially than the Agency gives. We cannot spend money as they can spend it. We do not attempt to do anything on their scale. We must be all the more careful, therefore, that what we do attempt is done as thoroughly as it can be. And, because what we do is so small, it is far easier for us than it is for others to attain at least this.

The Suba group were at the top of our list. There are thirty-five families of them. The problem which they presented was different in many ways from that of the Rafat group. To start with, they were

K

not one family association or sept. They had no mukhtar, only an unofficial leader, Abu 'Ali. Secondly, there was no mere question of moving them all from one dwelling-area to another close by. The members of the group were living in various hovels and caves in different parts of Bethany. Many of them had lived for some years in tents, scattered here and there. But with the decay of the tents, and the onset of their fourth winter, Mahmud helped them to obtain more permanent shelter, wretched as it was; and expensive, too. They had to pay a pound a month for a room, and that pound could be come by only by selling part of their inadequate rations. Thirdly, the area in which we had decided to site the next village is almost a suburb of Bethany itself. It would be in full view of every-one: we could no longer work, as we had to some extent in our first venture, out of sight (except for that of the elders of Tur) and out of mind. For the second village is on a plot of land to the east of Bethany, about half a mile beyond the Greek church. It stands right above the Apostles' Fountain. From the main Jerusalem-'Amman road, it is clearly visible; it is on the sky-line, in fact, and every traveller, as his car winds its way down the hairpin bends below Bethany, must see the new village rising in front of him. It is a grand site. It has a view that includes not only the 'Amman road, but a whole panorama. It starts from the village of Bethany, with the Mount of Olives above it. Then moving east, appears the village of Rafat al Zayyim, and after it on the far horizon the mountains of Gilead and of Moab, with a glimpse of the Dead Sea below Pisgah. To the south, the roofs and minaret of Abu Dis close the scene.

The land belonged partly to the people of Bethany, and partly to private owners. The problem of how much to buy and how to use it was more complicated than on the first site. There, it was simply a question of buying enough land to build eleven blocks of houses, and to fit those eleven blocks on to the site. Here, we had no limit to the number we could accommodate if we could get the land, and the means with which to build. So we bought as much as we could, which was two and a half acres to start with, hoping to get some more later. On this two and a half acres we had to put as many houses as we could, without overcrowding or waste.

The plot is shaped rather like the edge of a waterfall. It faces north-east. There is a flat piece on top, and then it falls away sharply. There was a footpath which led to the top corner of it nearest to Bethany. We decided to widen this path into a roadway, because it would be easier to get our materials to the site, and in any case as the village was to be so near the road, it might as well have a road to it all the way. It was not hard to make. It is by no means a boulevard, now it is finished, but it is as good as many another *piste* in the country, and serves its purpose in all weathers.

It was in November, 1952, that we had decided to undertake a second village. That was just at what should have been the beginning of the rainy season. We did not think of building until the fine weather came in the spring, April or May; and we were in any case still fully occupied with Rafat. But there were some things that could be done during the winter. First there was the quarrying. This being piece-work, the quarrymen could work when it was fine, and stay at home when it was wet, and we should pay them for what they produced. Then there were two things which we had left till last in the first village, which we decided to put in before we started on the houses in the second, namely, the ring-wall and the cisterns, of which we should need at least two in the new village. So work on the road, the wall and the cisterns was started. The wall was soon finished, on the three sides of the village where our boundary was settled. The north-eastern side, that is, at the bottom of the slope, we have left open, because we hope to extend our holding there; the owners have agreed in principle to sell, but one of those who must sign the document is away, and we cannot take possession till he comes back. We are in no hurry (even if we were it would be fatal to seem to be) as we have enough land to keep us occupied for some time. The cisterns were tantalizing. As we have seen, a cistern must be given time to dry after it is dug and after the coating of cement. The Rafat cistern had been dug and finished during the months of December and January, both of which were abnormally dry months. The well-digger then moved on to the new village. But no sooner had he and his team begun work, than the rains came in good earnest. The cisterns, both of which are bigger than the one at Rafat, were dug; but when it came to cementing them, there was never an interval long enough for even the first coat to dry thoroughly. March was worse; it rained almost every day, and we had snow and hail as well. The fine weather only came with April. The well soon dried, and the cement too; but dry it was to remain, because no more rain fell. This was a considerable blow: we had hoped to use these cisterns to supply the water for building. We turned to U.N.R.W.A. for help. They have a number of large tank trucks, which deliver water to camps. They promised they would send us three trucks a week, and they have made it good. Our road is justified already: the trucks carry the water to the entrance of the village, where they discharge it through their hoses in the direction of the top cistern, into which it runs over the rock by gravity. U.N.R.W.A. thus supplies what the clouds have withheld, and the builders draw their supplies from the cistern as though it had filled by nature in the ordinary way.

Before I say any more about the construction of this second village, or even tell you its name, I must once again say how it is being paid for, because the money contributed for the first village, in response to the Bishop's appeal in *The Times*, had all been spent.

It happened that I had written some account of what the Bishop was trying to do to a friend in Kuwait, Richard Goddard-Wilson, who had recently become English secretary to the Secretary to Government there. I had known him first in Iraq in 1941, when we were both on the staff of Sir Kinahan Cornwallis, I in the Embassy in Baghdad, and Richard Goddard-Wilson on his political advisory staff in Kirkuk. We were colleagues for six years. After a two-year interval, we again found ourselves serving in the same post, this time in Benghazi, where Richard was on the staff of the Resident, and I Adviser to the Ministry of the Interior. By this time, Richard had married Lavender Cassels. When Richard heard what the Bishop had done and was hoping to do, he declared that he would see what he could do to help. He consulted Christopher Pirie-Gordon of the Residency, who had formerly served in Palestine and Jordan. Between them, they decided to start a fund. This was to attract subscriptions, they hoped, not from the inhabitants of Kuwait, who were already being regarded as a general fountain of wealth, but from the British and Americans who were working there. It was a very generous, and also a courageous, plan. And vigorously did the two originators pursue it. There are, as I have said, large numbers of Palestinians at work in Kuwait; but for the reasons which I have indicated, the heavy personal responsibilities they have each and all to bear, Goddard-Wilson and Pirie-Gordon had not intended at first to include them in the scope of their appeal. But they soon found that the Palestinians insisted on coming in. And so a committee was formed which represented British, American and Palestinian employees, not only of the oil company, but of the big contracting firms as well.

When Richard Goddard-Wilson had gone out to Kuwait, Lavender had stayed behind in London to take a course of Arabic at the School of Oriental and African Studies. She thought, rightly, that in Kuwait, a knowledge of the language was more of a necessity than a luxury. It was only in December that she was to fly out to join her husband. She decided to break her journey at Beirut and to come down to Jerusalem, simply and solely to see what the Bishop's work was like, so that she could go on to Kuwait with a first-hand story of it. We had sent plenty of photographs of Rafat, but these, helpful as they were, were no substitute for the eye-witness. Lavender knows a good deal about refugee work. Immediately after the war she worked among refugees in Austria. She is the last person to claim to be an "expert" on anything; but the moment she came to Jerusalem, it was clear that she was facing a problem with which she was quite familiar, and about which she could teach us at least as much as she was so willing to learn. Together we visited frontier villages, and in each one Lavender had some shrewd comment to make, some helpful suggestion to offer. She made a careful and detailed study of Rafat, which at the time of her visit was nearly finished. On arriving at Kuwait, she was able, amid a thousand other avocations, to find time to encourage those who were working for the fund, her husband, Mr. Pirie-Gordon, and Mr. John 'Asfour, one of the leading Palestinian representatives. Soon it was clear that they would collect more than a thousand pounds. In the end, the Kuwait contribution reached the magnificent total of £1,250. It also transformed the basis of the Bishop's relief work.

In January of this year, the building of Rafat being finished, I decided to motor across to Baghdad, where I had not been for six years, to enjoy some hunting with the Royal Harithiya, the pack which the Prince Regent had started in 1945. While I was there, the Goddard-Wilsons invited me down to Kuwait, where I was able to visit the Oil Town, Ahmedi, and to meet many of those who direct it. I also visited the two schools where the pupils, American, British, Indian and Palestinian had all given their contributions to the village. As the headmaster of one of them said to me: "they are so proud of their house," meaning the house at Rafat which their contributions had helped to build. And I met the members of the committee who were organizing the fund in Kuwait. Quite by chance, I also met an old friend, Mohammed Ghussein, who now occupies a senior post in the Near East Arab Broadcasting Station in Cyprus. This station was formerly in Jaffa, and the majority of its staff are Palestinian. Mohammed asked me what I was doing. When I told him, he said, "what a good idea." He then explained that the staff of the Station were anxious to do something practical to help their less fortunate brothers in Jordan, but had been unable to decide what form their assistance should take. This plan of the Bishop's, he said, seemed to him practical and sound. Mohammed went back to Cyprus. Soon afterwards, the Bishop received a letter enclosing a cheque for £150, as a first contribution from the staff of the Station towards the new village. The initiative had been taken by a Moslem, and many of the contributors had been Moslems. The station magazine published an article by one of its staff who visited the villages together with photographs of them: and shortly after, along came another cheque for £50, making £200 in all subscribed in less than six months by the staff of this one station, all of whom have their own family commitments and burdens. One of the leading contractors of the Middle East is Mr. Emile Bustani. Mr. Bustani directs many companies, and is the agent of many others. His most famous one is the Contracting and Trading Company, known as CAT, of which a sleek and lucky-looking black cat is the symbol. CAT operates not only in Lebanon, but in Kuwait, Jordan, Qatar, Iraq, and Aden as well. Mr. Bustani, when he heard about the Bishop's plans, asked his 'Amman representative to look into them on the spot. A fortnight later, Mr. Bustani commended the scheme to his staffs in all his various branches as "a very human project." As a first instalment of his Company's support, he sent the sum of £200, £50 each from himself and his three associates, Messrs. Shammas, Khoury and Darwish.

What began as an experiment on the part of the Bishop has now become something much larger. It is now a co-operative enterprise with Arabs and Britons, Moslems and Christians, as partners.

This development has softened the attitude of the opposing deputy, and others like him who affected to see in the plan a wicked imperialist scheme for inducing the refugees to forgo their rights. In the face of such widespread Arab support, they have been constrained to change their tune. The deputy recently told an assembly of refugees living in his constituency that the plan was a good one, and did not in any way affect or curtail their right of ultimate return.

The foundation stone of the first house of the second village was laid by the Bishop on the 22nd April. With him in the top picture (page 144) appear Mahmud and Abu 'Ali. In the middle picture, the Bishop is inspecting the upper cistern. To the left of him, beyond the group in the middle, appears Abu Musa, holding his cloak in his right hand: all the men of Rafat had come over, dressed in their best, to wish godspeed to the new village. Also, perhaps, as a later conversation on their side of the valley seemed to suggest, to satisfy themselves if possible that the new village would not be better than theirs. In the background of this picture is Mrs. Stewart, talking to me. Above our heads, on the horizon, can just be made out the houses of Rafat. Many an anxious look is directed across the valley, many an earnest enquiry is made on the subject of the new village: surely, it cannot be better than their own handiwork? Did we not call it a model village to all the world? Across the ravine, the same question is being asked the other way round: surely their new and improved village must be better than that little experiment over the way? That will depend on them, we answer. It is a feeble answer: but truth to tell, we are by no means sorry to see this friendly emulation growing between the two sides of the valley.

The first twelve houses of the new village are placed at the very top of the site, right against the boundary wall. As in Rafat, we have avoided the straight line, the uniform spacing and the identical orientation. The main street does not in this case run in front of the houses. As you come into the village from Bethany, you find yourself in a circular open space. From this, on the right, a path runs along in front of the top houses. The main street slopes and curves down from the circus to the lower, eastern cistern. There it turns on itself in a hairpin bend, and runs back to the west, in front of the third range of houses. The houses themselves are of the same design as in Rafat, where they have proved successful. But they are a little larger—four metres square—and there will be improvements in detail here and there: they will be Mark II, instead of Mark I. The siting of each house is done first of all on the spot. Then we go round in a car to the Jericho road on the other side of the valley to see whether it looks just right. If it does not, we adjust it.

Once again, the I.P.C. have helped us. Mr. Littledale suddenly announced one day that he was sending over to us 2,021 sheets of corrugated iron, and seventeen steel doors. The iron will provide roofs for almost one hundred houses. And just before he left for England, Mr. Littledale promised us another 250 sheets. It looks as though, somehow, we shall have to go beyond our limit of one hundred houses this season.

Before I end this account of a village which is still being built, it will be well to say a word about the first of its new inhabitants. The village of Suba lies a mile to the south of the Jerusalem-Jaffa road just before it reaches Abu Ghosh, at a distance of six miles from the city itself. It is one of those pretty villages set in groves of olives, which soften the harsh outlines of the Judæan hills. Its citizens are typical hill-men, enterprising, canny and active. They were by no means all farmers like the men of Rafat. Some are masons, and some found employment in Jerusalem, like so many other hill villagers, for Suba possessed only 500 acres, mostly planted with olives and fruit trees; by no means enough to sustain all its inhabitants. The leader of our group is called Musa Ghazzaleh, or Abu 'Ali. I asked him how many people lived in Suba before the flight. Seven hundred, he said. And where were they now? In a hundred cities, he answered.

Abu 'Ali is an intelligent man; and his own history makes it specially pleasant and fitting to help him. I have mentioned Ahmed al-Khalidi. His family claim descent from Khalid ibn Walid, one of the earliest and greatest commanders of Islam, after whom Ahmed named his first-born. Now it happens that the people of Suba claim descent from Ja'far al Tayyar, a contemporary of Khalid's, and like him a military leader, who fell at the battle of Muta, in 629, the only battle which was fought by Moslems against Christians in the lifetime of Mohammed. Muta is a village a few miles south of Kerak, and the tomb of Ja'far is still venerated nearby. It was Khalid who rescued the discomfited forces of Islam after the death of Ja'far, and led them back to Mecca. Abu 'Ali's ancestors remained behind. They settled at Rabbeh, a village just north of Kerak, where the Government now has a flourishing agricultural station. Some centuries ago, seven, Abu 'Ali says, his people left Rabbeh, and came across the river (as so many tribes have done since the days of Joshua) and settled in Suba. There in the fulness of time, descendants of Ja'far and of Walid were in their turn to be partners. In 1938, Ahmed al-Khalidi decided to found boys' and girls' villages, to house and train the orphans of some of those who had lost their lives in the Arab revolt which had started in 1936. With his usual energy, he made the scheme a success. The children were brought up to fend for themselves, to attend school, to work on the land, to be clean, agile and self-respecting. The villages were built on some 500 acres of waqf land near Deir 'Umar, an old ruin two miles to the south-west of Suba, where in days gone by we would go to shoot partridges. The institutions were a model of their kind, and until the end of the Mandate, were among the places that every visitor to Palestine who was interested in education and the training of the young would visit. The buildings were admirable; sound and solid, but not too "fancy" in comparison with the standard of those the children might be expected to inhabit when they went out into the world. Abu 'Ali was the foreman in charge of building them. In the flight, like most refugees, he lost nearly all he possessed. But he somehow managed to bring away with him a photograph of Ahmed al-Khalidi. He still has it.

Now, it is the turn of those who believe in the liberal tradition of which Ahmed was such a conspicuous example to do what they can for Abu 'Ali and his people. But he is by no means leaving it to them. Already he is installed in a temporary shelter on the site of the new village; he looks after the work day by day just as he did at Deir 'Umar, and he is always on hand with a useful suggestion for where the next house is to be placed, or how the street is to be aligned. It is to be his village, and he wishes to shape its design from the beginning. There are ten of his people working there with him. Again, there was a difference from the people of Rafat. The Suba folk are not farmers without farms. As I have said, they had other professions and callings. Those of our group were mostly builders and labourers; and they had found some work when the new village was begun, though they were not earning the sum of £14 a month which would disqualify them as refugees and mean that they would lose their cards. To ask these men to forgo their one meagre source of income for themselves and their families, even to build their own homes, did not seem fair. So we made a compromise: we pay them for five days, and they give two days free. We employ ten of them; and five from Qastel (a village a little nearer Jerusalem). That is half our total labour force, the other half being drawn from Bethany and Tur, on the principle stated earlier on, that relief work must benefit not only refugees, but those whose fellow-citizens they are as well.

Already the villagers are talking of which house shall be whose.

The allocation at Rafat we simply left to the Mukhtar, and we heard of no differences. In our new village, there may be some, because Abu 'Ali, although he is a leader, is not an official one. But for the present all we say is that there will be no allocation till the whole village is finished.

The villagers of Suba are scattered; and our group did not feel that they were entitled, in the absence of both the mukhtars, to carry on the village's old name. What was the new one to be? We thought of many; finally, we settled on that of the caliph who founded a great and famous Arab city, Baghdad. He was called Al-Mansur. We felt that his name would be a good omen. Partly that, and also because of the signification of the name; for the meaning of "Al-Mansur" is "The Victorious."

Chapter Nine

*O how amiable are thy dwellings: thou Lord of Hosts! One day
in thy courts is better than a thousand.*

PSALM lxxxiv. 1, 10.

Our feet shall stand within thy gates, O Jerusalem.

PSALM cxxii. 2.

"*H*IEROSOLYMA, longe clarissima urbium orientis, non
Judaeae modo*"—Jerusalem, by far the most famous city
of the East, not of Judæa only. Thus does Pliny the Elder
describe the Holy City (*Nat. Hist.*, V, xv, 70). At the time when he
wrote, Jerusalem was a "*bustum*," a heap of ashes, having recently
been destroyed by Titus, but he spoke from personal evidence, for
he had been in Palestine a short time before the war. What a tribute,
from a pagan and a foreigner, a member of the race which had
humbled that very city.

For two thousand years, through good report and ill, Jerusalem
has held that primacy, has in fact augmented it. In Pliny's day,
Christianity was in its obscure infancy, Islam had not been born.
To-day, more than ever, despite all its tribulations, Jerusalem is, in
a way that no other city ever has been or ever can be, "by far the
most famous city of the East," and of the West too, for Pliny's own
Eternal City has for long acknowledged Jerusalem as the Queen and
Mother of us all.

The veneration of Jerusalem has been perpetual. But the modes
of its expression have been as various as human nature itself.

The Christian attitude to Jerusalem has seen many changes. Before
we consider what Jerusalem is for Christians to-day, it may be of
interest to contemplate the vicissitudes through which their affection
and reverence have passed. In a sense, the value which successive
generations of Christians have placed upon Jerusalem, has been a
key to their interpretation of their Faith.

The first Christians regarded Jerusalem less as a place whose
stones had a special virtue than as the place where the Apostles
lived: it was the men and women, not the things, that were

important and vital. They were in no sense bound to this or that building, as the scene of any particular act in the life of their Lord. The first Christians were Jews; as Jews they revered the Temple; but within a generation of the Crucifixion, even that great link had been severed, and the Christians of Palestine were exiles in Pella, beyond Jordan. There, the veneration of holy places was physically impossible, even had it been considered laudable. Apart from this accidental reason, there were three others, of far more weight, that made topography a minor or even wholly disregarded factor in their religious profession. The first is to be found in the injunctions of Christ Himself (John iv. 21-24) that neither in the sacred mountain of the Samaritans "nor yet at Jerusalem" should men worship the Father, but—and the command is repeated—"in spirit and in truth." And at the Last Supper, He instituted a Sacrament which is, even on the least sacramental view of it, wholly and essentially independent of place.

The second reason is that the man upon whom more than upon any other the Faith depended for its early propagation had received the faith individually and immediately. St. Paul had so far as we know never even seen Christ in the flesh: he was as unlikely as it was possible for anyone to be to associate with Him, even from a distance. None of the sites of the Gospel story meant anything personal to St. Paul. And it was he, strict Jew though he was by birth and training, who long before the destruction of the Temple deliberately divorced the Christian faith from Judaism.

The third reason is that until Christianity became a "permitted religion," it would be extremely difficult for any Christian from Europe or Asia Minor to make a pilgrimage to Palestine.

This does not mean that the Church of Jerusalem did not maintain and transmit the record of the places in which the scenes of Christ's early life had been passed. It did; in the gospels, in that of St. John even more than in the synoptic gospels, the precision of description is notable. Take for instance the story of the pool of Bethesda: "there is at Jerusalem by the sheep market a pool, which is called in the Hebrew tongue Bethesda, having five porches" (John v. 2). What could be more definite? Or, "He went forth with his disciples over the brook Cedron, where was a garden, into the which he entered, with his disciples. And Judas, also, which betrayed him, knew the place; for Jesus ofttimes resorted thither with his disciples" (John xviii. 1, 2). Scores of people must have known exactly which garden it was. And they would have told their children. These sites, and the acts which were done in them, would have become part of the tradition of the infant church. But that is quite a different matter from their becoming places of veneration or worship. The same sort of thing constantly happens in secular lives. There was never any doubt, for instance, about Shakespeare's birthplace. But it was only in the eighteenth century, more than two hundred years after his birth, that it began to be a "place of pilgrimage."

So it was with Jerusalem. When the time came, the traditions which had preserved the identification of the sites became public knowledge, and no longer merely the property of the local church. We have seen in the case of the Gate of the Pillar how tenacious tradition is in Palestine. The Jerusalem church would have been as least as zealous as popular hearsay to preserve and transmit the history of its holy places.

Despite all difficulties, despite the contrary reasons given above, the cult of pilgrimages gradually asserted itself; as early as the beginning of the third century, in fact. The list of the first sites to be regarded as holy is significant: it includes neither the Temple nor the Holy Sepulchre. The pilgrims were strangers to Palestine, men and women from Europe or Asia Minor, to whom Christianity was far more the complement and perfection of their own philosophy and natural piety than the fulfilment of Judaism. To them, the Temple, if it stood for anything, was merely the symbol of an outmoded dispensation: its site became first neglected, and then odious to the Christian Church. It was left to the Moslem conqueror Omar, in the year 638, to rescue the Temple area from neglect and defilement, and to make it once again, what it has been ever since, a centre of veneration.

The neglect of the Holy Sepulchre is harder to explain. Eusebius, who wrote in the early fourth century, preserves a tradition that the Emperor Hadrian had built a temple of Venus over the site of the Tomb of Christ. The fact that this site was the very first to be exalted and sanctified by the Empress Helena, and the previous absence of recorded access to it, seem to me strong proof that the tradition which Eusebius records is nothing less or more than the truth. No pious Christian would approach the shame and humiliation of a temple of Venus; every pious Christian would desire that Calvary and the Sepulchre of his Lord should be freed and purified before all else. The birthplace of Christ at Bethlehem was known and venerated as early as the third century: but the orientation of the early pilgrims to Jerusalem is a curious mixture of the "Catholic" and "Protestant" attitudes of a later day. "All believers in Christ," says Eusebius, "flock together from all quarters of the earth, not, as of old, to behold the beauty of Jerusalem, or that they may worship in the former Temple which stood in Jerusalem, but that they may abide there, and both hear the story of Jerusalem, and also worship in the Mount of Olives over against Jerusalem, whither the glory of the Lord removed itself, leaving the earlier city. There, also, according to the published record, the feet of our Lord and Saviour, Who was himself the Word, and, through It took upon Himself human form, stood upon the Mount of Olives, near the cave which is now pointed out there." (Eusebius has already dropped the pagan name Ælia Capitolina, in favour of the old name Jerusalem, though it was as "Iliya" that the first Moslems knew it three hundred years later. This simultaneous use of an older and a newer name for the same town is not without a parallel: the old capital of Malta for instance is to-day known both as "Mdina" and "Notabile.")

When, during the early thirties of the fourth century, as a result of the Empress Helena's visit to Jerusalem, the principal shrines were embellished with magnificent churches, not only were Calvary and the Holy Sepulchre and Bethlehem so distinguished, but two churches were also built on the Mount of Olives on the sites of the Ascension and the Teaching of the Lord's Prayer.

Once the Faith was free, once the shrines were open to worship, and under royal patronage, too, the flow of pilgrims was continuous. Even while the churches were still building, in 333, a pilgrim from Bordeaux had come to worship at them. He was the first of many such pilgrims to leave us some account of his travels. By the end of the fourth century, many men and women, fleeing the troubles and confusions of the temporal world, retired to Palestine to lead the lives of hermits and coenobites. St. Jerome was the most famous, the Empress Eudocia the most influential. Throughout the fourth and fifth centuries the churches and convents of Palestine increased in number and riches. The great Justinian was a liberal benefactor. He built not only churches, but a hospital and a hospice for pilgrims, the first of which we have record. Antoninus Martyr, who visited Jerusalem about 570, says that he stayed in the hospice, and that the hospital had more than three thousand beds.

These glories were soon to wither. In 614, the Persians under Chosroes II invaded Palestine. For nearly five hundred years Palestine had enjoyed peace, the Pax Romana which Hadrian had bestowed upon it. Never before, and never since, in all its recorded history, has Jerusalem known so long a period of tranquillity. The Persians were joined by many thousands of Jews, who were eager to regain what they regarded still as their own city, and to take their revenge on the Christians who had excluded them from it. Jerusalem was pillaged and its inhabitants massacred. Of the churches, only that of Bethlehem survived, because, it is said, a mosaic over the west door represented the Three Kings arrayed in the national dress of Persia. Thirteen years later, this disaster was avenged by Heraclius. But his victory gave only fourteen years' respite. Already the star of Islam was lord of the ascendant; and in the year 638, the caliph Omar entered Jerusalem.

After the first shock was absorbed, Jerusalem began once more to exert her undying attraction. But with a fundamental difference. Before the invasion of Chosroes, Jerusalem had been a Byzantine city, and its Church had been Byzantine. The sumptuous buildings of its churches and convents all proclaimed the Greek tradition, of architecture as of faith and practice. It was Greek of the Greeks, in aspect and in essence. It would not be so again. Only a few of the churches were rebuilt and those on a far smaller and less costly scale than of old. Of some, the very sites have disappeared. Others were to be rebuilt centuries later, but by Western Christians of the Latin rite, not by Greeks.

It is the glory of the Greek Church that after every disaster, whether it be of fire or war or earthquake, they have somehow contrived to preserve unbroken the tradition and existence of the major shrines of Christendom. The fabric of the Churches of the Holy Sepulchre and of the Nativity is still largely, chiefly, their responsibility and burden. They have never deserted their post, never given up their charge. But by a strange paradox, it was the Persians and the Arabs, the champions of the East against the West, who ensured that the West should in future have its part and lot in Jerusalem; and that the Holy City should be the property neither of the East nor of the West, but the mother city of the Church Universal.

Of the growth of the habit of pilgrimage, and of the cult of relics which went with it, an excellent account is to be found in Chapter III of the first volume of Mr. Runciman's history of the

Crusades. The Crusaders themselves have naturally left many relics in Jerusalem; there are fragments of their secular architecture to be found in the Old City, in the vegetable market, and in the covered suqs. Portions of the Church of the Holy Sepulchre and of the present Lutheran Church of the Redeemer, the grille which surrounds the Rock in the Haram, and the whole of the Church of St. Anne bear witness to their zeal. But it is the small human things, the unofficial relics, that are the most touching, and that most poignantly recall those strange men and women who organized and maintained Europe's first missionary and colonial venture. There are the mangers and tethering holes cut in the piers of Solomon's stables, into which you can see the poor Templars riding through that arched doorway of theirs, their faces of an alien pallor, their bodies weary from the weight of their iron brigandines. Above, in the Haram museum is a scrap of parchment, written in Latin, which came to light between the flags of the floor of the Aqsa mosque during restoration in 1926. It is a relic of the era when the mosque was used as the headquarters of the Templars. One day, in the Spring of 1184, Preceptor Eudes de Vendôme received a little note from Gerard de Ridfort, a future Grand Master and at that time Seneschal of the troops, saying that Rodbertus de Surdis Vallibus, or Robert de Sourdeval, had disembarked at Tyre. They had court-martialled him at 'Afule, stripped him of his insignia, and had confined him at Acre to await repatriation by the first available ship. The Preceptor read the report, crumpled it up and flung it away: thank goodness that tiresome little affair was settled. Poor Robert! I often wondered what happened to him, the Crusader who went wrong. I wondered, too, where Sourdeval was. That I found out in 1944. When the Allied Armies invaded Normandy, the name Sourdeval flashed in and out of an Eighth Army communiqué as having been occupied in passing by British troops. A far cry from Jerusalem in space, but not in spirit. Of only one Crusader is the tomb now preserved in Jerusalem, Philip d'Aubigné, an English knight, who after being tutor to King Henry III went to Jerusalem with the Emperor Frederick, and died there in 1236. His grave is just outside the Church of the Holy Sepulchre. More eloquent, of suffering and of sacrifice, are the hundreds of little crosses which you see carved or scratched on the columns at the side of the doorway, or on the walls of the slope that leads down to the chapel of St. Helena, or on the colonnettes of the entry to the Grotto

Official entry into Jerusalem of Michael Solomon Alexander, first Anglican Bishop, 21st January, 1842. Bishop Alexander is the middle figure of the group of three immediately behind the soldiers; Mrs. Alexander follows in the litter.

PAGE 170

"Jerusalem from the West," by Edward Lear, at 5 a.m., 3rd May, 1858. On the right of the Citadel rising above it. On the right of the Citadel minaret "David's Tower" of the Citadel rising above it. On the right of the Citadel minaret is the Armenian convent and gardens, on the site of the gardens of the palace of Herod the Great.

(R. Walmsley)

The Church of the Nativity, Bethlehem, from the west.

PAGE 158

Another version of the preceeding sketch, done three hours later—a characteristic
example of Lear's method of work. The minaret of "Nebi Daud" appears beyond
the south-west corner of the walls. In the valley of Hinnom below is Bishop
Gobat's Boys' School. It was founded in 1853, and was the first secular building
to be erected outside the walls. In the foreground are a group of Arabs on the left
and two Armenian monks on the right.

PAGE 170

"Jerusalem and the Valley of Jehoshaphat from the South," by Thomas Seddon,
1854. Except for the buildings of the Hebrew University and the two Churches in
Gethsemane, this view has undergone almost no change in a hundred years. From the
minaret on the Mount of Olives, the best panorama of Jerusalem and its surroundings
is still to be obtained.

at Bethlehem. Because they are so small, and because they say nothing of who made them or whence they came, they speak to the imagination more eloquently than any lettered memorial, of the perils of that long journey, and of the joy and peace of having carried the cross to these very shrines where the Lord had been born and had suffered. Very occasionally, there is a name and a date, sometimes a coat of arms. In Bethlehem, the pillars of the nave bear pictures of helmets with crests and mantling, mostly German, with well-known heraldic devices, the twin horns, the swan, the Moor. And on one pillar kneels a palmer or pilgrim, with his hood at his back, his cockleshell on his scrip, and his hands raised in supplication to his patron saint, St. James. There he is, in his habit as he lived. He is a human being, like us; and yet of a world that is not ours.

Pilgrimages did not end with the end of the Latin Kingdom. If anything they increased. Does not Chaucer tell us that his redoubtable Wife of Bath had been to Jerusalem three times? The Franciscans had established themselves in Jerusalem at the beginning of the thirteenth century; but, as we learn from a German pilgrim called Burchard who was in Jerusalem about fifty years later, it was the Greek monks who still maintained the hospices. He speaks very highly of their piety and good discipline, but says that the Latins were "worse than the other people of the land."

In the next century, we begin to notice a change come over the motives of those who visit Jerusalem; and it is in a Venetian, not unexpectedly, that we first observe it. Marino Sanuto presented the record of his travels to Pope John XXI in the year 1321. Sanuto, though still a pilgrim, is already a traveller. His work has maps of Palestine, and even a plan of Jerusalem. This is only a sketch, and a rough one at that, but it shows us the general lie of the city, and that, for instance, the south wall in those days once again included the whole of the western hill, or "Mount Zion" and the Cœnaculum. A little later, in 1336-41, a German, Ludolph von Suchem, was travelling in the East and stayed for some time in Jerusalem, of which he gives a detailed description, excepting, of course, of the Moslem buildings, into which no Christian was then admitted. Ludolph found the Franciscans installed on "Mount Zion," and says, "Foreign merchants, and even Saracens, praised them much, for they did good offices for all men." By this time, many holy places had been grouped together, including even the place of the election

L

of St. Matthias, under the roof of the "Mount Zion" Convent, since
the convenience of pilgrims was accounted of more importance than
topographical accuracy. It was the same in the Holy Sepulchre. The
strangest story that Ludolph has to tell is about prisoners of war; it
has a hauntingly modern tone. Speaking of the country near the
Dead Sea he says: "Here in my time there were Templars who had
been made prisoners at the fall of Acre, who sawed wood here and
there in the mountains for the Sultan's service, and did not know
that the Order of the Templars had been suppressed; for they worked
here and there in the mountains, and had seen no man from this side
of the sea (i.e. Europe) since they were taken prisoners." They must
have been prisoners for more than forty years. Not long afterwards,
the Egyptian sultan granted a petition for their release, and they
returned home with their wives and families.

The fifteenth century continued to produce pilgrimages and
pilgrims' records. Among them is that of Felix Fabri, a Dominican
who visited Jerusalem in 1480 and again in 1483, when he stayed
for six weeks with the Franciscans on "Mount Zion." The thorough-
ness with which Father Felix examined every place of note, and the
completeness with which he recorded his findings, are a foretaste of
what in our own time the great Ecole Biblique of the French
Dominicans was to achieve. The "Wanderings of Felix Fabri" are to
be found in volumes vii-x of the Palestine Pilgrims' Texts Society,
and his description of Jerusalem alone occupies 1,033 pages. In
those days and for many years after, admission to the Church of the
Holy Sepulchre was free only at Easter and the Feast of the Finding
of the Cross. At other times a fee of five ducats a head was demanded
by the guardians. The pilgrims were assembled—in Ludolph von
Suchem's day it was in the morning, but by Fabri's in the evening—
and then admitted two by two into the church, which was locked
behind them. They spent the night—it had formerly been a day and
a night—there, and were then turned out again. In the forecourt
of the church there were stalls at which bread, eggs and fruit could
be bought to eat during the visit. Fabri was taken all round the
church which, except for the destruction of the tombs of the Latin
kings, beginning with Godfrey de Bouillon, by the Greeks after the
fire of 1808, was much the same then as it now is. He later, being a
good Dominican, went round a second time by himself to examine
things properly. Then he felt tired and "went down to the place of
the Finding of the Cross and read my Matins there. I took great

delight in that underground place because it was quiet and suited to me" after all the bustle and noise above. But some of the pilgrims were looking for him to hear their confessions. "At last they came down to where I was, and I heard them there, sitting in the chair of St. Helena." At sunrise Mass was celebrated on Mount Calvary. "After the service my lords, knights, and all the pilgrims received the sacrament with great piety, and the service lasted until the hour of eight in the morning. At the very instant when we had finished, the Saracens came to turn us out."

The year is 1483. It is farewell to "my lords, knights and all the pilgrims," farewell to the Middle Ages. The Turks are in Constantinople; printing has been invented; the New World will soon be discovered, the Reformation will rend Europe. In the *Gerusalemme Liberata* of Tasso the old romantic Jerusalem will live; but in future, more and more of those who visit the earthly Jerusalem will come as travellers rather than pilgrims.

The first of the new sort was an Englishman. George Sandys had close ties with both the Reformation and the New World. He was the youngest son of Edwin Sandys, who became successively Bishop of Worcester and London and finally Archbishop of York. His elder brother was one of the founders of Virginia, and in later life George was to be treasurer to the Virginia Company, and a member of its first Council when it became a Crown Colony. As a young man, while still a student, he made a lengthy journey into Turkey and its dominions, including the Holy Land. That was in 1610. He published an account of it five years later.

Sandys was the first of a long and illustrious line, the English authors of travel books. You find in him all the qualities which have distinguished so many English travellers in all parts of the world; the humour, the charming paradox of their (often unconscious) insularity even when most inflamed by the gad-fly of travel, their love of precision, and above all their talent for keeping their eye on the ball, for observing and recording the manners and cities of men. Sandys has all these. He was at Jerusalem for Easter. He attended the Holy Fire, which he found an "impostury." He gives an exact description of the ceremony, including the interesting detail that in his day "the Æthiopian priest first enters (without whom, they say, the miracle will not fadge)." Sandys stayed with the Franciscans, whose "Pater-guardian" was "a reverend old man of a voluble tongue and winning behaviour." He was locked inside the Sepulchre for three days, but being prudent, he had taken a pillow and a carpet. He spent much of the time in the Franciscan quarters inside the Sepulchre. The Church, he says, was built by the Empress Helena "of whom our country may justly glory"—no ambiguity about her birth for Sandys. He gives precise details of all the different communities, the "Grecians, Armenians, Copties, Abissens, Jacobites, Georgians, Maronites and Nestorians." He tells a rather Chaucerian story about a young female worshipper who was so devout that, in prostrating herself she "showed more than she intended," and of what befell her thereafter. Sandys is the first visitor to Jerusalem who had the modern outlook, which holds that in a travel book an ounce of measurement is worth a pound of epithets. His measurements are recorded not only in figures in the text, but in a series of numbered and lettered plans and illustrations. They are beautifully drawn and notably accurate. Sandys was the founder of the school that over two hundred years later was to be brought to perfection by Robinson, Wilson and Warren. His book remained popular throughout the century.

In 1696, the chaplain of the British factory at Aleppo decided that he would take a party of gentlemen up to Jerusalem for Easter. They rode down the coast past Tripoli and Beirut to Acre. Maundrell was the first traveller to observe the now famous inscriptions at the Dog River. He saw "several Tables of figures carv'd; which seem'd to promise something of Antiquity." He examined them and found that "The figures seemed to resemble Mummys." From Acre, the party then went through the hills via Samaria and Nablus. Maundrell was struck by the bareness of the countryside—not a tree between Lubban and Bireh. Like Sandys, he was shut inside the Holy Sepulchre for three days at the Latin Easter. He paid fourteen dollars as fee. This year, the Greek Easter was a week later than the Latin so Maundrell stayed over for the Holy Fire. Like Sandys (whose account he may have read) he says that the worshippers behaved more like Bacchanals than Christians. His English phlegm was affronted by their "tumultuous, frantick humour." On Jerusalem itself Maundrell adds little to what Sandys had already published; Herod's Gate has been reopened; and St. Anne's church, which Sandys found used as a mosque, had become derelict by the time of Maundrell's visit.

The Golden Age of travel was beginning. The eighteenth-century English traveller was a man of culture and wealth. He also, for all his enquiring zeal and his humour, preserved nevertheless a deep sense of reverence for antiquity. As Samuel Johnson put it:

> "The grand object of travel is to see the shores of the Mediterranean. On these shores were the four great empires of the world: the Assyrian, the Persian, the Grecian, and the Roman. All our religion, almost all our law, almost all our art, almost all that sets us above savages, has come to us from the shores of the Mediterranean."

During the eighteenth century, it was the Mediterranean that principally claimed the attention of the English traveller, eager as he was to acquire Italian pictures, and the marbles and "medals" of ancient Greece and Rome. Wood's visit to Baalbek and Palmyra made a sensation in polite circles, who were quick to transform his drawings into stone, as may be seen, for instance, in the renowned gardens of Stourhead. Palestine itself attracted only one notable English traveller. He was a Fellow of the Royal Society, Doctor Richard Pococke, who visited Jerusalem in 1757. He was a man of discernment, and was apparently the first foreigner to realize the existence of the famous Siloam tunnel, though without making any attempt to trace its course.

By the time the nineteenth century dawned, England was approaching the apogee of her moral and political greatness. She was well equipped to make her own due contribution to the eternal riches of the Holy Land and of Jerusalem. During the period of her primacy, that is to say between the years 1850 and 1880, England conferred greater benefits upon the Holy City and Palestine in general than any people had ever bestowed before. If, in the future, any foreign nation aspires to do as England did a hundred years ago, it will have set itself an exacting standard indeed. At a time when our misdeeds prevail against us, it is well to recall an epoch when the name of England was admired, respected and honoured. The dates I have named cover the period from the time when England, as the ally of Turkey, not only helped her to repulse Russian aggression, but was able to persuade her progressively to liberalize the administration of her empire, until Mr. Gladstone's fatal "bag and baggage" tirade and the occupation of Egypt convinced Turkey that England was no longer a friend, and drove her into the welcoming arms of Germany.

From the beginning of the century, a stream of Englishmen and women had been visiting the Holy Land and many had written of their experiences. As Europe settled down after the storm of the Napoleonic wars, travel became a popular diversion, particularly with the introduction of steam ships. With the turn of the century the ominous word "tourist" had entered the language. Many of those who came to Palestine were tourists; but there was still a proportion, which was steadily to diminish as the twentieth century drew nearer, who were pious, intelligent, and well-educated— "travellers," in fact.

Between 1830 and 1835, three young Englishmen visited Jerusalem. All three of them wrote books which are still read with pleasure. The first of the three was Benjamin Disraeli. As a Jew, he was moved, in so far as that strange nature was ever moved emotionally, by the scenes of Bible history. But the plight of the Palestine Jews must have made Disraeli more glad than ever that he was an Englishman, and confirmed him in his belief that it was through adoption and assimilation that his ancient people were to find their destiny. This belief he was to make good in his own career; but few could have discerned the future Prime Minister of England in the young dandy of the 'thirties. The result of Disraeli's tour was *Tancred*, a romantic novel with Palestine as a background, but a Palestine of its author's own fashioning. The book has memorable characters in it, the mysterious Sidonia, for instance, generally believed to be modelled on Rothschild, and it has, as anything of Disraeli's must have, memorable phrases. Was it he or Kinglake who, recalling Leviticus xxvi. 19, gave us the classic description of Palestine in summer, "an earth of iron beneath a sky of brass"? It was certainly Disraeli who made "the moon sink behind the Mount of Olives," i.e. in the east; but many a novelist has had trouble with the moon. The famous last sentence of *Tancred*, "The Duke and Duchess of Bellamont had arrived in Jerusalem" is not so snobbish a bathos as it sounds: they were, after all, Tancred's parents. The most important result of Disraeli's voyage was not his novel, but the personal knowledge of the Levant which it gave him, and which, reinforcing his hereditary instinct, was to make Disraeli the first English statesman to comprehend the Near East and its problems. So far, he has proved to be the last as well.

The second of the trio was a young nobleman called Robert Curzon. He describes himself as "a sort of biblical knight-errant." For it was as "a devout lover of old books" that he travelled in Egypt, Palestine and Greece, between the years 1833 and 1837. He was the typical English traveller of his time, endowed with humour, simple piety, a good education and private means. He did not publish his book until some years later, but it was an immediate success, and its fourth edition appeared in 1851. It is called *Visits to the Monasteries of the Levant*. Curzon apologizes for "presenting to the public another book of travels in the East, when it is already over-whelmed with little volumes about palm-trees and camels, and reflections on the Pyramids." Jerusalem was only one of the places he visited, and only sixty-five of his 420 pages are devoted to Palestine. But his record has two outstanding points of interest—the Holy Fire and Ibrahim Pasha. As we have already seen in the cases of Sandys and Maundrell, the ceremony of the Holy Fire has a characteristic fascination for Englishmen. It is a sporting event spiced with danger, and an opportunity to feel superior. Even to-day, when the Holy Fire is a mere shadow of what it once was, it has the same attraction. (I have seen it six times myself.)

In 1834, Ibrahim Pasha, son of Mohammed 'Ali, and then ruler of Palestine, attended the ceremony. It ended in an appalling catas-trophe. After the fire emerged, "the smell was terrible; and three unhappy wretches, overcome by heat and bad air, fell from the upper range of galleries, and were dashed to pieces on the heads of the people below. One poor Armenian lady, seventeen years of age, died where she sat, of heat, thirst and fatigue." But this was only the prelude. As Curzon was leaving the church and came near the door, "I made my way between them as well as I could, till they were so thick that there was actually a great heap of bodies on which I trod. It then suddenly struck me they were all dead! I had not perceived this at first, for I thought they were only very much fatigued with the ceremonies and had laid down to rest themselves there; but when I came to so great a heap of bodies I looked down at them, and saw that sharp, hard appearance of the face which is never to be mistaken. Many of them were quite black with suffocation, and farther on were others all bloody and covered with the brains and entrails of those who had been trodden to pieces by the crowd." Curzon had to struggle for his life with one of the Pasha's staff. "As the officer was pressing me to the ground, we wrestled together among the dying and dead with the energy of despair. I struggled with this man till I pulled him down, and happily got again upon my legs—(I afterwards found that he never rose again)." Ibrahim Pasha himself had a narrow escape. He fainted twice, and was only rescued by his guards. More than four hundred people, some of whom had been pressed to death as they stood, died that day. Most of them were strangers and pilgrims. Ibrahim Pasha did all that he could to help, and saved the lives of many others. Curzon had a long interview with him afterwards, and "the conversation turned naturally on the blasphemous impositions of the Greek and Armenian patriarchs, who, for the purposes of worldly gain, had deluded their ignorant followers." "The Pasha was quite aware of the evident absurdity, which I brought to his notice, of the performance of a Christian miracle being put off for some time, and being kept in waiting, for the convenience of a Mahommedan prince." Curzon shrewdly comments that, had Ibrahim been a Christian, that would probably have been the last of the Holy Fire; but "the interference of a Mahommedan in such a case as this would only have been held as another persecution of the Christians." Twelve years later, Curzon met Ibrahim again, this time in London, at Mivart's (now Claridge's) hotel. He was much impressed with England. "In France," he said to Curzon, "there is more fantasia; in England there is more roast beef."

The third of the young travellers was Edward Kinglake. He visited Jerusalem the year after Curzon, in 1835, at the age of twenty-six. Nine years later he published *Eothen*. The name, "From the Dawn," is a stroke of genius. The book at once became, and has ever since remained, a classic. Kinglake was to become the author of a vast history of the Crimean War. Nobody reads it now; but everyone has at least heard of *Eothen*, and most people have read at least part of it. The portrait of Lady Hester Stanhope is the best, among many good ones. In style, Kinglake is much like Curzon, only more succinct. He has the same photographic receptivity to impressions of people and places, and the same humour. He also had a share of Disraeli's prescience. Disraeli, in *Tancred*, foretells the British occupation of Cyprus: Kinglake in *Eothen*, the British occupation of Egypt.

Not again would three such brilliant young men visit Palestine within so short a space. But the stream of writers continues. It is now to be enriched by female contributions. In the last century, it was

not considered modest for a female to write a travel book: it took
the twentieth to produce women like Gertrude Bell and Freya Stark.
Women must write journals, for their families and friends, and only
publish them when begged to do so. This convention applied even
to the Queen. She was the authoress of two of the most vivid and
engaging travel books of the century: they appeared under the title
of *Leaves* (and *More Leaves*) *from the Journal of our Life in the High-
lands* (1869 and 1885). Her Majesty's advisers would not suffer her
to publish a third. Lady Francis Egerton in 1840, Mary Eliza Rogers
in 1855, and Miss Emily Hornby in 1901, all wrote their books
as private journals, which only later were given to the world.
Even Isabel Burton's *Inner Life of Syria, Palestine, and the Holy
Land* (1875) is said to be "from my private journal." It is
pretentious and sloppy, but has one good illustration by Frederic
Leighton. Harriet Martineau is not really an exception. She was the
first European woman to visit Petra; but her *Eastern Life, Present and
Past* (1848) is concerned less with travel than with the promotion of
"philosophic atheism."

Lady Francis' work is slight. It tells us little about Jerusalem,
but a good deal about Lady Francis. A notice at the beginning of the
book announces that the profits arising from it "are for the benefit
of the 'Ladies' Hibernian Female School Society,' which was formed
in 1823, having as its sole object, the temporal and eternal interests of
the *female* population of Ireland, by uniting a Scriptural education
with those necessary arts of domestic and humble life of which they
were, at that time, almost universally ignorant. The Society's labours
have been much blessed. Many thousands of girls have, through its
instrumentality, been fitted to fill the stations allotted to them by
Providence, with respectability." The party consisted of Lady
Francis with her husband and one of their sons, two friends, her
maid, an English footman, a Maltese servant, and a Cypriot cook.
No Holy Fire for Lady Francis. "We are come too late for the
Easter ceremonies here. I am glad of it. They present a most disgraceful scene of violence, superstition, fraud and schism." "Oh!
for the simple purity of our own Church, and that it were set forth
here instead of this most corrupt and disgraceful one." Lady Francis
makes the interesting note that at the time of her visit "A wheeled
chariot or carriage of any kind is unknown in Syria; not even a
wheel-barrow is to be found there!" She was much affected by her
first view of the Mount of Olives. It "had a strange effect upon me,

which I shall never forget. Had I been alone, I should have cried; but one must not give way to these emotions in public, whatever one may do in the silence and solitude of one's own chamber."

The chief value of this little work is the illustrations, which are lithographs from sketches by Lord Francis. In feeling, they are not unlike the work of David Roberts, who had been in Palestine two years earlier. Roberts was inaccurate, but his records of Palestine and Syria and of Egypt and Nubia are of value to-day nevertheless. An artist of less technical ability, but of far greater feeling for the country, was Edward Lear, who came to Palestine in 1854, and again in 1858. Only of late years has Lear come to be appreciated. In translating the line of Palestine, and the feel of its landscapes, he has so far had no equal. Another young English painter, Thomas Seddon, worked with Holman Hunt in Palestine in 1854. He was only thirty-three, but produced work which Ruskin pronounced to be "the first landscapes uniting perfect artistical skill with topographical accuracy; being directed, with stern self-restraint, to no other purpose than that of giving to persons who cannot travel trustworthy knowledge of the scenes which ought to be most interesting to them." His "Jerusalem and the Valley of Jehoshaphat," reproduced in this book, was purchased by public subscription and presented to the National Gallery. The last great English artist (if we may so call him) to paint in Palestine was the American, J. S. Sargent, who was here in 1902, and again in the winter of 1905-6. Most of his sketches are in private collections in America and England; but the Tate possesses two canvases, and the Fitzwilliam Museum at least one water-colour. They have all Sargent's mastery of light, which in the bare Palestine landscape is the key to the whole setting. The rocks seem at first to be so dead and immutable. In fact, they are continually alive and changing. Sargent was fascinated by them.

The English artist whose Palestine pictures are best known is beyond question Holman Hunt himself, and that brings us back to Miss Rogers, for she met him here. Mary Rogers was the sister of Edward Thomas Rogers, who was at the time of her visit assistant to the famous Consul Finn, and vice-consul at Haifa. She spent four years in Palestine. Her *Domestic Life in Palestine* is one of the best books ever written about the country, because Mary Rogers really knew the people, and would go to visit them in their houses. Her description of the Abdulhadis of 'Arrabeh, whose descendants of to-day are still held in high regard, is delightful. She had become fluent in Arabic, and had the gift of attracting the sympathy and confidence of her Arab friends. Children of all races loved her. She took quite naturally to Arab ways. It was summer time when she arrived in Jerusalem, and it was then the custom, started by the Finns, for European families to move out of the town and to camp on the hills to the west of it. The Finns always camped at Talbiyeh, to the south-west, the Bishop and Mrs. Gobat in an olive grove near Lifta, on the Jaffa road.

"There was no house on the grounds to serve as a retreat or shelter in the heat of the day, as on the Talbiyeh, but the trees under which Mrs. Gobat's pretty drawing-room or day tent was pitched, served almost as effectually as a protection from the sun. Sofas, cushions, easy chairs, writing tables and work tables, children with their dolls or lesson books, made the place look quite homely and took away the idea of the transitory nature of tent life. Mrs. Gobat gave me a hearty welcome there, and introduced me to her friends who came from the surrounding tents, and to the children, who left their studies or their play to welcome us. Quite a large party was soon assembled in the tent and on the sofa under the opposite tree. After a luncheon of fruit and bread, olives, and cheese, &c., Mrs. Gobat smoked a narghilé, evidently enjoying it, and I date the taste which I acquired for tumbac from the experimental pipe which I smoked with her." "A beautiful white goat followed us wherever we went. It was the goat which Mr. W. Holman Hunt used as his model while finishing the well-known picture of the scapegoat. Two had died in his service, but this one became quite tame, and would answer to his call; he gave it to these children when his picture was completed."

(Among many other subjects, Holman Hunt also, as was to be expected, painted the Holy Fire.)

But we must leave this picture of domestic life and art to return to 1838. In that year two important events occurred: the foundation of the British consulate, and the first visit of Dr. Robinson.

Hitherto there had been no consuls in Jerusalem. The British consulate was the first. It was followed in 1841 by the foundation of the Anglican bishopric. There was as yet no church building. An attempt had been made to start one in 1838, but permission to build had been refused both by Mohammed 'Ali and by the Porte, on the ground that to allow the erection of a new church would be to infringe the terms of the capitulation of the Caliph Omar! Three years later, the London Jews' Society started to build, without asking any questions; but the Pasha immediately stopped them. It was only in 1845 that a firman was granted for the building of a "consular chapel," and thus Christ Church arose and was consecrated in 1849. Until 1857 the consul lived in part of what is now the parsonage. By that time tolerance had so far advanced as to make the legal fiction no longer necessary. In 1855, Christians were, for the first time, admitted to the Haram. In 1856, the Edict of Toleration for all religions in the Turkish Empire was promulgated.

James Finn became British consul in 1846, and held the post until 1863. He was a Victorian Englishman of the highest type. He was deeply pious, spoke and wrote a number of languages, including Turkish, Arabic and Hebrew. He was energetic and honest, and un-flinching in protecting the interests of those committed to his charge, who included, by an instruction given by Lord Palmerston to the first consul in 1839, "the Jews generally." Finn was no intriguer, and he had no wish, as other powers and their consuls had, to work against the Turkish Government. On the contrary, he considered that the welfare of all sections of the inhabitants of Jerusalem and Palestine was best to be guaranteed by allowing, encouraging and helping Turkey to liberalize and reorganize her government. To Finn, Turkey was a friend in need of help, Russia a menace. Finn's views and methods were fifty years ahead of his time. His belief that Turkey was capable of rejuvenation, and that Russian expansion was the danger, has been substantiated by the events of our own day. His determination to obtain justice by force, not of arms, or intrigue, or threats, but of character, endeared him to both ruler and subjects, and raised the name and influence of his country to their zenith. In 1878, after his death, when Turkey and Russia were again at war, his widow published *Stirring Times, or records from Jerusalem Consular Chronicles of 1853 to 1856 by the late James Finn.* This book is still the main and wholly trustworthy authority for the state of Palestine a century ago. It gives a picture of turbulence and of neglect, out of which peace and prosperity are gradually emerging, not least as the result of Britain's moderate and disinterested policy.

Dr. Edward Robinson was an American divine, who, having been appointed Professor of Biblical Literature at the Union Theological

Seminary in New York, decided that before he took up his duties, he would see Palestine for himself. He had devoted fifteen years to the study of his subject. He was an accurate observer, a man of good judgment and without any prejudice as to the authenticity of this or that site. His *Biblical Researches in Palestine*, published in 1841, mark the beginning of modern scientific archæology. The results which Robinson achieved are all the more remarkable in that he was unable to make any examination below the surface; he worked solely on his profound knowledge of the Bible and of Josephus. Robinson is best remembered to-day as the discoverer of "Robinson's Arch," the name given to the remnant of the viaduct that joined the Temple cloisters to the Upper City; for it was Robinson who first realized that the skewback still visible on the eastern side must be the spring of one of its arches. His theory was proved to be correct when Wilson and Warren excavated the site. Robinson revisited Jerusalem in 1852. But he did not live to write his projected Historical Geography. Where Robinson led, others soon followed. There were other Americans. Lieutenant Lynch has already been mentioned. His report became the standard work on the Dead Sea. Dr. W. M. Thomson's *The Land and the Book* (1859) is a classic. Dr. Barclay, whose *City of the Great King* appeared in 1858, added to Robinson's discoveries. He is fittingly commemorated by "Barclay's Gate" in the western wall of the Temple. The relations between the British and American explorers were always excellent, so that it has been quite natural in this century for them to conduct joint expeditions. In early days, the particular preserve of the Americans was the then almost unknown land on the east of the Jordan. French explorers, too, were active. De Saulcy, de Vogüé, Clermont-Ganneau are all names famous in the annals of Palestine. The rebuilding in 1888 of St. Stephen's Church, and the foundation there of the Ecole Biblique of the French Dominicans, has bestowed upon France the unquestioned leadership among resident Biblical scholars. The long and fruitful partnership of PP. Vincent and Abel was broken alas! this year by the death of Père Abel. But their great works on Jerusalem and its topography live; and under the direction of Père de Vaux, the School is as assiduous and authoritative as ever.

In 1841, the first survey of Jerusalem had been made by Lieutenants Aldrich and Symons of the Royal Engineers, who found themselves in Syria in connection with the operations which

restored the country to Turkish rule after Mohammed 'Ali's usurpa-
tion. In 1864, a new and more extensive survey was undertaken.
Jerusalem was short of water. Miss Angela (afterwards Baroness)
Burdett-Coutts decided to remedy this lack. Having learned that
the first step would be an accurate survey of Jerusalem and the
neighbourhood, she gave the necessary money, £500, to the
Director-General of the Ordnance Survey; and Captain (afterwards
Major-General Sir Charles) Wilson with a party of Royal Engineers
was sent to Jerusalem to do the work. Wilson not only carried out the
survey, but also prepared plans of the Church of the Holy Sepulchre
and of the Haram, and made some underground excavations near
the latter. These investigations led, not to the renovation of the
water supply (which had to wait until Allenby arrived fifty-three
years later) but to the foundation of the Palestine Exploration
Fund. The project attracted support from every rank of society.
The Committee of nearly one hundred members included both
Archbishops, three dukes, many bishops and deans, and such famous
laymen as Lord Dufferin, Lord Shaftesbury, Lord Lawrence, Samuel
Gurney, Sir Moses Montefiore, G. Gilbert Scott, R.A., Professor
Rawlinson, Professor Palmer, Dr. Pusey and the Speaker. The
Queen was Patron.

Queen Victoria took a close personal interest in the Holy Land.
A visit to Palestine was regarded as part of the education and
training of the Prince of Wales, and of the Prince of Wales's sons.
When the Jerusalem Literary Society was founded in 1848, Prince
Albert sent a donation of £25. Prince Alfred, afterwards Duke of
Edinburgh, whose visit to Palestine in 1859 preceded that of his
elder brother, was the first English prince to enter the Holy Land
since Prince Edward, afterwards King Edward I, had left it in 1272.
Prince Arthur, later Duke of Connaught, was here in 1865. The
font in the English Cathedral of St. George in Jerusalem is Queen
Victoria's gift.

The Committee decided to continue the underground exploration
of Jerusalem, which Wilson had so ably begun. The work was started
in 1867, by Captain (afterwards General Sir Charles) Warren,
assisted by three corporals, one of whom was to take photographs,
one to take charge of the "dig" as we should now call it, and the
third to complete the ordnance survey. They worked for three
years, mostly below ground. The results of these astonishing labours,
carried on always in discomfort, often in danger, were published

in 1871 under the title *The Recovery of Jerusalem*. It was a proud but wholly merited title. The levels of practically the whole of ancient Jerusalem, particularly in the vicinity of the Temple, had been plotted by these painstaking men. To-day, visitors talk of "Wilson's Arch," but few have seen it. Fewer still could tell you the contours of the city, which became familiar to our countrymen almost ninety years ago. Their shafts are filled up, and there is no memorial of them to be seen, except here and there a broad arrow bench mark on some ancient stone. But in their day they were widely known and revered. Not only the great in the land supported the Fund for whom they were working, but local associations were formed throughout the United Kingdom, and lectures delivered up and down the country to further its aims.

The Fund's second achievement was the survey of Palestine. This took many years to complete. It was, like the former ventures, entrusted to an officer of the Royal Engineers, Lieutenant Conder, with whom, in the last stage, was associated Lieutenant Kitchener. The Survey was published, on a scale of one inch to a mile, in 1881. It covers twenty-six sheets. It is accompanied by three volumes of memoirs, which form a priceless archæological gazetteer of the whole country, one of special papers, one on Jerusalem, one on the flora and fauna of Palestine, one on its geology and one of name lists. All later maps have been based on this great undertaking.

As I said earlier on, archæology has come up in the world of late. It has become a purer and purer science, and has extricated itself from the web of politics and pride that formerly bound it. British archæology has continued to flourish in Palestine despite the decay of British policy. The "P.E.F." could not again achieve two such masterpieces as the *Recovery of Jerusalem* and the *Survey of Palestine*; nor could anyone else. But it continued to add to our knowledge of the country and of the Bible. In the days of the Mandate, the work of Richmond on the Dome of the Rock, of Crowfoot on Ophel, Samaria and Jerash, and of Petrie in the south, to mention three of many, was to maintain the good tradition. The guide books written by Hamilton, Iliffe and Johns of the Antiquities Department, the exquisite maps of Roman Palestine, and Palestine of the Crusaders, produced by the Surveys Department on the initiative of Colonel Salmon, its director, and by Mr. Gerald Harding, of the Antiquities of East Jordan, showed that British archæologists were still among the best. The work of Professor Dorothy Garrod has already been referred to. In our own time, during this very year, Miss Kathleen Kenyon in her second season at Jericho has produced results which have astonished the world. Of all these achievements, the foundations were laid by those pioneers in the 'sixties and 'seventies.

How vast had been the progress of Palestine, how bright its prospects had become, may be read in the pages of Laurence Oliphant. Oliphant was an eccentric. He had long known Turkey and the Turks. It was he who, after the Crimean War, had introduced the cigarette into London drawing-rooms. (It had been invented, thirty years before, by a resourceful Turkish gunner of the Acre garrison, who finding that the quartermaster had sent them tobacco, but no pipes to smoke it in, had the bright idea of wrapping the tobacco in rolled up fuse-paper.) In later years, Oliphant became a member of a strange and austere American sect, interested himself in the return of the Jews to Palestine, and settled on Mount Carmel. While living there, between 1882 and 1885, he wrote a number of letters to the New York *Sun*, by whose editor they were published in 1886. They give a wonderful picture of activity, of new colonies, founded by Germans, by Bosnians, by Jews, of new projects for railways and irrigation. There are pictures of the Turcomans and of the Druses. There is an unforgettable sketch of General Gordon. Already, with Oliphant, you are in modern Palestine. He is almost the last of the great English writers on Palestine, but not quite. There was still to come one of the greatest of all: George Adam Smith, whose *Historical Geography of Palestine* (first published in 1894) was to be the great work of which Robinson had dreamed.

All travel was spoiled, and its values prostituted, by the advent of the internal combustion engine. In days gone by, no one would dream of rushing through Palestine in a day, or even in a week. When the late King George and his elder brother visited Palestine in 1882, five weeks was thought a fitting period for all that they had to see; and Royalty had not even then the leisure that subjects can command. Who would now think of spending a month on a trip to Palestine? Yet modern brains are no more receptive, no quicker than those of our grandparents. When, after the First War, the motor-car came into Palestine, people were always boasting of how easy and speedy it was to visit Jericho or Jaffa or Hebron. What they overlooked was that the coming of the motor had seen the disappearance of the horse, and that though a few places could be seen more easily, that is more superficially, a large number could never be seen at all. I have mentioned Miss Hornby. With her sister and another female companion, Miss Hornby spent six weeks in Sinai and Palestine in 1899, and seven in Palestine and on a journey to Petra in 1901. These three women spent nine days alone in Petra, which says Miss Hornby, no traveller had been able to visit for five years. They climbed Mount Hor, and had their tea there. One sister sketched, the other kept her journal, the third lady took what Miss Hornby calls "kodaks." They visited Kerak, and Rabbath Moab, and the tomb of Ja'afar (the ancestor of Suba). They even visited Machaerus, the fortress-palace where Salome danced and St. John the Baptist was beheaded.

They knew how to spend their time, those Victorians. And they had money to spend, as well. Who now can afford enough of either to visit Machaerus, or 'Arrabeh, or Dothan, or a score of other places famous in Bible history? Who, for that matter, succeeds in leaving the worn groove of the main road?

The golden age of travel is past. But the pilgrims still come and go. They are not sightseers, they "look not at the things which are seen, but at the things which are not seen: for the things which are seen are temporal: but the things which are not seen are eternal." They come from the East and from the West. No longer as before the First War are the streets of Jerusalem thronged with thousands of Russian pilgrims; nor, as during the second, with Poles and Africans, peoples unknown at the first Pentecost, yet to whom Jerusalem, the ideal Jerusalem, had been the great reality since the days of their infancy: their feet, too, now stood within her gates. This year, the Way of the Cross on Good Friday was trodden by pilgrims from all over Europe and America, each group shepherded by a priest who could lead their devotions in its own language. There was, too, a group of Orthodox Cypriots. They were all old folk. They were worn and pinched. Their clothes were worn, too. They were very poor people, who had saved up for years, in order that before they died, they might have the supreme experience of visiting the scenes of their Lord's earthly life. Their faces were beautiful to behold.

Gibbon records that it was the sight of the bare-footed friars singing their vespers in the ruins of the Temple of Jupiter in Rome that suggested to him the idea of writing the *Decline and Fall of the Roman Empire*. A scene similar to that which suggested to Gibbon

M

the decline of a worldly empire—namely the Franciscans in the crumbling Holy Sepulchre—has often suggested to others the rise of a heavenly one. You do not come to Jerusalem to witness the Church Victorious. That may be seen in any part of the world, in Rome, in Washington, in China or Peru. In Jerusalem, you see the very origins of the Church, the very rock, as it were, from which it was fashioned. What seems so neglected, so squalid, is but original humanity, what seems conflict, is but the state of man untouched by grace. From that same squalor, that same conflict, sprang the Twelve, who were themselves so changed that they went forth to change the history of mankind. That is the miracle which no man can deny, the miracle which makes all others seem secondary. And it took place here in Jerusalem. It is that which draws the pilgrims, now as ever.

On May the 2nd of this year, two young kings came of age, King Husein of Jordan, and King Feisal II of Iraq. They are second cousins, great-grandsons of King Husein of the Hejaz who in the First War roused the Arabs to fight on the side of England and her allies. They are princes of the House of Hashim, the world's oldest reigning dynasty, and lineal descendants of the Prophet Mohammed himself. Throughout their kingdoms, which are neighbours, and far beyond their frontiers, there was great rejoicing at the advent to power of these two young sovereigns, not only because of their youth, but because they embody the principle of a Faith. King Husein of Jordan is now not only a living representative of the Prophet, but the Guardian of that Sanctuary, the Haram esh Sherif, which is venerated by millions for its association with the Prophet (Quran, xvii, 1). One of the young King's first acts was to visit it. Under his protection and that of his government are also the Holy Places of Christendom. This is no new thing, Islam has ruled Jerusalem before—longer in fact than any other Faith or nation, for 1,187 years altogether.

The Queen of England is a friend of these two young Kings, both of whom have been students in her country. She sent her uncle, the Duke of Gloucester, to greet them on their assumption of their constitutional powers.

A month later, on June 2nd, the Queen of England herself was crowned. King Feisal of Iraq sent his uncle, the Prince 'Abdulillah, who had for fourteen years been his devoted regent and guardian, to bear his good wishes and those of his House to the Queen of

England. Here in Jerusalem, a great company assembled in St. George's Cathedral to pray for God's blessing on the Queen. There were high officers of the state, the Minister-Resident, the Mutaserrif and the Commandant among them, and there were prelates and priests of every branch of the Christian Church. There were Greek Orthodox, Armenians, Copts, Abyssinians and Syrians. The Church of the West was represented by Dominicans, Franciscans, White Fathers and Benedictines. The Lutheran Propst was there, and so were the Abbesses of the two Russian convents of Gethsemane and of the Mount of Olives. The service was a wonderful act of unity. Later, as with millions of others in all countries of the globe, we listened to the Queen of England dedicating herself to the service of God and her peoples, the feeling of unity was overwhelming—the knowledge that God had chosen this royal servant of His to be the leader of all men and women of good intention and desire. Here in Jerusalem we heard it and felt it, in this very city where Zadok the priest and Nathan the prophet had enacted the prototype of that very coronation. So eternal, so perpetually renewing, is the spirit of Jerusalem.

In this book I have tried, however imperfectly, to express the thoughts that possess an Englishman as he contemplates Jerusalem in the year 1953. They are thoughts of grief at what has befallen the city, of shame at the part which his country has played in allowing such tribulation to fall upon so many innocent people. But they are thoughts too of faith in what his countrymen and women are now doing to alleviate Palestine's distress, of faith in the great and beneficent tradition which they inherit from their forebears who lived and worked for this country, of faith above all in the eternal destiny of the Holy City to give light to them that sit in darkness and to witness for ever that

THE ONE REMAINS

Appendix I
U.N.R.W.A.

Month: June, 1953   JORDAN DISTRICT

MONTHLY DISTRIBUTION RETURN OF REFUGEE POPULATION

Area and Place	CAMPS				VILLAGES		TOWNS		TOTALS		
	IN TENTS		IN BUILDINGS*								
	No. of families	No. of persons	No. of families	No. of persons	No. of families	No. of persons	No. of families	No. of persons	Total no. of un-rationed babies	No. of un-rationed families	No. of persons
'Amman Area											
'Amman	—	—	—	—	—	—	6,912	34,405	1,216	6,912	35,621
Zerqa	—	—	—	—	—	—	999	4,855	156	999	5,011
Salt	—	—	—	—	—	—	827	3,985	235	827	4,220
Madaba	—	—	—	—	—	—	1,242	6,256	184	1,242	6,440
Karak	—	—	—	—	—	—	570	2,757	88	570	2,845
Tafeeleh	—	—	—	—	—	—	7	27	—	7	27
Ma'an	—	—	—	—	—	—	36	195	15	36	210
Aqaba	—	—	—	—	—	—	112	509	32	112	541
Zizia	—	—	—	—	97	523	—	—	5	97	528
Na'our	—	—	—	—	417	2,150	—	—	40	417	2,190
Sweileh	—	—	—	—	274	1,526	—	—	36	274	1,562
Sahab	—	—	—	—	111	605	—	—	43	111	648
Wadi Essir	—	—	—	—	137	710	—	—	42	137	752
Fheis and Mahes	—	—	—	—	107	545	—	—	31	107	576
Battir	—	—	—	—	10	44	—	—	3	10	47
Rashadieh	—	—	—	—	113	610	—	—	9	113	619
Azraq	—	—	—	—	73	288	—	—	6	73	294
Jabal Hussein Camp	1,316	6,460	158	873	—	—	—	—	439	1,474	7,772
Zerqa Camp	261	1,347	764	3,674	—	—	—	—	295	1,025	5,316
Total	1,577	7,807	922	4,547	1,339	7,001	10,705	52,989	2,875	14,543	75,219
Irbed Area											
Irbed	—	—	—	—	—	—	1,618	8,081	523	1,618	8,604

The column headings for this statistical table are not present on this page (they appear on the facing/previous page). Values are transcribed in their grid positions; a dash (—) reproduces a printed dash in the source. The first place name ("Mafrak") and its data are cut off at the top edge of the page.

Marrak (Mafrak)									
Kufrenjeh	—	—	—	—	6	22	1	6	23
Ajloun	—	—	—	—	17	76	1	17	77
Jarash	—	—	—	—	37	170	5	37	175
Huson	—	—	—	—	59	281	21	59	302
Ramtha	—	—	—	—	151	722	36	151	758
Um Qais	—	—	40	169	—	—	6	40	175
Malka	—	—	103	451	—	—	10	103	461
Samar	—	—	29	141	—	—	3	29	144
Deir Yousuf	—	—	19	81	—	—	8	19	89
Rasiyeh	—	—	240	1,095	—	—	13	240	1,108
Kfarat	—	—	45	230	—	—	8	45	238
Sareeh	—	—	56	305	—	—	25	56	330
Huwara	—	—	22	105	—	—	11	22	116
Samma	—	—	115	596	—	—	32	115	628
Taybeh	—	—	50	263	—	—	17	50	280
Shajara	—	—	25	78	—	—	12	25	90
Deir Abu Said	—	—	128	637	—	—	28	128	665
Shuneh	—	—	640	3,156	—	—	132	640	3,288
Saal	—	—	50	253	—	—	13	50	266
Mughayer	—	—	47	217	—	—	11	47	228
Bushra	—	—	38	185	—	—	10	38	195
Waqqas	—	—	337	1,645	—	—	70	337	1,715
Anjara	—	—	22	112	—	—	7	22	119
Manshiyeh	—	—	95	401	—	—	18	95	419
Bashatweh	—	—	245	1,241	—	—	67	245	1,308
Baqoura	—	—	278	1,370	—	—	62	278	1,432
Ghour Arba'in	—	—	454	2,066	—	—	77	454	2,143
Soum	—	—	16	80	—	—	4	16	84
Qumeim	—	—	102	472	—	—	30	102	502
Harima	—	—	88	995	—	—	20	88	415
Wadi El Yabes	—	—	224	1,024	—	—	30	224	1,054
Kraymeh	—	—	185	850	—	—	9	185	859
Irbed Camp	630	3,115	—	—	—	—	246	630	3,361
Total	630	3,115	3,693	17,618	1,950	9,617	1,578	6,273	31,928

Month: June, 1953

MONTHLY DISTRIBUTION RETURN OF REFUGEE POPULATION

JORDAN DISTRICT

Area and Place	CAMPS IN TENTS No. of families	No. of persons	IN BUILDINGS* No. of families	No. of persons	VILLAGES No. of families	No. of persons	TOWNS No. of families	No. of persons	Total no. of un-rationed babies	TOTALS No. of families	No. of persons
Jericho Area											
Jericho	—	—	—	—	—	—	1,444	6,934	281	1,444	7,215
A.D.S.	—	—	—	—	8	35	—	—	3	8	38
Auja	—	—	—	—	220	1,101	—	—	46	220	1,147
Rameh	—	—	—	—	34	174	—	—	—	34	174
Shuneh	—	—	—	—	27	124	—	—	8	27	132
Kufrein	—	—	—	—	11	55	—	—	2	11	57
Ghor Nimrein	—	—	—	—	5	19	—	—	1	5	20
Aqabat Jaber	465	3,164	5,320	24,302	—	—	—	—	1,546	5,785	29,012
Ein Sultan	1,238	6,196	1,209	5,111	—	—	—	—	824	2,447	12,131
Karameh	544	2,852	3,356	16,555	—	—	—	—	812	3,900	20,219
Nuweimeh	429	2,043	717	3,428	—	—	—	—	368	1,146	5,839
Bedouins	1,174	5,286	—	—	—	—	—	—	86	1,174	5,372
Total	3,850	19,541	10,602	49,396	305	1,508	1,444	6,934	3,977	16,201	81,356
J'lem and B'lem Area											
Jerusalem	—	—	—	—	—	—	3,969	19,106	540	3,969	19,646
Bethlehem	—	—	—	—	—	—	1,905	10,060	358	1,905	10,418
Beit Jala	—	—	—	—	—	—	794	3,961	180	794	4,141
Beit Sahour	—	—	—	—	—	—	648	3,486	143	648	3,629
Bethany	—	—	—	—	168	970	—	—	25	168	995
Abu Dis	—	—	—	—	254	1,297	—	—	60	254	1,357
Silwan	—	—	—	—	303	1,621	—	—	56	303	1,677
Tur	—	—	—	—	138	800	—	—	17	138	817

Table of population statistics (column headings are cut off at the top of the page; values read from the rotated page).

Locality	(1)	(2)	(3)	(4)	(5)	(6)	(7)	(8)	(9)	(10)	(11)
Bedouins (J Jem)	1,024	178	32	–	–	992	178	–	–	–	716
Beit Fajjar	146	27	12	–	–	134	27	–	–	–	125
Husan	528	85	29	–	–	499	85	–	–	–	151
Wadi Fukin	695	124	39	–	–	656	124	–	–	–	–
Beit Safafa	154	27	6	–	–	148	27	–	–	–	–
Sharafat	1,004	199	51	–	–	953	199	–	–	–	–
Battir	1,465	272	72	–	–	1,393	272	–	–	–	–
Sur Baher	549	111	1	–	–	548	111	–	–	–	–
Jabalin Bedouins	–	–	284	–	–	660	–	–	–	–	–
Muascar	4,951	888	242	–	–	–	–	4,631	888	3,425	–
Dheisheh	4,018	768	33	–	–	–	–	351	52	573	–
Aiyda	652	130	42	–	–	–	–	46	5	–	–
Beit Jibrin	838	151	–	–	–	–	–	–	–	796	–
Total	**59,653**	**11,335**	**2,225**	**36,613**	**7,316**	**10,993**	**2,082**	**5,028**	**945**	**4,794**	**992**

Ramallah Area

Locality	(1)	(2)	(3)	(4)	(5)	(6)	(7)	(8)	(9)	(10)	(11)
Ramallah	7,308	1,427	314	6,994	1,427	–	–	–	–	–	–
Bireh	4,181	825	212	3,969	825	–	–	–	–	–	–
Aboud	793	143	43	–	–	750	143	–	–	–	–
Abu Qash	88	10	7	–	–	81	10	–	–	–	–
Abu Shukheidem	1,139	215	45	–	–	1,094	215	–	–	–	–
Ajjoul	82	15	3	–	–	79	15	–	–	–	–
Anata	24	6	–	–	–	24	6	–	–	–	–
Aroura	80	14	1	–	–	79	14	–	–	–	–
Atara	151	29	3	–	–	148	29	–	–	–	–
Bir Nabala	66	14	3	–	–	63	14	–	–	–	–
Bir Zeit	2,469	429	120	–	–	2,349	429	–	–	–	–
Beit Duqqo	157	53	4	–	–	153	33	–	–	–	–
Beit Hanina	93	19	4	–	–	89	19	–	–	–	–
Beit Illo	1,075	198	55	–	–	1,020	198	–	–	–	–
Beit Ijza	531	99	38	–	–	493	99	–	–	–	–
Beit Inan	819	153	52	–	–	767	153	–	–	–	–
Beit Our Foka	172	34	6	–	–	166	34	–	–	–	–
Beit Our Tahta	352	74	22	–	–	330	74	–	–	–	–
Beit Liqia	206	39	6	–	–	200	39	–	–	–	–

MONTHLY DISTRIBUTION RETURN OF REFUGEE POPULATION

| Area and Place | CAMPS | | | | VILLAGES | | TOWNS | | Total no. of un-rationed babies | TOTALS | |
| | IN TENTS | | IN BUILDINGS* | | | | | | | | |
	No. of families	No. of persons	No. of families	No. of persons	No. of families	No. of persons	No. of families	No. of persons		No. of families	No. of persons
Ramallah Area (Cont.)											
Beit Nouba	—	—	—	—	49	219	—	—	19	49	238
Beit Sira	—	—	—	—	65	283	—	—	18	65	301
Beit Rima	—	—	—	—	114	569	—	—	34	114	603
Beit Ixa	—	—	—	—	154	710	—	—	14	154	724
Beitin	—	—	—	—	39	194	—	—	12	39	206
Beitounia	—	—	—	—	116	616	—	—	32	116	648
Biddo	—	—	—	—	192	905	—	—	66	192	971
Bil'en	—	—	—	—	17	91	—	—	6	17	97
Budros	—	—	—	—	153	658	—	—	30	153	688
Burham	—	—	—	—	4	20	—	—	—	4	20
Deir Ammar	—	—	—	—	34	167	—	—	11	34	178
Deir Abu Masha'al	—	—	—	—	77	324	—	—	15	77	339
Deir Dibwan	—	—	—	—	64	339	—	—	13	64	352
Deir Ghassaneh	—	—	—	—	130	690	—	—	19	130	709
Deir Ibze'i	—	—	—	—	20	91	—	—	5	20	96
Deir Ijreer	—	—	—	—	17	68	—	—	4	17	72
Deir Nizam	—	—	—	—	2	5	—	—	—	2	5
Deir Qaddis	—	—	—	—	79	394	—	—	12	79	406
Deir Soudan	—	—	—	—	2	8	—	—	—	2	8
Doura Qare'	—	—	—	—	31	153	—	—	4	31	157
Ein Arreek	—	—	—	—	23	103	—	—	12	23	115
Ein Qinia	—	—	—	—	26	130	—	—	10	26	140
Ein Sinia	—	—	—	—	56	269	—	—	17	56	286
Ein Yabroud	—	—	—	—	78	420	—	—	24	78	462

Ibwein	188	30	7	—	—	181	30	—	—	—
Imwas	852	183	28	—	—	824	183	—	—	—
Jammala	100	24	6	—	—	94	24	—	—	—
Jania	30	9	4	—	—	26	9	—	—	—
Jeeb	189	31	8	—	—	181	31	—	—	—
Jebia	21	5	—	—	—	21	5	—	—	—
Jifna	871	193	32	—	—	389	193	—	—	—
Jilijlia	39	7	1	—	—	38	7	—	—	—
Jdira	105	19	6	—	—	99	19	—	—	—
Kh. Bani Hareth	273	55	20	—	—	253	55	—	—	—
Kh. Musbah	142	34	11	—	—	131	34	—	—	—
Kh. Abu Falah	82	12	2	—	—	80	12	—	—	—
Koubar	80	20	2	—	—	78	20	—	—	—
Kufr Aqab	50	8	—	—	—	50	8	—	—	—
Kufr Ein	50	29	12	—	—	154	29	—	—	—
Kufr Malek	240	50	12	—	—	228	50	—	—	—
Kufr Ni'meh	183	37	9	—	—	174	37	—	—	—
Lubban	169	34	6	—	—	163	34	—	—	—
Mazare' Noubani	198	39	4	—	—	194	39	—	—	—
Mazra' Qiblieh	574	98	32	—	—	542	98	—	—	—
Mazra' Sharqieh	287	50	10	—	—	277	50	—	—	—
Mikhmas	74	12	6	—	—	68	12	—	—	—
Nabi Saleh	231	35	6	—	—	225	35	—	—	—
Nabi Samuel	35	8	1	—	—	34	8	—	—	—
Ni'leen	844	182	34	—	—	810	182	—	—	—
Qalandia	172	29	6	—	—	166	29	—	—	—
Qarawa	167	29	10	—	—	157	29	—	—	—
Qibya	558	110	34	—	—	524	110	—	—	—
Qubeibeh	408	76	19	—	—	389	76	—	—	—
Rafat	270	44	11	—	—	259	44	—	—	—
Ras Karkar	135	28	1	—	—	134	28	—	—	—
Ramoun	214	40	13	—	—	201	40	—	—	—
Rantis	446	85	22	—	—	424	85	—	—	—
Saffa	465	98	28	—	—	437	98	—	—	—
Shibtine	108	24	7	—	—	101	24	—	—	—

Month: June, 1953   JORDAN DISTRICT

MONTHLY DISTRIBUTION RETURN OF REFUGEE POPULATION

Area and Place	CAMPS				VILLAGES		TOWNS		Total no. of un-rationed babies	TOTALS	
	IN TENTS		IN BUILDINGS*								
	No. of families	No. of persons	No. of families	No. of persons	No. of families	No. of persons	No. of families	No. of persons		No. of families	No. of persons
Ramallah Area (Cont.)											
Shuqba	—	—	—	—	76	354	—	—	16	76	370
Silwad	—	—	—	—	242	1,248	—	—	85	242	1,333
Sinjel	—	—	—	—	18	87	—	—	1	18	88
Surda	—	—	—	—	16	68	—	—	2	16	70
Taybeh	—	—	—	—	66	325	—	—	14	66	339
Tireh	—	—	—	—	123	642	—	—	29	123	671
Turmos Ayya	—	—	—	—	34	177	—	—	8	34	185
Um Safa	—	—	—	—	19	99	—	—	5	19	104
Yabroud	—	—	—	—	12	66	—	—	2	12	68
Yallo	—	—	—	—	116	570	—	—	26	116	596
Beit Surik	—	—	—	—	35	164	—	—	10	35	174
Qattaneh	—	—	—	—	284	1,179	—	—	41	284	1,220
Am'ari Camp	257	1,044	91	468	—	—	—	—	108	348	1,620
Deir Ammar	390	1,888	105	570	—	—	—	—	159	495	2,617
Ein Arik	24	96	275	1,273	—	—	—	—	84	299	1,453
Jalazone	803	3,898	42	240	—	—	—	—	277	845	4,415
Qalandia	286	1,332	116	586	—	—	—	—	140	402	2,058
Total	1,760	8,258	629	3,137	5,874	28,855	2,252	10,963	2,742	10,515	53,955

	(1)	(2)	(3)	(4)	(5)	(6)	(7)	(8)	(9)	(10)	(11)
Nablus Area											
Nablus	—	—	—	—	—	—	3,134	15,282	749	3,134	16,031
Jenin	—	—	—	—	—	—	1,501	7,364	340	1,501	7,704
Tul Karem	—	—	—	—	—	—	812	4,303	356	812	4,659
Villages	—	—	—	—	13,286	63,887	—	—	2,558	13,286	66,445
Askar	497	2,613	10	67	—	—	—	—	174	507	2,854
Balata	825	4,610	12	64	—	—	—	—	251	837	4,925
Far'a Camp	489	2,761	350	2,184	—	—	—	—	148	839	5,093
No. 1 Nablus	322	1,949	2	17	—	—	—	—	59	324	2,025
Nur Shams	484	2,772	114	730	—	—	—	—	153	598	3,655
Tul Karem	592	3,082	410	2,274	—	—	—	—	250	1,002	5,606
Total	3,209	17,787	898	5,936	13,286	63,887	5,447	26,949	5,038	22,840	118,997
Hebron Area											
Hebron	—	—	—	—	—	—	5,840	28,570	1,302	5,840	29,872
Idna	—	—	—	—	293	1,567	—	—	96	293	1,663
Tarqumia	—	—	—	—	353	1,721	—	—	82	353	1,803
Beit Aula	—	—	—	—	292	1,674	—	—	87	292	1,761
Beit Ummar	—	—	—	—	236	1,232	—	—	78	236	1,310
Yatta	—	—	—	—	62	331	—	—	24	62	355
Si'ir	—	—	—	—	108	617	—	—	21	108	638
Doura	—	—	—	—	707	3,274	—	—	242	707	3,516
Dahriyeh	—	—	—	—	571	2,604	—	—	136	571	2,740
Halhul	15	59	—	—	214	1,148	—	—	95	229	1,302
Fawwar	952	4,385	—	—	—	—	—	—	257	952	4,642
Arroub	1,050	5,177	—	—	—	—	—	—	314	1,050	5,491
Total	2,017	9,621	—	—	2,836	14,168	5,840	28,570	2,734	10,693	55,093
GRAND TOTAL IN JORDAN	14,035	70,923	13,996	67,444	29,415	144,030	34,954	172,635	21,169	92,400	476,201

Appendix II

FRONTIER VILLAGES

TABLE I
Land Lost to Israel

Sub-District	Population excluding refugees	Original area in dunums*	Present area in dunums	Percentage of original area lost
Jenin	10,260	311,110	114,008	63·3
Nablus	7,500	327,912	305,883	6·8
Tulkaram	39,020	267,424	109,153	59·2
Bethlehem	6,230	30,741	20,742	32·5
Jerusalem	7,230	31,107	21,673	30·3
Ramallah	2,850	28,647	22,887	20·1
Ramallah (ex Ramle)	11,430	139,146	58,708	57·8
Hebron	34,630	709,699	490,556	30·9
Total	119,150	1,845,786	1,143,610	38·0

NOTE:—Nineteen frontier villages which have lost only a negligible proportion of their lands are excluded and also the larger towns.

TABLE II
Classification of Remaining Lands in Frontier Villages

Sub-District	Present Area in dunums	Cultivable Land in dunums	Non-Cultivable Land in dunums	Percentage of present area classified as non-cultivable
Jenin	114,008	39,698	74,310	65·1
Nablus	305,883	105,217	200,666	65·6
Tulkaram	109,153	93,291	15,862	14·5
Bethlehem	20,742	9,474	11,268	54·3
Jerusalem	21,673	8,934	12,739	58·8
Ramallah	22,887	14,705	8,182	35·7
Ramallah (ex Ramle)	58,708	27,671	31,037	52·9
Hebron	490,556	168,438	322,118	56·7
Total	1,143,610	467,428	676,182	59·0

NOTE:—These tables originally appeared in the November 1953 issue of *The World To-day*—published by the Royal Institute of International Affairs—and are here reproduced by kind permission of the editor.

* 1 acre = 4 dunums.

Index

M 13

JERUSALEM
1954

Demarcation lines
No Man's Land

SANHEDRIYA

Jerusalem
Water Supply

Home for
Aged

KARM ES SILA

Mand

Hospital

Cinema

Hospital

Italian
Hospital

Hospital

College

Hospital

Cinema

Cinema

Cinema

Cinema

Police
HQ

Cathedral

Central
Prison

RUSSIAN COMPOUND

Courts

G.P.O.

New Gal

Museum

Cinema

Girls'
College

Ratisbonne
Monastery

Mamillah
Cemetery

Govt
Offices

Ja

Jewish
Agency

French
Consula

Terra Santa
College

YMCA
Stadium

King David
Hotel

YEMIN MOSHE

Greek Monastery
of the Cross

SHAM

TALBIYA

Capucin Monastery